PENGUIN BOOKS

hermit

'Beautifully observed . . . piercingly lyrical.'
Sunday Times

'Her tone throughout is conversational, mostly buoyant and
occasionally rapturous at the pleasure of living in isolation.'
Times Literary Supplement

'Fitton brings heart, body and soul to this compelling story
of deliberate living. A book about solitude – hers and other
people's – that runs rich with love for the natural world.'
Tanya Shadrick, author of *The Cure for Sleep*

'Written with often startling beauty, *Hermit* is an intimate
account of the healing power of solitude. Though deeply
personal, it explores universal truths about society and the
human condition. A brave, brilliant and important book.'
Lee Schofield, author of *Wild Fell*

'A dreamy, beautiful book about the consolations of solitude.
In *Hermit*, Jade wanders a sunlit, windswept, delicately drawn
landscape of loss and longing, and in doing so finds the stillness
at the centre of herself. Hopeful and open-hearted.'
Cal Flyn, author of *Islands of Abandonment*

'A compelling, engrossing memoir that beautifully
encapsulates the human experience (both the misery
and the magic) of suddenly finding yourself rebuilding
life from the ground up, alone. I loved it.'
Emma Gannon

hermit

A memoir of finding freedom in a wild place

JADE ANGELES FITTON

Dear James,
So sorry this is so late in
getting to you — a small
token of thanks for granting
permission to use beautiful words
of Jarman's from Blue — chapter 18.
Always grateful.

PENGUIN BOOKS

PENGUIN BOOKS

UK | USA | Canada | Ireland | Australia
India | New Zealand | South Africa

Penguin Books is part of the Penguin Random House group of companies
whose addresses can be found at global.penguinrandomhouse.com

First published by Hutchinson Heinemann 2023
Published in Penguin Books 2024
001

Typeset in 11.40/14.02pt Dante MT Std by Jouve (UK), Milton Keynes
Printed in Italy by Elcograf S.p.A.

The authorised representative in the EEA is Penguin Random House Ireland,
Morrison Chambers, 32 Nassau Street, Dublin D02 YH68

A CIP catalogue record for this book is available from the British Library

ISBN: 978-1-804-94052-5

www.greenpenguin.co.uk

For my parents: thank you for my life.

For my wife Ghada, and my life...

Prologue

The first moth of the year has flown in through the open sky-light from a starry-clear night in early March. I imagine how far this silver thing might've flown to reach the island, to reach the false moon of the illuminated computer screen on my bed. How far we have both come.

The skylarks and puffins have started arriving, but for months here the only birds I've seen or heard are ravens and herring gulls. For months the island has been shut down and there has not been a single visitor; it is still another month before anyone will be allowed to return. We have been utterly alone on this little rock. For someone searching for isolation, and who has been searching for many years now, this is a bitter-sweet taste of it.

Here, gorse flowers dangle from sheep like golden bells. Turds from the Highland cattle pile up high as dolmen. Hundreds of gulls are swept from the cliffs and over the sea, like drifts of snow. The puffins dig their burrows into the soft mud, under clods of pink thrift, moss and grass, lining their nests with bracken and the occasional bit of plastic. We cook in one pot on a hotplate, and have now for months. I dream of avocados and watercress, of pizzas and tortellini, of dim sum and sushi.

Lundy is a three-mile-long windswept island twelve miles off the North Devon coast. It lies directly opposite Croyde, the village where I used to live. Further inland, where the fields turn rugged and into slate-slicked moors, is the converted barn where I began this journey. Not once imagining that the wind would blow me here, to a kind of isolation I have never experienced, onto an island where I look back on myself.

As evening draws down, the lights on the mainland begin to flicker and the lighthouse at Hartland Point beams at us. Further north, the Bull Point lighthouse flashes, a handful of miles from the barn, as if to say, *I'm here, I'm here.* Like a heartbeat, *I'm here, I'm here.*

The island is off the national grid and runs on generators. Every night these are turned off from 12 a.m. until 6 a.m., so the night sky is gin-clear. Waking up before six requires a more primitive way of living – lighting candles to see by, wrapping up or making a fire because of the lack of heating, and, the hardest part, living without coffee until 6 a.m. Except for the call of the herring gulls, the distant rush of the sea, it is as quiet as the earth ever can be, and there's something precious to be found in that silence. That's why I'm here.

At night the wind rises, animates like a supernatural force. Every evening in the winter and throughout spring, without fail, the wind is there like a dark creature scouring the land. Desperately searching for something, whipping backwards and forwards so as not to miss a single blade of grass, a single rock, a single star. But it never finds what it is looking for, and every night it returns. Every night I open the big red door and there is the wind creature, searching frantically for what it has lost.

The Barn

I.

Big City Blues

Eyes down. Eyes down. Eyes down. This has become my mantra. Never look another man in the eye on the street, in a café, even with friends. Even when he is not with me. Eyes down. Eyes down. Eyes down. Follow the path of least resistance that is the dark marks of the pavement, the ghosts of chewing gum guide me home. Eyes down. Eyes down. Eyes down. Even then, if someone else's look lingers too long on me, you can bet I'm going to hear about it later.

'You hear that? He said you look like a slut.'

Eyes down eyes down eyes down. Render me invisible.

It has worked its way back to me that friends and acquaintances have started calling me 'geisha girl' because I don't talk to anyone any more, not without permission. At some point, I broke. I was born in the year of the tiger but I skulk around the edges of rooms like a smacked cat. I do everything to hide myself. I am not as I once was. I just want it all to stop. I just want us to be happy. Yet still he tells me strangers whisper that I look like a slut.

I came here chasing the shadows of my parents, looking for this big, exciting life I'd heard about: wild and revelatory and liberating. An existence full of colour and visions. Long before I met him, when I was a waitress in a market town two hundred miles from here, I looked up at the stars on a cigarette break and told myself I was destined for more. Bigger, grander things that I had yet to discover; things that were beyond my comprehension. But it doesn't matter that I was born here, that London is in my veins; the wild is in my bones now, and when you fall in the city, it's not on grass, it's on concrete. I am always falling these days.

It's around 4 a.m. I want to drop to my knees screaming for something to save me. I want to rip this life off me; it feels like a skin I was not born to wear. But I follow my training. Eyes down. Eyes down. Eyes down.

Within a year, the combination of unstable, self-proclaimed genius and drinking, taking and smoking too much of everything has led him to announce he is psychic, predicting when he will die, when I will die. He is suspicious of most things, but particularly of me.

I've been kicked out of his flat, where I am supposed to be staying, not for the first time and certainly not for the last. The evening started with him telling me, as he often does, that he wants to make a life with me but, as usual, it's ended with another vicious fight about who I am and who I have been talking to; everyone is a suspect for my infidelities, even the postman. The crack of a can makes me flinch. I know once he starts drinking he will get angry, sooner or later. I go to bed to avoid exacerbating the anger further and he plays Elvis's 'Suspicious Minds' on a loop at full volume for hours as he drinks. He is desperately trying to fill a hole that only seems to get bigger the more that he consumes. Everything falls into that hole, and there it is flipped on its head, and then flipped back; everything I think I know, everything I think is real, I come to doubt. We have entered an alternate reality and I can't seem to find my way back out. He walks around East London pretending to be blind or homeless, for attention, yet he tells me that I am the one who is mad – to even entertain this, coming from someone behaving as he is, means that, indeed, my grip on sanity is slipping.

I think I *must* be the mad one. I must try harder to be a better human being. Although I'm not even sure I know what a human being is any more. I can't do anything right and I feel like an alien. Everyone keeps telling me how this story will end, offering cautionary tales of people they have known or heard about, and yet I think I am different, that my story is not like anybody else's story, I will not let it end in disaster. It's this belief that means I have not been willing or able to end it. Like a gambling addict, I have lost control. I keep trying to make up my losses only to get further in debt, until eventually I will have nothing left to lose and the game will be over.

I have become someone I dislike. I know I am being lied to all of the time and it is slowly driving me mad. I have also started to lie because every time I tell the truth I am screamed at, or told I am lying. I scream and I scream a lot. Everything that he once praised me for – my confidence, my looks, my writing, my laugh – has quickly become what he hates about me. And God, does he hate it.

The city is all hard edges and orange skies. I have left my body and it is slaloming between traffic on Kingsland Road. I live in Clapton, it's miles from here; I'm never going to make it and I don't want to. I'm not crying. I'm gone. A double-decker bus narrowly avoids me, the driver is annoyed.

How long will it take for something to happen?

A group wandering home from a night out sees me in the road and pulls me onto the pavement. I'm sitting on the ground, weeping over my life story like every other drunk in the street. But I'm not drunk. I won't remember the words they say but I know they were kind. It must have been them who call the ambulance. If they called the police, instead of being treated with the care I desperately need, I would be arrested on a public order offence, as plenty of other desperate people have been. I am lucky, I just don't know it yet. I won't remember the journey but I will remember the feeling of embarrassment I experience on arrival. Even in a state of acute hysteria, I feel like someone who has had the coastguard called out for floating out to sea on a lilo. It makes my desire to vanish stronger. He can never find out about this. This is bad.

The next thing I know, my friend appears in the psychiatric ward of Homerton Hospital. He is at the top of my recent calls list and the doctors have phoned him. I spoke to him hours ago, talking about a music video we'd made, feeling fine. Now I am in a small, light grey room, absorbing as little as possible in the hope that if I don't let this reality in, it won't have happened, I won't really have allowed someone to rack me into a psychiatric ward. And yet, even I can't deny the walls are very real. There is no escape. I have been holding my breath in the hope I will pass out and wake up in a new life. I discover making yourself pass out is a lot harder than you might imagine. My life has become unbearable, and yet I have been unable to escape it, time and time again. Found myself too weak to change it at the crucial moment, time and time again. In the last couple of years I have developed a habit of punching my head when no one can see me, or at least only when the people who are screaming at me can see, to try to stop it all, all that pain up there, how the fuck do we turn it off?

I am falling very fast now. But the room tightens its grip.

My friend assures the doctors that I don't need to be sectioned.

He assures them that he knows me, he's known me for years and he can take care of me tonight. He tells them that I don't normally behave like this – he's never seen me like this. He drives me home, puts me in his bed and he sleeps on the floor. Before I pass out he holds my hand and tells me, as so many have, that I need to leave now before something really bad happens.

I agree, I do, but afterwards, it goes on. I go back because I think I'm lucky to be loved by him. Friends try to help me, tell me to leave over and over again, or when I am kicked out at least not to go back. They're upset when I do. I always do. People can't help me and I won't listen. Then I start losing friends. And when that starts happening, I just stop telling people.

I do make a sincere attempt at leaving. With the encouragement of a friend, I write a long letter saying it's over, and put it in his letterbox. I really think this marks the end of it, but I find ending this relationship is complicated in ways I had not anticipated. The complication I am finding with leaving is that I can be blackmailed or guilt-tripped into returning. It's almost impossible to be in a relationship like this for any length of time and to remain blameless – you will behave badly, sooner or later. I am not blameless. Anyone who says this situation is not about blame has not been in a relationship like this: a relationship like this is fuelled by casting aspersions, fuelled by a relentless defamation of someone's character, by a constant, remorseless barrage of accusations for which the benefit of the doubt is never given. It is bringing someone down to the point where they have no confidence in themselves and are shamed into obedience. A relationship like this survives on blackmail.

The first time, I didn't defend myself. It was early on in our relationship, we'd had a few glasses of wine, and I couldn't understand what was going on. My brain could not compute how we had got to this, me curled up on the floor by the front door, my nice brown leather satchel that my mum had given me over my shoulder, being kicked. Everything had happened so fast. We'd gone from having an argument about something I'd said to this: me literally being kicked out of his flat. But I've defended myself ever since. I always fight back now.

Why didn't I leave the relationship then? Because I felt like it had been my fault. I was made to feel that, despite his violent reaction, he was the victim of my behaviour – this is how the story always goes, and I end up apologising. He's like the characters in the comic books he reads: either the hero or the victim of any given situation – and he decides which. (Guess who's the villain?) In his defence, I should've known better. He's been sad from the day I met him, when he was drunk after logging into his ex's Facebook account and reading her messages, although it seems like he was born sad. How can you feel your own pain so acutely while disregarding someone else's? That's what I don't understand. He doesn't find living easy either, doesn't feel like he fits in, that's why I feel a connection to him. But he finds it difficult for different reasons. He thinks himself semi-divine, an anointed genius, a frustrated prodigy in a world that doesn't give him the respect he is due. Even as I write I can hear him asking, how was he expected to behave when I am so fucking infuriating?

In my new state of mind, the mind of an unhinged perfectionist, someone blameless in this relationship would be someone who doesn't push, shove or kick someone attacking them. In my mind, and his, someone blameless is someone who just lets a person attack them, someone with a Zen-like ability to overcome the natural instinct to defend themselves – that's what I am striving for, to overcome my instinct to survive. It's a form of enlightenment I can't seem to attain, but I'll keep trying.

In a moment of cosmic dissonance, he asks if I want to move into his mortgage-free flat. His flatmate left about a year ago now and he could do with someone paying him rent again. I jump at the chance of paying more rent than I do in my Clapton flat. My sister takes me to see a play, and when I tell her that I'm moving in with him she tells me she thinks it's a really bad idea. 'But I'm paying rent,' I say before the lights go down, 'so I'll be independent.'

'No, you won't be,' she says.

'Why not?'

'Because that's not how it works – he'll have you trapped, you won't have anywhere else to go.'

I won't listen. This comes just after I've been mugged and beaten up in broad daylight on the street where I'm living. The men in the barbershop I live above let the man who was beating me up walk in after me, lighting a cigarette, and when a woman eventually called the police the barbers played dumb, acted like they'd seen nothing. I don't want to be there any more. And it must mean *something* to him, asking me to move in. So I do move in, and when a girl comes round with some friends of his after his birthday party that I am instructed not to attend – which I don't, to show him that I can do what I'm told – I discover that he's telling people I'm only a tenant.

'Oh yeah, he said there was a girl living here at the moment,' she says.

That's me. Is the heart like the soul's seed? If you break it hard enough it will be released. (Mine must be a coconut.)

It might not be the wisest move, but I keep being given reasons to ask him why it's one rule for him and another for me, or, rather, no rules for him and all the rules for me. The fighting gets worse, to the point where, even with all my bravado, I get scared. We have a fight where I call the police and we break up.

Away from him, I am depressed and partying too much but I am making new friends, and I've found somewhere nice to live. I have regular waitressing work and am becoming established as a journalist at fashion weeks, and I'm writing more – I've started getting articles and poetry published. I've also started having panic attacks, but I'm ignoring that.

Then, after about a year, he calls me saying he thinks he's dying. Please, I must go and see him; he really thinks he's dying this time. Not like the last time he dumped me and then texted me quoting the statistics for male suicide and told me he was dying, when I left my own party to cycle to his to check in on him and I found him at home taking GHB with his friend, completely fine, save for the fact he was taking GHB. This time is different, he's alone, he's so sad, smoking some plastic when he was a teenager is killing him, he's sure, he just wants to see me one last time, he'll be dead in a few months. It's as if he can always sense when I am turning a corner, starting to feel all right again without him. Sometimes I really do believe he's psychic – best not to think a bad word about him, just in case.

One of my best friends, who saw us fighting the night I called the police, cries when I tell her that I'm getting back together with him. I think she is being dramatic. She doesn't talk to me for a couple of months but I'm so busy trying not to put a foot wrong with him that I hardly notice. I want to be perfect this time, I want to be faultless. I will lead by example, back into the dark, familiar hole. It only takes a few weeks for me to lose any agency over my life that I thought I'd gained. I've sleep-walked back to what I know, because I am lost and it recognises me. The shouting has started again. I've started hitting my own head again to try to make it stop. He's walking beside me calling me names, calling everyone in my family names. There's so much violence in his language, he has such a genius for it, such creative command over all the awful and extra-ordinary combinations of words he uses, that if it weren't so painful to hear I might find it impressive. As it is, I am begging him to stop. He gets inside my head and begins a sustained attack. This is torture.

I punch my head as hard as I can in an attempt to knock myself out. Of course, I fail. I can't feel the pain yet but there's a high-pitched tone in my ears and my saliva tastes like metal. I'm crying and he's laughing at me – no wonder he's laughing, I've become a joke and I know it. And yet, as I watch him laugh at me, spit at me what a fucking lunatic I am, I think there is something very perverse about watching someone in this state and encouraging it, like starving a snake and then paying to watch it eat itself alive.

Ah, there's the pain. Remember when I shouted at him on the street in Spain that I deserved better than him, only to quickly retract it out of fear that I was wrong, what was I think-ing? How can I ever deserve better than this if I behave like this, if I hurt myself like this, because when I behave like this, it makes it so easy to accept the judgements he puts on me like weights. Yeah, I am a piece of work, but God, do I want to change. I want to pull what is left of this spirit of mine out of my body and throw it into the sky, hope it's caught by one of the gulls that eat the blood and bones from the butcher's on Kingsland Road and finds its way to the coast. I'm back here all over again, trapped in my own body.

When I was about seven, my mum went to the market in the local one-horse town and bought Kit Williams's book *Masquerade*, an illustrated children's book following the adventures of a hare, which sparked a nationwide treasure hunt. She bought several copies: a couple to cut up and frame the pictures – she still has the swimmer in her bathroom – another to read, and another to lose.

Hours upon hours were spent poring over the book and the treasure Williams had designed to accompany it, the 18-carat gold hare inlayed with ruby, turquoise, mother-of-pearl and moonstone that he had hidden somewhere in the land. But it was the book that really took hold of me, its illustrations of moons and dandelions, fire and water, young and old, players and fools, patchworks and honeycombs – all the weird and wonderful trippy folk-art motifs that I recognised from the trippy country life we lived. Morris dancers and mummers came to our favourite pub out in Iddesleigh on May Day to dance and mime and put on plays. People with a hangover from the sixties, still full of love for the world and humankind, reviving ancient identities in the late eighties and early nineties, digging deep into the mud of our collective psyche to uncover things that used to bring joy when we had so much less. These people came to the pubs with the hope that they could still bring joy, simple and out of place as their treasures were in a quickly modernising world. In a photo, I stand outside the pub in Iddesleigh aged about four, staring up at the semi-circle of mummers around me in wonder. *Masquerade* stirred my belief that nature and magic are interlinked, and that humans, at their best, at their least guarded, can act as intermediaries.

For a long time now, I have been looking for something: a breakthrough, self-actualisation. A divine purpose, a calling, an awakening. Whatever you want to call it. I have tried to achieve it through partying and laughing. I have tried through throwing love where it does not belong. I tried through experiencing minimal success in a producing career. I have listened to friends' stories of taking ayahuasca and acid and wondered if that's how I'd break on through to the other side, but can never get my act together to score any. I tried to achieve it by pushing my body to run for as long as it could in an ultramarathon. But there is never anything that can satisfy me.

I have wanted to get out of London for a while, but now it has become a matter of urgency. I have hurt myself so frequently and so badly, physically and mentally, that I don't know if I will ever recover. I want to be able to let my guard down again. I want to fall back on the land I grew up in. I have to leave this place.

A couple of weeks later, with his blessing, I leave London for Devon. My mum puts me up on her sofa, and while there, I read something about the Christian belief in being willing to turn your hand to anything. Although some Christians seem to have forgotten this belief, as I have been working in circles where humility is scarce and everything is geared towards elevating yourself – towards getting yourself in as high a position as possible, so you can delegate to others and turn your hand to as little as possible – this seems a rather elegant notion. I also desperately need money, so I get into cleaning holiday cottages for the tourists, as many women down here do.

Early in the job, I am told by one of the older workers that there was once a point in time when guests would strip the beds and even leave a small tip for the cleaners. In the here and now, we have been given two neighbouring party-houses to clean, where large groups come down to get shit-faced on long weekends. The house I and another cleaner are assigned is in a state, but by comparison, we've lucked out. As the cleaners next door are finishing up and getting ready to go back to their kids, they quickly check the bedroom drawers for old ear plugs or lost underwear and find one full of vomit. That's how grockles get a bad name.

Despite this, I am grateful for the work, and while I'm cleaning a toilet the woman who owns the two places makes a surprise visit and finds me holding a bog brush over her loo. She chats to me for a few minutes, says I seem 'bright', gives me her number and says she wants me to be her assistant; she has too much on with summer coming and needs some help. I'm not feeling very bright but I gladly become her assistant. I cycle to work and back on the Tarka Trail every morning and evening, listening to the curlews and the oystercatchers, inhaling the smell of seaweed, mud and buddleia, and think that this – even sleeping on my mum's sofa in a tiny one-bed flat – is a better life than the one I've been living in London. Just for how the views on these cycle rides to and from work make me feel. This is home, here, and I feel a pang of regret when I think of home being anywhere else. I didn't realise until now that home could be a whole landscape; I thought it had to be a building.

I can't really enjoy being here though, because now that I cannot be monitored at close proximity except on the weekends I see him, he calls all the time and, despite knowing I have a nine-to-five, if I don't answer the first time he calls, I am interrogated when I do pick up. Where was I? Why didn't I answer? Who was I with? Why am I lying to him? I am constantly on edge. A doctor advises that I start taking medication for my depression and anxiety, and I do for a while but it doesn't change how he treats me and so my anxiety and depression don't change either. My mum gets irritated by my sustained defensiveness about almost everything, my manic paranoia; she is sick of listening to me on the phone in the next room crying and grovelling – she lost her patience with the situation a long time ago. 'Just tell him to fuck off!' she shouts through the wall.

Within a couple of weeks of working for her, my boss gathered something was up. Eventually, she gleaned enough information from me to understand that, despite my protests, all is not well in my life – crying in the back room all the time is kind of a giveaway. I do know there is a possibility that I am in complete denial about the reality of the situation I am in, about the effect it is having on me. But I tell myself that I can endure it. After a few refusals, she drives me to see a therapist with whom she has made an appointment for me, knowing I won't go of my own volition. My trouble with therapy is that everything's theoretical: what I should do, how I should react, or shouldn't. It's much harder to put it all into practice, especially now my fight-or-flight mechanisms are working in overdrive. I tell the therapist everything I can think of that is wrong with me, every flaw in my being, so that she gets a good idea of what he has to put up with, and that I won't leave – so how can I do better? It's a short-lived experiment, but I do take something away from it. The one thing the therapist keeps repeating to me is 'boundaries'. I have to 'create boundaries'. This is the only way I can protect myself and stop this cycle of self-loathing.

Unfortunately, my boss has heartache of her own, and after six months of me working for her she leaves the country for a while. I return to London and immediately realise it's a mistake. The weather is beautiful, noticeably so, and I walk around wearing pastel shades listening to happy songs but things are worse than ever; we're fighting all the time now. I'm waking up to the realities of his heavy drinking, him staying out all night, having fights with strangers. Then there are the physical side-effects, things I tell him I don't want him to feel humiliated about but which are concerning and unpleasant for both of us.

While he's shouting at me for suggesting he might have a problem, I have a moment of inspiration. I will try to reach out to him, I will try to build a bridge between us by confiding in him – that's how you build trust, isn't it, by trusting someone with your vulnerability so that they feel safe to be vulnerable with you? I tell him that life deals everyone blows we struggle to recover from, that before I met him I was raped. He rips me to shreds. Wishes obscene violence on me that I can't bring myself to write down. I slap him. Surprisingly, it's the first time I've ever slapped him. I tell him that he has been spoilt rotten, that he really is just a nasty little prick. He accuses me of abuse. What? Me? Yes, me. But what about him? What about every time he's lost his temper and hit, slammed, grabbed, ripped, shoved and kicked? It's never him. How could I forget even for one moment that I am always the one at fault, without exception. How dare I get on my high horse. How dare I point fingers at a genius. I should be ashamed of myself. I am.

Why can't you just be kind to me, I ask, why is it so hard? You're so nice to me when you want to get back together, why can't you stay nice? He does stay nice. It's me, it's me, it's me. Repeat after me until I believe it. It's me, it's me, it's me. It's all my fault and I do believe it. I will always believe it's my fault, I will say I know it's wrong to other people but I will still secretly believe it. Now, I'm further under his boot than I've ever been; I've trapped myself here. I don't know what I was thinking, telling him. I only know I am desperate. Desperate for him to show me kindness, but I knew even as the words were falling out of my mouth that telling him was a stupid thing to do. It's just more ammunition against me in arguments, further proof that I am 'damaged goods'.

I would like to say that this is the moment I realise that he will not, cannot, love me as I want to be loved, that there is a divide between us that cannot be bridged, but this isn't that moment. I've seen what happens in the world where people split up and it all falls apart. I grew up in that world and have an unconscious, uncompromising, all-consuming drive to find out what happens if you see it through to the alternate ending. What is the reward for clinging on to the white-knuckle ride – is it beautiful beyond the bone-crushing waterfall?

2.

God Knows Where We're Heading

Just when I least expect it, there is talk of getting engaged. I'm working in Milan, about to go on to Paris for two weeks on a job that, after much negotiation, will be the most I've ever been paid. I quit. Because he says if I come back to London he'll ask me to marry him. Even though I know it won't make me happy, we both know it's an offer I can't refuse; it's all I've wanted from him, validation. I come back imagining an emerald ring waiting for me, but it's bullshit, of course it is. He's quite open about it – he was never going to marry me, he just wants me to be somewhere he can keep an eye on me, and now I'm here, he's shouting at me for not having enough money. I appreciate that pain has a way of cracking us open, and that through the cracks we see everything differently, but I am completely shattered. There is no ring and there never will be and I'm starting to get really tired now. I'm so tired of being told a shit is a rose. I'm tired of my head hurting from the crying and shouting and punching. I'm tired of putting cucumber and wet cotton pads from the fridge on my eyes to calm the swelling. I have to find some peace.

This is an SOS.

God, do you read me? I have been losing for too long. I really think I will kill myself soon if something doesn't change. If I am helped, given a breakthrough, a drastic change in fortune, I will do something good with my life, I promise. Yes, I am bartering with God now. Telling God that I really mean it, I'll do anything, just give me a sign. I am offering my life up for some scraps of benediction. Wandering into churches and crying at the ceiling, putting my fingers in holy water and wiping it across my brow and my heart. Throw me a fucking bone, please.

It's early and there's a blackbird in the tree outside. Previously its song was a warning that I'd stayed out too late; now it's my alarm clock. In my need for peace and quiet I have started getting up very early, before anyone else is conscious, and in feeling like I have nowhere left to turn but death or God, I have advanced from just wandering into churches expecting a miracle and have started reading religious texts. Unlike the solace found in an empty church, I've found the Bible pretty unforgiving and, although I was into Revelation and its unclean spirits coming out of frogs' mouths, the Bible's actually quite scary, particularly towards the end – an awful lot of 'wrath' and general 'fearing of the Lord'. I'm already terrified, so my attentions have instead moved towards the pretty pictures, the artifice of early Christian literature. Like a baby and a thief, I have been drawn to what shines. I've become fascinated with illuminated manuscripts and the medieval monks who painted them. I have no discrimination in my preferred style of illumination. I moon at the beauty of them all and the hours of someone's life that it took to create them. Were the monks who created these manuscripts searching for something, and did they find it in the lives they led? I'm fascinated by their rituals, their devotion, their routine, the comparative simplicity of their lives. The austere, isolated toil around which their existence rotated. The sanctuary of their own private cell. From here, it looks like another planet, one I have tried to emulate as best I can in East London in the twenty-first century by getting up early to paint improvised commandments in the style of illuminated manuscripts, one of which reads, *When Offered . . . Always Accept An Exorcism.*

Do I need an exorcist? Don't rule it out.

In the quiet of these early hours before the bottles start smashing in the bar next door, I have been dreaming about another life, allowing myself to get lost in fantasy. I wonder if there is such a thing as the 'right path', some invisible channel you travel down as you make right and good decisions, that protects you from harm and takes you to better places, because I seem to have gone down a garbage chute. What might the other life that runs alongside this one look like – the life I can't seem to break into? It would have chickens and a view; I would have a home in which I felt secure; I would have the time and space to write; I would go outside in the mornings with a cup of coffee and listen to the birds. I want a good life, a calm life. I don't want fame and fortune like he does, I just want a little life in which I am safe – nothing big, nothing grand, not any more. I want to hide away, busying myself with the day-to-day. I want the life I left behind, searching for something better.

His parents sell the London flat they bought him outright, and as they have always done in the hope of making him happy, they give him money: the profit, which is well over a hundred thousand pounds. He doesn't have a job any more, and after the flat is packed up I say to him that at least it's cheaper where I want to go. I can't keep up with the rate he's spending money. He's frittering it all away, knowing that more will come, and every time I suggest he might want to invest his money in something sensible – like somewhere to live – he accuses me of trying to steal from him, so I've given up on that; but a hundred-odd grand could last him a very long time where I want to go. Does he want to move to Devon with me?

If he doesn't want to come then I'll sleep on my mum's sofa again, but I am going. I'm not sure for how long this time, but I have to go now. I might lose my remarkable powers of recovery soon. It's taking me longer and longer to bounce back from each argument. I can't stand near the edge of train platforms any more because I'm worried I will follow an impulse and throw myself off. A friend tells me a story about a woman she knew who committed herself to a convent after a break-up. It's tempting and I wonder how you go about doing that – getting oneself into a nunnery. I do think I'd enjoy aspects of convent life, and decide that, like jail, it can remain an option if all else fails, because I'm not sure the nuns would want me, I'm not sure I'd want them either, and I already devote my life to a man who thinks he's the Messiah and I can't say it's been much fun, so going back to Devon just seems a lot easier.

He doesn't have anywhere else to be and maybe the fresh air will do him good, and he supposes his money will last longer there. So he will come with me, and the presence of his bank account makes it a lot easier to rent a converted barn in the middle of nowhere from an estate agent than if I'd been on my own, for which I am very grateful.

A few days before we leave for Devon I stay on the sofa of a friend. She has a new lodger living with her. This woman is a telephone psychic and doesn't seem entirely connected to reality. However, as detached as this woman might be (she will go on to paint herself entirely gold from head to toe and claim she is an Egyptian queen), she is also good at her job.

I've never been much into tarot or psychics, not because I doubt that some people have the ability to divine the future – I don't doubt that – rather, the couple of times I've consulted them they've been accurate but never had good news for me; it's always been about him, and I'd rather live in false hope. But I'm stuck in a house with her, and having told her a little about myself, she insists on pulling a few cards for me. She pulls the same card twice. It's a card with an illustration of an astrolabe. An astrolabe is an ancient navigational device that tracks celestial bodies, but I have no idea what an astrolabe means in this context. The card is the Three Chalices. Upright, it signals the end of hardships, good times ahead; reversed, it means isolation, taking charge of the situation and leaving the community. I don't know any of this, at this point in time I have no idea whether it is upright or reversed, or both, but she is telling me I need to leave the relationship; it is time now. She says I have to stop living this same pattern every lifetime; I have been living this pattern, this relationship, for many lives, and it is finally time to break the cycle. I am twenty-eight and ancient.

As she tells me this, my mind races back to a few months ago, when an eccentric friend of my mum's called me up and said, 'I've spoken to a witch I know, and she said you have to leave him, he's not the one for you.' The man in question was sitting right next to me and I was worried he would hear what was being said and get angry. I didn't ask who the witch was. I didn't want to hear it. But here I am with this woman and she is saying the same thing. Every witch in Christendom knows this is going to end, one way or another. Her blue eyes and peroxide-blonde hair glow in the afternoon light; she has that diaphanous quality people who have truly clairvoyant abilities always have, as if they're not entirely here, just hanging in suspension like dust in sunlight, projected into being with the weight of a hologram. She is saying, 'Sometimes, you have to get rid of someone so you don't see them again in the next life.'

Not another life, I think, not like this one. But the only way for souls to leave purgatory is through a passionate reliving of their experience. We leave London for Devon.

After a night at a picturesque beachside hotel where he throws crab sandwiches at me, we move into the converted barn on the Exmoor hills. I'm deluded enough to think there is a minute chance something might change drastically, but beyond that I can't explain why I'm doing this with him, other than I know it's a bad idea but I also know it needs to happen anyway.

The barn is set facing hills and is surrounded by fields and a small country lane dotted with houses, and a little way down is the farm from which we rent it. In the field directly in front of the barn are the farmer's sheep. Inside, it's characterless downstairs, with depressing little bedrooms that seem to catch the light at all the wrong angles and a windowless magnolia bathroom that does at least have a bath, which is all I care about. But upstairs is a big kitchen-living room, with wooden beams, a fireplace, and big windows through which the view pours into the room. I could look out onto this view for the rest of my life and be content. He is not so enthusiastic; the beams and the view aren't enough. He regrets the decision to move almost immediately and makes this very clear.

With no one else to confide in, I start a journal. Early in the mornings before he wakes up I secretly write, wishing, wishing, wishing. Praying I won't have to be the one to leave this time. I like it here. I could be happy here. But not like this. It's not beautiful to him here, it's just the middle of nowhere – the land of the failures, the nobodies, those who are 'dead to the earth' – and he blames me for him being here. I'll take the blame for that. I write, 'My instinct tells me to sit tight and wait. At some point, some time, I'll know and it'll make sense.'

I start work as a cleaner again while it's still holiday season and he looks for jobs online, but none of them down here are good enough as he sits on the sofa smoking joint after joint. At least he's drinking less, I guess, but he's acting pretty strange. Tracing every number that calls him. Finding people's IPs. Creating multiple accounts on social media. As autumn creeps in, the cleaning dries up and I have to sign on while I apply for other jobs – mostly receptionist jobs, but I also start applying for online writing work.

There is a comical disparity in our wealth but we share the bills. I may be delusional but not so delusional that I'd rely on him for money, and anyway, I'm here a lot more than he is. It didn't take long for him to start spending more time back up in London. I leave him to it because I'm getting windows of calm, a glimpse of what life could be like if I were alone here all the time. But just when I'm starting to really like it, he comes back from staying with friends in London and shows how kind he can be when he wants to be. He gives me a pair of slippers from the Ritz. Because he knows how much I like hotel slippers, he says, he went to the Ritz and asked for a pair especially for me. It's such a sweet gesture, such a nice surprise after so much bad. I never doubt his story. It never even enters my head that maybe you don't simply walk into the Ritz and ask for a pair of slippers at reception. It doesn't occur to me that there might be another reason for the slippers, like him staying there. To me, staying at the Ritz is unimaginable. Look at me walking around in my posh new slippers, so happy that he thought of me while he was away. How does he keep a straight face?

The anger returns with the slippers. We're miles from most things here, but only about ten miles from a farm where a woman was shot by her jealous husband, and the story has been echoing in my head since we arrived. I like to think I will survive this relationship, but I know in my gut that if it carries on I will end up dead, by my hand rather than his – by accident, a cry for help that's just a little too loud. Even here, in all this beauty, I am hurtling through space towards one catastrophe or another. I am still in the cosmic garbage chute, making the wrong decisions and fending off the endless stream of galactic detritus that appears as a result of them, and I'm on my last legs. The next thing that hits will break me. I am not responsible for my actions any more. Neither is he. I am turning twenty-nine and life no longer seems infinite; I don't have any more years to waste on being suicidal and unfulfilled. I try something new and brace myself for impact. I play dead. I stop defending myself and allow myself to be condemned. I become mute, just like he wants. As with a Chinese finger trap, I have to stop fighting if I am to get out of it.

After a few days of this he seems to lose interest in picking at me. But the absence of anger creates a vacuum that is filled only with the fear of when the anger will return. Even the air in the barn feels tight, pulled to its limits, and I must walk and talk as carefully as I can so that I do not split the silence stretched over the house. But, one night, it ruptures. Every mistake I've ever made is turned on me, as are the ones I haven't made, the ones he's imagined, and I can't help but stand up for myself. I shout back and we have a fight that scares him more than it does me.

I'm only scared if I've done something wrong, not if he has, and this time I do everything right, in my mind – I don't defend myself. Maybe it's the adrenaline, but I'm not scared when I end up slammed against a wall, then another wall that my head hits. We know by now that I've got a thick skull – I'm still standing, his face in mine as he screams. I scream back. I could do fifty rounds of this and stay standing. I've been beaten up plenty in my life; I was put in hospital for talking back to a group of townies when I was a teenager. Compared to that, his attempts don't even touch the sides. If he was bigger this would be a different story, but physically I just won't be knocked down any more, not by him. It's the psychological bullying that will get me one of these days, but just so long as it's not today, because today I am doing what I have been trying to do for so long. I keep my hands behind my back and let it happen, because it was going to happen anyway.

I've got used to this, this rhythm: we'll both calm down, I won't speak, and it'll be fine again, for a few hours. But this time when he calms down he says he needs to leave before there's an accident and he really hurts me. I hear myself disagree, almost automatically; I say that it'll be fine, I'm not hurt, I'm never hurt, a few bruises, a few cuts, never anything more, it's not a big deal. When I called the police in London that time they didn't think it was a big deal, and that was much worse than this time, so why make a big deal out of it? In fact, when the police arrived it did seem like I was to blame; my lame story of falling over was enough to satisfy them, to my surprise. Despite my blood on the walls of the staircase up to his flat, the call-out seemed to be an inconvenience to them. I listened from two metres away while he put the blame on me and they believed him. I let him tell them how awful I was. I could see them, glancing at me, like *poor guy, what a nightmare she must be*, and I nodded and agreed. It was me, it was me, repeat it until I believe it.

Why am I like this? Then, it was because I wanted to prove I was better than this, that we could be better than this, told myself that this would never happen again, and even if it did, next time I wouldn't react. I had also realised once I called the police that if I told the truth I'd have nowhere to live, just as my sister had warned, and anyway, I learned that I can't tell the truth as convincingly as he can lie, so why bother trying?

Now, I don't know what my excuse is. I've been writing day after day how much I want him to leave, and now he offers to go and I feel duty-bound to give fair warning. I say that if he leaves then this is the last time, we will never get back together, and I mean it. I know he doesn't think I mean it, that he'll be able to twist my arm once he's got bored or lonely like every other time, but I do mean it. For the first time, I mean it. But the thing is, I'm not sure I want him to go. He's taken up my whole life, every thought, and if he's not there any more then I don't know what is. I am completely convinced that if I do get really hurt along the way then it will be my own doing, and maybe I don't deserve any better than that. Some lives just don't work out. But it's out of my hands now; life is moving incredibly quickly all of a sudden.

After dozens of fruitless job applications, he is offered a job doing what he wants to do, hundreds of miles from here. This changes everything: if he leaves now it won't be on me – I won't have to feel guilty about that, at least. I encourage him to take the job, although I know he's going to take it either way, and he does. I get up early and I go to sleep early, giving him a wide berth and saying as little as possible, wondering what will happen next, almost scared to move for fear that I might disrupt whatever is in motion here. I watch the events unfold in disbelief.

When the day that he is leaving arrives, I remind myself that this is what I have been praying for – this is deliverance, it just looks more familiar than I'd imagined. It's overcast and the cold air feels thick. The sparrows are chirping, the sheepdog is barking somewhere in the fields, the winter sun is already high in the sky – life has important things to be getting on with, nothing is waiting for us. There is no breeze and we don't argue today. Reality has flipped again, and he is behaving more maturely than I am about this – he's even being nice, he's being generous. Sometimes I wonder if he isn't a physical manifestation of life itself: one endless learning curve. I can never predict what is coming next – where has this calm and measured person been? I find the re-emergence of this facet of his character, a facet I usually only get to see displayed for others these days, extremely frustrating, having needed it for so long, but better late than never, I suppose.

He packs up his computer and some clothes he likes and says he'll be back to collect the rest. All this time I've been beating myself up for thinking about leaving someone who made out that they couldn't live without me. People can always live without you, especially when they say they can't. I'm a little hurt to realise this but I am tired of being moved. I accept it all and keep breathing. Somewhere in the ruins of me, a resourcefulness is rising. If I can believe that I have deserved everything bad in my life, then I can now choose to believe that I deserve better. I watch him out of the back door, smoking and texting, and think that this is it now, and I know it. I have to keep myself together, that's my only task this year.

I make him a sandwich for the drive because it seems weirder not to. There is no shouting, no tearful goodbye – not even from me, I've done that already. He just turns on the engine and drives away while I'm not looking. Our old life falls flat at my feet. The ending of it all feels like a punchline to a joke no one was listening to: *wrong crowd, man.* That's what did us in, a complete sense-of-humour failure about it all. If I'd had a better sense of humour, I would have laughed at him the first time he called me names, and left. But what can you do when you're too scared to laugh? Scream.

The sound of the car fades down the road as I walk back into the barn. I open the door and stand there looking around. It rained in the night and I can smell it on the air, even inside.

Outside, it's dark and empty, save for the mizzle-soaked rooks blown from the trees, the dark passing clouds, and the voles that creep through the damp undergrowth. Below the barn floor on which I lie, there is a field full of mushrooms, some of them magic, and dreaming sheep. Further still is an ancient woodland with a river running through it, and ten miles north there are cliffs and the much-contested feral goats of the Valley of the Rocks, and there's the sea that's blowing in this old and salty wind that slaps the walls of the barn. I stare at the beams above me. Tears run into my hair and cool on my skull.

I have a saying I once illuminated: 'If all else fails, just lie on the floor and wait for something to happen.' This time, the something that will change the course of my life has already occurred. I am on the moors with no car, no public transport, no shops. The wind is blowing gusts of rain that slap the windowpanes. It is so dark outside. Not dark like the city where the sky glows, but black-dark. Not a light in the sky, not even the moon. Just a cluster of stars that I can make out even without my glasses.

They aren't tears of grief that are cooling. I've grieved every time I have been dumped, which must be approaching a hundred times in the last four years. I don't know what these tears are, because this time I do not feel resentment, I do not feel love. Strangely, I do not even feel loss. Now that I have finally let go, it's as if what I was holding on to had already gone so long ago it never was. I have lost nothing and I have nothing left in me. I'm still alive, though, so I must find some courage, enough to start behaving with a little dignity from here on out. It would be nice if I could emerge with that – surprising too. But I'm waiting for the aftershock; should I be worried about what comes next? He always threatened to ruin my life and I can't put anything past him, but I can hope that his interest in me is over now. It's never been over before. My thoughts are spinning. I get up off the floor and write in a scrawl in my notepad: 'This was it all along, that feeling of foreboding.'

It feels like a bomb's gone off inside me and I'm too scared to look at the damage. What is the damage? I don't know if it's too soon for my body to process it all, too soon to realise I have been conditioned to live in fear and to fear people, their anger and their disapproval. But if this is the end that I have been dreading all these years – what I am experiencing now – then maybe I don't have to look at the damage yet. Maybe I've escaped unscathed and I'll never feel the pain; it will never manifest in ways I do not expect. Maybe I won't feel like a fraud every time someone says something nice about me. Or, maybe, just maybe, in being abandoned it is me who has escaped. It is me who has got lucky. Out here, I will never see anyone else. I only meet the farmer who owns the barn once, as he shouts over the fence, and the estate agents only twice: once to rent it, and once before eventually leaving. They don't notice the dent in the wall.

3.

Lightning Tree

Outside is still dark and the stars flicker, making their light seem as fragile as a candle's. If I exhale too hard I will blow them out. The birds are yet to start their chorus and the land is as silent as a hand on glass. I am filled with a childlike excitement at the prospect of being able to enjoy this place in peace. I went to bed at 9 p.m. last night, so getting up at 6 a.m. is easy. Despite the darkness I don't turn on the lights in the bedroom, they're too bright and bleak, so I use my phone's torch to shuffle out into the hall and flick the stair lights on and walk up to the high-beamed kitchen. It might be easier getting up at this hour if you've gone to bed early, but I can't find pleasure in it without the promise of coffee. I wait for the kettle to boil and look out of the kitchen window and down onto the land, sinking into the view.

In the fields are white bubbles of pregnant sheep. Behind them are the winter hills where the aged sun will rise in a couple of hours. Down past the sheep and to the woods my mind's eye travels. I'll go for a walk later, into the view that stands so tall in my days. First, I have work to do. I had a stroke of luck a few weeks before he left. Writing was never something I was able to do for a living, until now. Based on some art criticism and some journalism I've had published over the last couple of years, I've got a part-time writing job. It's working from home, writing daily art news for an art website, and this, accompanied by the odd script-editing job and copywriting work, means I can come off benefits and support myself here through writing, and I feel determined. I will apply the dogged persistence that I furnished the relationship with to my career for the first time and see what, if anything, comes of it. Aside from being what I want to do, this job is also what I desperately need, since I can no longer work anywhere but my desk on the kitchen table. This job is my lifeline.

I light a candle. Except for this and a lamp, the room is in half-darkness and it gives working a conspiratorial air. Listen to that: silence. No one calling up for me to make them a coffee. No one getting up in a bad mood again, still angry from the night before. I left the kitchen tidy last night and there isn't someone else's crap to clear up that's appeared while I've slept, and only my washing-up to be done. When I take out the bins, and it was always me who did it, it's only going to be my rubbish. The back doormat isn't covered in ash and spliff butts for me to sweep up. When I smoke, I put it out in an ashtray. I don't have to be careful of what I do or what I say. I'm finding the experience of being on my own so pleasing it feels revelatory.

I do fear he will come back unannounced and this new feeling of freedom will have been a ruse. I am nervous to check my phone in case there are hundreds of missed calls and messages accusing me, or threatening to humiliate me, as there have always been when he's not around to say it to my face. But when I check my phone there are none. As I make some porridge and another coffee, watch the oats steam in the pan and inhale the scent of fresh nutmeg while the blue-black sky turns grey, I can't help but feel a little hopeful. What if life could be this simple?

★

I didn't prepare for life alone here without a car. I didn't stock up on food and there has been an immediate shift in my priorities, from focusing on emotional tribulations to more essential, practical needs. A spotlight on my physical survival forces a much-needed distraction from my feelings, like in acupressure when force is applied to one part of the body to help relieve pain in another. Maybe that's why I'm not resisting the situation, why I'm prepared to run my supplies down to the last. I have enough coffee, porridge and spaghetti for now. There are some wrinkled carrots, a couple of other vegetables that are past their best and some crusty Cheddar that I'll make do with. If I were more adventurous and had a better knowledge of fungi, I would be foraging, but I'm not. I don't need any more than I have. There will not be any more until I ask my mum to drive out and do the hour-and-a-half round trip to go shopping. But I haven't told anyone he's left yet. I have no idea what to say. I need to feel steadier on this new path before I can deal with anyone questioning its integrity.

For now, what I do have is enough bread in the freezer to make a cheese sandwich for lunch, which I'll take and have as a picnic on my walk – and I can just go for a walk, on my own, with no questions asked, no accusations, no suspicious minds. I keep reminding myself that there is no one monitoring my movements. I must remember how to think without it being a portent of a conversation with someone; I don't need to prepare my defence. I must absorb more and give less.

Much of the land surrounding me is owned by farmers or landowners, most of it empty of livestock and not planted for crops. There are 'Keep Out' signs further down the road and, as is often the case, they can limit the freedom to roam considerably, until you choose to ignore them. As I am renting the barn, I figure I am allowed to roam the nearest fields, and slowly I will figure that, seeing as I was born on this planet, I am allowed to roam into further fields and further woods and valleys.

In these fields, for the first time in years, I am the only figure in the landscape and it is a surreal experience. I am *alone*. Walking over the damp grass, I keep looking over my shoulder to see who is watching me. No one is, ever; there is never anything out here but my shadow, which no one treads on any more. My shadow follows me through the fields I walk through, the field I sit in, floored with relief. It mimics me as I lean back on the old drystone wall and feel the earth support me. This land has known me all my life. It has known the lives of my parents, my grandparents, my great-grandparents, and on and on and on, and there is something to that. You can have a connection to a place through something that happened to you, or someone you know, through an animal, or a song, but my connection to this landscape is my dead, and they see me clearly. To be known by the land is all the company I need.

My dad's family in the south-west goes back as far as the eye can see – the Oliver name was everywhere round here, carved into the rocks. We were wreckers, miners, milkmaids, labourers and housewives up until my great-grandfather, Adam Oliver. He was born in St Minver, Cornwall. The son of a stonemason with aspirations, he slowly worked the family up to comfortable middle-class, founding a carpentry factory in Barnstaple called the Barnstaple Cabinet Company, which later merged with the arts and crafts company Shapland and Petter, with Adam Oliver at the helm. Back then, in most people's eyes the

Olivers were posh, they had made it; but, like a bed, it would be much quicker to unmake. None of this interested me when I was growing up here; the Oliver Buildings that once housed the factory (built by the unrelated William Clement Oliver) were boarded up and left by developers to crumble by the river, which seemed symbolic of the Oliver legacy to me. But there is a reason we seek out our roots, and maybe the reason is a feeling, and the feeling becomes stronger when we've felt lost.

Previously, I'd doubted Devon was home because I was born in London. My dad was a special-effects technician there; my mum had been an actress, a model, a waitress, an antiques trader, a saleswoman of strange velvet paintings, a care worker, and many things in between, but had never really claimed to be anything other than trying (and frequently succeeding) to have a good time.

I spent the first few years of my life living on Archer Street and, later, Brewer Street, in Soho near I Camisa, the Italian deli where I was given sugared almonds that my mum always worried would break my teeth. There is a family portrait of my elder sister, Charlotte – who was by then at university – and myself in our flat, and behind us out of the window, a sign in pink neon reads 'Girls, Girls, Girls'.

We left when I was three. I would soon be starting school and my paternal grandparents and great-aunt were living in Devon, as my maternal grandfather had in his last years. He had recently passed away, leaving a small, timber-frame bungalow with a large garden next to a farmer's fields and a wood in North Devon. We moved in. My dad continued working in London in the week and drove down to Devon every Friday night, while my mum took care of me, worked part-time and managed the building site our bungalow became. Both of them were tired, but happy for a while.

Slowly, over the years, my parents transformed the tiny bungalow into a large house. One of the builders had a genius for structural design, which meant that we didn't need an architect. Skilled builders were interspersed with some of the other builders Mum found – the men of the nearby town who drank vodka from the bottle all year round on a bench in the town square, slowly turning redder as summer came on. But given a chance and something to do, they worked hard. They helped build a house that was testament to my parents' imagination. My parents had ignored suggestions that they should build as many bedrooms as possible, and instead a sitting room was created that was one outrageously big room with a ceiling twenty-five feet high and big windows of recycled stained glass. Old pews taken from refurbished churches were turned into a daybed, metres of bookshelves were made by a friend's father, and there was a wood burner at the heart of the room. The 'big room' led onto a veranda of railway sleepers that looked onto an old well, with a hammock that swayed beside the woods.

My room also backed onto the woods, the trees framed by another stained-glass window, and beside the window was a bunk bed my dad had made that we painted cornflower blue, the same colour as the hall. My parents' bedroom had French windows that were left open all summer, and through them the breeze and the bats would pass through the house. My parents painted our tiny bathroom navy blue and stencilled it all over with silver and gold stars. Towards the end of his life, my paternal grandfather moved into the original part of the house, and I would come home from school to find him leaning out of his kitchen window asking me how my day had been. They painted the outside of the house a deep red, and wisteria – what I called 'the mysterious' – grew all over it. 'The mysterious is in bloom.' There was a drive that ran from the spinney our house was named after at the bottom of the garden up to the front door, and to hear the gravel crunching under the wheels of a car meant we were home, or Dad was coming back from a week working in London, or he was leaving again. When the house was finished, a family friend and her husband came down from London to see it. After a few drinks, while being shown around, the husband said to my mum, 'It's the best £40,000 you'll ever spend. Now you just need the perfect life to put in it.'

I didn't hear him say it. I was as feral as they come – a miniature hillbilly, bare-chested in dungarees, making bonfires in the back garden, always out in the neighbour's woods or in the garden, where there was a decrepit, ivy-covered munitions hut that, during the Second World War, the old boys of the village had sat in while they polished their rifles, played cards and drank homebrewed cider. The garden was wide and full of wildlife: toads, dog roses, ducks, crab apples, treecreepers, red admirals, woodlice, rats. I would spend all day on my own with the world. I caught the bats that flew into our house and studied them before releasing them again. My small hands were called on by my parents, to pick out dead birds that had flown down the chimney into the stove. On walks down to the river, deer would run past me, so close I could feel the air move between my body and theirs. I wasn't allowed to eat sweets, but no one could stop me sucking nectar from the honeysuckle that blossomed over the old garden wall. In the summer the verges would pulse with the sweet smell of decay from a dead badger, fox or vole. Huge rats the size of small cats started invading the house, and my dad shot one while on the phone to a bank manager and still swears that's what got him the loan we needed.

I knew we were struggling for money; we'd always been struggling for money because, despite having a wonderful life, we always needed to reach for a bit more in order to sustain it. I knew my parents were arguing, they'd always argued, but they were wild – that was part of how they loved each other and how they had loved each other for over thirty years. I thought, *This is our interpretation of a perfect life.*

Things were on the decline, the mood in the house was bad, but when my grandfather died my parents' arguing got worse. There had always been epic parties at the house, but the shouting was no longer jubilant, it was pain-filled and angry. I started smashing things to make the shouting stop. A clock. A glass. One night, I threw a whole packet of eggs at the wall, one after another, to try to get my parents to stop arguing. It didn't work. They had decided to send me to a private secondary school that they couldn't really afford and were often late paying the fees – were chased down for them on many occasions, and the threat that I might have to leave hung over all of us. This was a constant source of argument and something I felt guilty about. I loved the school's wild location but got on with very few of the teachers there and was regarded as trouble, bred of trouble. Excepting a few friends, my parents and I were generally frowned upon by the aspirational and avaricious cohort that populated it. I felt unwelcome and out of place. I started acting up and was assigned a counsellor at school to whom I refused to say a single word – saying anything would have felt like a betrayal of my parents. I knew how this went, I knew that the counsellor wanted me to say how hard things were for me because of our fracturing life at home, and I was never going to give them that because that wasn't how I felt. I was grateful for the life my parents had given me and I guarded them like a dog. The counsellor didn't come back the following week, and for reasons I wasn't party to, I didn't see them again.

I was approaching fifteen when my parents split up, and in just over a year the charmed life vanished. Like magic, the life of privilege and apparent abundance was turned into a life of very little. The house had to be sold, and the people who bought it knocked down the ivy-covered munitions hut. The house was painted cream like every other house in the village. They built a box-like extension that covered the window my grandfather would lean out of. I left our home one day thinking I would come back; I didn't even pay attention to the sound of gravel under the wheels, or the sound of the big wrought-iron gates creaking as I closed them for the last time and got back into the car with Mum. It wasn't real, what was happening; soon, someone would call this farce off. There was a part of me that believed that if fortune could change to such a degree for the worse, then it could change for the better and somehow, through some miracle, we would be able to buy the house back, maybe next year, or the next.

In the meantime, my mum rented a bleak little studio flat above a shop in the nearby town. Despite the sale of the house, my dad only very narrowly avoided having to declare bankruptcy, and after the divorce there was nothing left. My parents now living in respective rooms in Devon and London, with no space for me, they rented me a room in a family friend's attic while I left the school and attended the local community college. Half of the attic room was taken up by my parents' queen-sized bed that I now slept in.

I could see how much my parents were suffering and felt a duty to keep myself together as best I possibly could. It was the least I could do for them and for myself. I was trying to focus on my A levels and was busy telling myself I was fine, because I really wanted to be fine in spite of it all. In a bid to reconcile myself to the new situation I would ask myself questions like 'What would you rather have, the house or your parents?' The answer was obvious; the answer made me feel that I had got lucky when so many people, including good friends of mine, had a home, they might've even had two homes, but had lost a parent. I was very aware that I was fortunate to have mine. They had brought me into a world where I had everything I could have dreamed of, for a while. The situation had simply got out of hand, we were all collateral damage, there was no one thing or one person to blame; we had all contributed to the end, just by existing.

Regardless of what I told myself, the impact of losing the house was catastrophic. Once the shock dissipated and the reality of our new, precarious life started to dawn on me – no childhood bedroom to retreat to when things went wrong, as they invariably would, no bedrooms anywhere in fact; no money, the impossibility of ever recouping our losses, the endless struggle that life had become – I started to get angry about everything we'd lost, until I realised the futility. So I pushed the place I belonged to the back of my mind, where it only escaped in sleep. I still dream of that house – every couple of weeks, at least. The world will be ending and I'll run from wherever I am to find my parents in their bedroom and offer them a bottle of water. Or I'll simply be walking down the blue hall towards the yellow kitchen with all its wood engravings, over the floorboards and past the Pre-Raphaelite print of Proserpine and her pomegranate, to the stove in front of which I used to sleep on the floor with my dog . . . and then I'll wake up and feel disorientated. Now, thirteen years later, I still wake up disorientated, but I would rather that than not dream of it. We can drive past the house as many times as we want, look through the wrought-iron gates and up the drive, over the garden, to our home, but in the end, all the money in the world couldn't buy back what we've lost. And yet, a whiff of silage anywhere and I am home again.

It was towards the end of our time at the house that I recognised that my experience of loneliness is relieved when I am alone; there is symmetry in it. I thought countless times in the intervening years that it must be nice to finally stop trying to belong, to walk away from it all, from them all. I thought that, rather than missing out, there must be something to gain from leaving so much behind. When someone takes things from us that we don't really need to survive, if we look at it another way, they are relieving us of a burden.

In my early twenties I was given a book on alchemy, the art of transmuting matter – typically base metals into gold, but equally the self into the higher, perfect self. The latter transformation was what interested me. Alchemy was practised by solitary men and (particularly impressive) solitary women who sequestered themselves away for years, even decades, as they searched for a cure for the human condition, a way to reunite with the divine while still living. I became fixated on alchemists, and by the time I was imitating the isolated monks painting illuminated manuscripts, which often featured hermits of one form or another, the symbolism of the solitary figure was already extremely powerful to me. In retrospect, my obsessions scream of escapism, but that was all I wanted to do – I wanted to escape. Going out alone into the world didn't seem weird to me; it seemed radical, exciting, an act of defiance, full of the potential for discovery. I admired these people. I wished I had the kind of self-belief, or faith, that the solitary figures I had become fascinated with had – figures encapsulated by Hieronymus Bosch in his painting *The Crucifixion of Saint Wilgefortis*.

Wilgefortis (or Liberata in Italian) was a folk saint who took a vow to live alone, and when she was threatened with marriage by her father she miraculously grew a beard to appear unattractive to her prospective husband, and so her father had her crucified. In Bosch's painting, beside her feet as she dangles from the cross there is a hermit, who sits in front of a city on fire, his expression disappointed but not surprised; then there is the prophet who stands apart from the crowd, pointing to her, as if warning the executioner beside him that there are bad times ahead.

I didn't have the diligence of the alchemist, the courage of the bearded lady, the conviction of the hermit or the foresight of the jabbering prophet, wandering barefoot from the crowd. I had to be left on my own – I had to be physically put on this path to take it.

Now, I'm here. And out here, it seems obvious that it's always been enough for me to be alone, pressed up against the glass of the world, just happy to be looking in. I head further afield, past the sheep, over toadstools, through a gate and down into a wide and wood-bookended valley with a river running through it. It's like walking into a secret garden but on an epic scale. A stream runs from the hill to the right, where there is a still-autumnal spinney, and down into a river, where a darker, older woodland lies. By the stream, under the shelter of the trees, the grass is still covered in frost. Everything glittering.

I stand rooted to the ground, staring. A lightning tree in a field of green. This new life that is unfolding, that I feel as if I am stumbling into after so much praying and wishing and hoping it would happen, it has materialised so suddenly that I can't help but feel that no matter how many times I look over my shoulder to find no one there, something has my back.

4.

Book of Hours

I've started praying for luck. Does that make me religious or superstitious? At night, before I go to sleep, just in case. I don't ask for much – only to wake up. A few years ago I was told that I have a heart murmur, and I've started to think about my heart stopping in the middle of the night. Elephants just die if they get lonely. An elephant stranded or abandoned on its own can't deal with the idea that it might be the only one left, and its heart breaks. Up on this hill, it does feel like I'm the only one left; I sit here like Methuselah, and in the silence I find myself imagining conversations with all the people I've known who have died. Or less conversations and more me telling them things, what I've been up to, like I'm writing postcards from some exotic location and I'm telling them back home what it's like. I say sorry a lot. Sorry for not having got to this point – this realisation of how precious life is – sooner, while they were alive.

There was no frost this morning but I could've guessed that. I fell asleep with the window open and, despite it being January, it wasn't too cold when I woke at 5 a.m.; the air in the barn smelled cool and fresh. It's almost three o'clock now and I've finished most of my writing work for the day and can afford to take a break. Exploring land I'm not sure I'm supposed to be on is what I look forward to most in my days.

I walk down through the fields, to the cold stream and over a small wooden bridge that arches over the winter river. The tall, bare, willowy alder and hazel that bridesmaid the river soon become thick and gnarly oaks covered in silky forklet-moss, ordinary moss, old man's beard, silver-green cartilage lichen and mint-green monkshood. Lichen pulses from the ground and over tree bark and stone. In a moment my surroundings turn to ancient woodland. Soon, the air smells of damp wood, fungus and moss.

Temperate rainforest still exists on Dartmoor as Wistman's Wood, but much of the rest of what was rainforest in Devon and Cornwall is now the bleak, bracken- and heather-scratched moorlands of Dartmoor, Bodmin and Exmoor, cleared by Bronze Age settlers and medieval tin miners. Looking at this dripping, twisted woodland, I feel pretty certain it was once connected to the disappeared rainforests. Part of understanding this landscape, of understanding any living thing, is seeing what's no longer visible.

In 1977, Ralph Whitlock wrote in *The Folklore of Devon*: 'The county, the third largest in England, has as its nucleus the huge, austere, and almost uninhabited massif of Dartmoor, around which the more fertile countryside is arranged as a frame. On the north it is fenced by another bleak plateau of almost equal altitude . . . Another maze of steep-sided hills serves as a barrier between Devon and south Somerset and west Dorset. Nor are the intervening vales flat plains but rather a tangle of lesser hills, many of them buried in woods. It is a secretive, half-tamed countryside.'

I am in the secretive, half-tamed borders of arable farmland on that other 'bleak plateau', Exmoor. This is the land of the exiled and the unwanted – about ten miles from here is the Valley of the Rocks, where the Romantic poets Wordsworth and Coleridge set an unfinished work about the sorrows of exile called *The Wanderings of Cain*. It was also in the Valley of the Rocks that I ran the ultramarathon on a weekend away from London three years ago, in one of my many bids to experience something else, something ecstatic. All this yearning and searching for a breakthrough has led me back to this place. So if nothing else, I figure it is a sign to stay.

I'm back.

Where have I been?

Ostensibly, little has changed in the years that have passed since the marathon: I still don't have a stable form of income, I don't have kids, I have no savings, no property, no husband, no career, no horse, no dog, no piano. I have none of the things I thought I wanted but, in the end, it's the absence of these things that is affording me the freedom to live like this – and not only that, their absence necessitates an alternative way of living. Our connotations of people living alone, particularly with regard to women, are hardly favourable. Fairy tales teach us that women living alone in the woods are evil. Society instructs us that they are sad, lonely and crazy – I was all of those things until very recently, but I'm finding I am none of them now I'm alone. The harassed life I led before this one surely plays a large part in why an isolated life is appealing to me right now. But I know that isn't all there is to it. It goes deeper.

Deeper in the heart of Exmoor, there was another woman who lived alone on the moors. Her name was Hope Bourne. I've heard family friends talk about her before as a kind of mythological figure. Now I'm so close to where she used to be (in many senses) that I find myself picking up the phone, wanting to know more about her, wishing I could better emulate her. I want to know what the sequence of events was that drove her to end up on the moor. Was it like mine? Because she doesn't give much of a clue in her books.

Aged fifty-two, Hope started a new, solitary life – not as a recluse (someone who actively avoids human company), as she was frequently at pains to stress, because she welcomed company and sought it out frequently, but as more of a hermit. Hermits – though they live a reclusive existence that, historically, has often (but not always) been part of religious discipline – are traditionally encouraged to embrace company and conversation when it comes along, despite their often-isolated posts. Bourne was of this ilk rather than an antisocial recluse, but as she despised order in any form I wouldn't want to organise her solitude into a tidy category. To my mind, however, if there ever was a hermit of the woods, it was Hope Bourne.

Hope spent her early years in Hartland on the North Devon coast before moving to the Cotswolds with her mother. Hope's mother then died, leaving a lot of debt, which forced Hope to sell their family home. With no qualifications, no money and nowhere to live, she returned to the county she had known as a child, and after a series of increasingly isolated cottages she moved into a leaky caravan in a valley at the burnt-out Ferny Ball farmstead, surrounded by a small wood in Exmoor National Park. She would live there for twenty-four years.

This was where John Mitchell, a local farmer who now lives in my old village, got to know her. He recalled how he would often be riding in the middle of nowhere and 'Hope would just pop up out of the heather, miles from anywhere'. Because she knew the moors so well, he would leave his children with Hope for the day and she would walk with them for miles, teaching them about all the moorland flora and fauna.

Where Hope lived was remote, but she was never unwelcoming to the friends (and, later, film crews) who visited her, and she frequently paid unexpected visits to others. John says she was 'more sensitive than most people realised. She didn't have a bad atom in her head, she always trusted you until you gave her reason not to.' Before she moved into the caravan at Ferny Ball, it's said that she fell in love with a younger man from the area who ultimately married someone else. It's reported that she sought solace in the wilds of Shetland and then in the nearby village of Withypool while she recovered from the heartache. When she eventually went to live at her caravan she resolved to be emotionally and financially independent.

Hope once wrote that she lived as she did simply to follow a 'natural urge'. Other than this, there is little mention as to what the catalysts were for this new, extreme life. It is only in an unpublished manuscript discovered after her death that there is reference to a 'total breakdown'. While alive, Hope never addressed her heartbreak or any painful events in her past directly, and she never mentioned pain as a motivation for the life she led in her books. Heartbreak is solely an abstract, universal concept in *Wild Harvest*, one of several books she wrote about life on the moors. Heartbreak, she says, is one of the consequences of a lack of imagination, along with environmental destruction. But her words would lead you to believe that she never experienced emotional pain, only physical injury.

John says that she would never talk about her past. He tried on a couple of occasions to find out why she had ended up on the moors, what her life had been like before, whether she was divorced or never married, but she flat out refused to talk about it and made it clear he was not to pry again. To his knowledge, no one knew anything of her life before the moors, though it seemed as if something very painful had happened. One can only guess, but from what little I have experienced already in the barn, I would guess that Hope's extreme way of living helped her find perspective when it came to her emotional pain, whatever that might have been.

Rejection may have led her to the caravan, but without a doubt it was her love of the natural world that made her want to stay there, where fitting in didn't matter. Alone, we are accepted by our surroundings without a moment's hesitation. This is perhaps why I feel a little envious of her. I find myself so hungry for experience all of a sudden, so eager to become of the natural world and connect with it in as authentic a way as possible, but it seems incredibly unlikely that I'll be settling in a caravan in Exmoor National Park anytime soon. It seems unlikely anybody will. And if I'm honest with myself, I don't know if I could live very long without a bath or a shower. I'm not sure I could eat rotting meat and use newspaper for socks, as she did.

Friends have joked that in willingly living alone like this I've become a hermit, and I've laughed along with it. But until very recently I didn't quite see that in many respects I have. It wasn't a sudden realisation but one that materialised gradually, over the last couple of weeks until I thought, *oh God, maybe I* am *turning into a hermit*. If friends hadn't said it, it might not have occurred to me, because the hermit is an archetype and many of us cannot get past the physical appearance of that archetype. The hermit is a thing of the past. The hermit is male. The hermit is old, ancient even – he is Tolstoy's hermit who is 'very old . . . so old that the white of his beard is taking a greenish tinge'. The hermit lives in the woods and is probably still scratching away at a cilice. The hermit doesn't become a hermit by accident. Or this is what we think.

The archetype has never evolved, possibly because we have failed to pay attention to the reality of those who withdraw from society: we do not recognise them unless they are a bearded old man in the woods. So I'll keep looking for those who have withdrawn from society – from early history to the present day – who don't wear the habit or the facial hair in keeping with the archetype of a hermit. Distinct as I might like to think my experience of solitude and how it has come about, I know there will be parallels between my lonely life and the lives of others. There must be, because in seeking solitude in isolation, in willingly maintaining this state, we have all done something deemed slightly unnatural. Why am I really choosing to find comfort here, alone with the wild, rather than in people? What encourages someone to behave like this? Are all loners looking for perspective – to step back far enough that they can see the world clearly and be grateful to be here once more? Can the reasons ever be unpicked, and is there always a reason? Or is this, as it feels to me, a state of being that has been waiting for an opportunity to be? As a woman, I could easily be considered a recluse, but even the word 'recluse' became gendered as we lost its true meaning. Historically, 'recluse' referred to a hermit's isolation from the world once they had jumped ship.

Remote, off-grid living can be emblematic of seeking a very specific Albion of bygone years, where 'foreigners' were mistrusted, the village was your world and girls were pliable and rosy – an Albion that some chase in the futile hope that it can be caught and dragged báck into the present moment. But although prejudice certainly exists here in Devon, not everyone in the countryside was indoctrinated into homophobia, misogyny and racism at Young Farmers' balls. Anyway, I'm not here for that Albion. I'm looking for something beneath the surface. A much older, weirder Britain. Sometimes I think that all people like myself are looking for is the magic that has been snuffed out of us; the ability to see midges glowing in the sun and believe they're deities. These were the things my ancestors believed in, and I have a proclivity for magical thinking running through my veins. Like somewhere, deep in my blood, there is a proclivity to see a ship and will it to wreck.

Just as time passes slower at sea level than it does up in the mountains, time seems to pass at an altogether different rate when you're alone. Here, it's as if I can move within each moment at the rate at which time is really passing – not in minutes or seconds, but at the imperceptible speed at which life really moves most of the time. If the sun didn't rise or sink, my life here could be one long day – long enough, I hope, to start again. For decades, the world was moving so fast I couldn't process what was happening; I could only keep chasing the days that became increasingly rapid and disorientating. Now, Time lumbers over the fortress of hills but doesn't have the momentum to reach the barn.

In the barn's stillness I let in all of my yesterdays, one by one, year by year. Maybe it's all this sitting for hours without distraction, but I'm finding I have better access to my memories – voluntarily and involuntarily. Until recently, life was something to get through, not to savour and remember.

Now I'm experiencing flashbacks, both good and bad; I have been almost daily for the past two weeks. That many moments having been pushed aside was bound to create a backlog. Dreams of our old home are an almost nightly occurrence. If I am grieving anything right now, it seems to be that.

The high ceiling of the barn reminds me of home, and I am starting to see it for what it is – gone. I stare at images of the red house and its wide garden, tall trees and clematis-covered veranda on one of the many estate agents' pamphlets that my mum has kept all these years and still carries in her handbag, out of pride for what we achieved even if we didn't manage to hold on to it. I wonder how that life would have panned out if it hadn't imploded – I wouldn't be here in this barn now, that's for sure. And considering the materialistic tendencies I had as a teenager, I tell myself that if I hadn't had to learn how to live without, I'd have become a spoilt and oblivious adult with an unimaginative dress sense, so it's not all bad.

Sitting in the armchair in the late afternoon, the orange of the sun falls onto my shoulders and onto the page. I look up. In my kitchen is everything I need to survive. I have food – jars refilled with rice, lentils, spaghetti, coffee. I have the kitchen table which is both the table I eat at and the desk at which I work, which has quickly become an altar of twigs, stones, small jawbones, moss and feathers – bits I have collected on my walks. At the end of the table is the mess of my illuminated manuscripts. I'll be the first to admit that they're not very good – they'd never make it into a book of hours, or any illuminated medieval prayer book – but so obsessed was I that, before leaving London, I even held an exhibition of them. Despite being mortally depressed at the time, getting up early to paint them meant I could lose myself for a while in the peace of the city; before anyone else got up, life was gentle. Painting them created moments of escape, and there was the germ of this moment I am living now contained in those quiet hours, when everything was okay in the silence, when I had the space to daydream a different future for myself. That silence is what led me here. A friend said it best when he texted me about my current situation: 'A blessing, no disguise.'

The last month or so has taught me that there are practicalities to living alone like this, and it's going to take me some time to get used to the fact that I have no car, no bus, no ability to transport myself to wherever I might need to be, and there are no shops within walking distance, but I am finding this feeling of powerlessness strangely liberating. My agency is not being impeded any more. I just have the quiet dialogue of a routine that is the result of my free will. To panic over the limitations of my life here would serve its end, and for me that is not an option. So I accept these limitations as a compromise for living here, which is a compromise I am more than happy to make.

In order to survive in comfort, organisation is key. I am spending more time than I ever have devising meals and planning what can be eaten when. I'm learning to preserve things, to eat and cook more sustainably, to dry out chillies, mushrooms and herbs and freeze anything else. Nothing is wasted any more, everything is transformed into something. My mum and I have been arguing for a few years now, almost always about the relationship, so our bimonthly trips to the shops are acting as corrective. On the way back from our last trip she said, 'I wasn't sure last year, but I like you. I'll always love you, but I like you again.'

'What a relief,' I replied. That's what living here feels like, a relief of pressure.

Sometimes, though, be it the weather, that she's away or other circumstances, she isn't able to come, and when that happens I have to go without. Within the first week of being here alone and without a car, I learned to always have something – anything – in the freezer. I'd become accustomed to having a corner shop on every street I lived on for years. If I ran out of something, I just had to pop out and get it. If I fancied something, it was never more than a five- or ten-minute walk away, usually less. But where's the fun in that? Maintaining your own existence in a remote life requires practical self-sufficiency – not necessarily a prepper-style self-sufficiency with a full floor-to-ceiling larder, banquet-ready with pickles and gas masks, but it does require some organisational skills. And relying on myself more is helping me to restore some faith in myself. I have a budget I need to stick to: £25–£30 per week after rent. It's enough.

Whatever happens, I'm going to survive – it's not like I've found myself on the Stampede Trail in Alaska with no food, like Chris McCandless, the American adventurer, nomad and hitch-hiker who had to scavenge what little he could, mostly skinny rabbits and the potentially poisonous berries that were the sole subject of his last diary entry, which just read 'BEAUTIFUL BLUE BERRIES'. I am in a forgiving landscape with supermarkets a couple of days' walk away if I *really* needed to go, and there's a garage a day's walk. I haven't hitched down here for a while, but it remains an option in desperate times and, to me, living without a constant stream of convenience is worth it if it means I can be alone. That is the most important thing to me. I remind myself that as long as I have good health and a roof over my head then I am lucky, but in every other regard I'm not used to a comfortable life any more and I don't think I'd enjoy it. I seem to put myself in intentionally uncomfortable situations – not the ones that seem to come so naturally, like struggling to pay bills or having to set aside the money to buy superglue to put my boots back together, but rather the uncomfortable situations that lift my mind from these things, that transport me away from the day-to-day discomforts. I've wanted a break-through for so long, tried so many often-destructive ways of achieving it, and already I know that being alone out here will get me closer to it than anything else. The land will not try to shake me off like a burden, and I know beyond a doubt that I want to stay here. I know this will prove to be a rare opportunity to discover what I believe based on what the earth makes evident, to see and appreciate life at its most fundamental and allow that to influence how I think and how I feel.

Some people thrive on company. I don't.

5.

A Fire Was in My Head

The weather's been boisterous this week. The last few nights I've lain awake listening to the orchestra of telephone lines that run down the road opposite, howling and moaning in the wind like some damned symphony. It's brought a frisson of excitement to my evenings. Otherwise, excitement is derived from my dwindling food supplies. Lunch is defrosted toast with a fried egg, sunny-side-down, and tomato ketchup. It's surprisingly delicious and will become a Barn Classic. While I eat alone at the kitchen table that's long enough to seat eight, I stare out of the window at the hills, like un-crested waves, and want to transport myself there. I've turned the radio on for the first time in a long time and I'm finding it distracting. I turn the radio off. The quiet is restorative after all that noise.

I meant to look at the planets aligning last night but I fell asleep too early again. I'm a little disappointed, it was supposed to be *an event* in my otherwise eventless evenings, but at least I was awake early enough this morning to see the blue mist coming over the hills. Now I can hear the calls of the gulls that come from the coast in search of ploughed fields, between the chirping sparrows that are making a nest in the extractor fan. The morning mist has dissipated. The sky is threatening but I wrap up and head outside, marching up through the fields, thinking of work, of life, of this and that and on and on, until I find, after about an hour, that the thoughts have all dissolved and I have reached the highest point on the horizon seen from the kitchen window. I am among the trees that fringe the hills now.

From the brow of a hill, I can see the white giants of wind turbines a few miles to the west running, running, running. The wind today is big and old; it doesn't snap back and forward in direction, it's slow to turn and schleps on one way forever, in harmony with the rocks and trees and all things slow and old. Today, it is a wet westerly wind, and it heaves to the east as I wipe dew from the grass across my forehead and then open the neck of my jumper and wipe some on my chest. The places that have been hurt the most. I steal more dew and draw it along my forehead again to cool the fire. Embers now. Fading. Nothing to fuel it any more. It's a strange, unthinking reaction that I must've picked up from wandering into churches and dipping my fingers into whatever liquid was lying around, in the hope of experiencing salvation by osmosis. This is at once a blessing and an initiation; in order for the land to absorb me, I must first absorb it.

Moody clouds have slunk quietly over me while I've been standing, dazed; but the light remains laser-bright over the wind turbines that turn turn turn, and as rain begins to fall I resist the urge to pull up my hood and head home. I leave my hood down and turn my face up into the clouds. *Come and get me.* I've done this before in London, but could never quite get the notion of acid rain out of my mind and, even in a state of despair, had enough self-preservation to cover my head with a newspaper. Here, I will the rain to fall on me. The cloud consumes me until I am drenched, and then, within a few minutes, the downpour is nothing more than a few drops, and the air is silent in its new wet jacket until a blackbird sings from the blackthorn in jubilation for the passing cloud. The wind blows and the rain clouds move on to some other lonesome soul.

Like the megaliths in front of me, I feel charged, buzzing like I'm walking on a ley line. The well in our old garden was supposedly built on a ley line that went from the thirteenth-century church to another village well, just down a muddy lane from us. In King's Nympton, the village I grew up in, there were still people who talked about ley lines without scepticism; people had talked about these energy lines long before they were given a name in 1921 by Alfred Watkins, and long before they could be considered pseudoscience. Before ley lines had names, they were felt: currents of energy running like straight rivers across the entire world, often between ancient monuments of great consequence as well as many, like our garden well, of little. The old boys in the village could never accept that my name was Jade, not Jane, but they could accept much grander, more mysterious things, and I answered to both names, anyway.

The village was an inaccessible and isolated place for thousands of years, until the car. Some who lived there when I was young still didn't have a car; they would wait for the bus once a week to go to the market town. There were still old West Country boys who'd rarely left the county in all their long lives; men and women who lacked so much experience on one hand, but on the other had immersed themselves completely in the land around them – they were the specialists of this particular area. That there was good energy and bad energy in the land didn't need to be proved or quantified, it was felt; it was all around us and always had been. I was told about the lines as if they were a matter of fact. The earth has lines of energy; water can be found with a dowsing rod made from willow; if you run out of petrol, you piss in the tank. I accepted these beliefs as completely as a litmus test.

I follow the hedgerow, ushered by black plastic – once used to wrap silage – that's caught in the blackthorn, looking for a moment like a hunched highwayman emerging from the thicket of the past. As I walk through the soaked grass and feel the damp seep in through my boots, whether or not I'm walking on a ley line I feel like I've been plugged into something. Turned on. Tuned in. The simple pleasures of a quiet life are proving quite profound: in order to truly feel one thing, maybe sometimes we must feel another first. 'The deeper that sorrow carves into your being,' Kahlil Gibran wrote, 'the more joy you can contain.' I don't know about more joy, but certainly more gratitude.

As if to compensate for a sudden dearth of drama in the rest of my life, my dreams are becoming increasingly vivid and dramatic. I've been dreaming about our old house a little less these past few weeks and have started having nightmares: that I'm trapped in a room with him and have to escape without making him angry, have to be nice, keep smiling and nodding, terrified he will turn on me with that look before I can find a way to slip out and run. I dream he arrives unannounced and catches me off guard, wanting to see my phone, and keeps asking for a passcode I don't know. Or I'll be closing the front door behind me, and he'll appear, wedging his arm between the door and the frame, trying to force his way in – I guess the subconscious isn't always hard to read. The dreams never take place here but in dream versions of London flats, and, God, am I relieved to wake up alone here, to nothing but a bird or the sound of rain or sheep outside. I don't think I'll ever tire of that.

In his silence, I fear him, or rather I fear his anger. That's what I fear in my dreams – not him, but his anger. I fear an unexpected visit to the barn from the anger. I still fear a phone call from the anger, or a sudden influx of messages, but there's only silence. I've had notifications of him booking holidays using our shared Airbnb account, but I've turned those off now. I don't want to know. I want to let something that's been trapped in me rise like a bubble in a spirit measure. Enthusiasm . . . I remember this feeling. The more time passes, the more horrified I am by how hopeless my life got, and I worry that this optimism I've started feeling will prove to be temporary. Will the Bad Times find me again and escort me back to the hole?

When I hear other people talking about having suicidal thoughts I always assume they must have been more serious than the thoughts I had, that they were more earnest in their determination to end their lives. Was I suicidal when I walked in front of that bus? Was I suicidal when I contemplated the easiest ways of ending my life? Or when I wondered how I could get past the horror of throwing myself in front of a train? Or when I looked at the ground from his balcony and wished I had the courage to hit it, but instead threw my phone and watched it smash? Was I suicidal when I lay in the empty country roads after being screamed at on the phone for the sixth or seventh time that day, red hands covered in bleach from cleaning and knuckles aching from changing bunk beds, waiting for a car I knew was never coming? Was I suicidal? I have no idea. I do know that I was not sincere in my thoughts or my actions. How do you end a life when the world remains so beautiful in spite of your pain? I wanted the life I was living to end but I did not want to have to die to end it, and yet all signs kept pointing in that direction.

To be here, alive, is as much of a miracle as I should ever need, and I must always remember that from now on. But as I think back on it all, I'm frustrated by the lack of pragmatism I displayed when we both needed it most: if he did not end it, then I had a responsibility to end it, for good, and I can't seem to absolve myself of the fact that I did not live up to my responsibility. I can't help but feel angry at myself for being a part of it getting so out of control, for being so out of control, for doing the same thing over and over again and hoping for a different result. I don't think I should absolve myself, not yet. A guy I used to work with, who was not renowned for being the sharpest tool in the box, said to me once, after I'd returned to the relationship again, 'You're a smart girl, Jade, but you make bad decisions, and you make them all the time.'

He was right. But just by making the decision to stay out here in the barn, I feel like I have begun a conscious effort to make decisions that are not self-destructive. And one of the first steps in taking better care of myself is to accept every instance in which I have not done so and to learn from it. I work through the years in the safety of the barn, while the hills fend off the march of time.

The future is finding me, even here. The hedgerows are speared with the stems and leaves of daffodils, their yellow buds still hidden under green hoods. The new leaves of wild primrose, thick like a toad, promise the blossom of their flowers before too long. The snowdrops are in full bloom, white helmets bowed like melancholy knights, still lining the banks despite coming out a little early this year – there were snowdrops at Christmas. A cow parsley is flowering already, the only one for as far as I can see. It feels like I'm seeing a lot all of a sudden. On my own, it's like something dark has been peeled from my vision. And it's not only my perception; my behaviour changed the instant I was left alone here. I am no longer violent towards myself, probably for the very simple reason that there is nothing here encouraging that kind of self-destructive behaviour any more. I'm finally allowing myself to let my guard down, I feel at home for the first time in almost fifteen years and I'm sure this is part of the reason I now find myself identifying with the hermit. Yes, a hermit is an outsider, but a hermit is also intrinsically connected to home, to a place of safety and shelter, be that a cave or a house or a shed or a cell. That's all I have been looking for, above and beyond everything else. To be able to close the door on the world and everyone in it and withdraw into the sanctuary of somewhere, anywhere, that's out of harm's way. It's true that, as with many who crave isolation, I have come to distrust society at all its levels. I've wanted to get the hell away from it.

Retreating from society and seeking social and geographical isolation can be linked to a number of psychological factors such as post-traumatic stress disorder, social anxiety disorder, apathy, autism, depression, obsessive-compulsive disorder, narcissism, intellectual disability, schizoid personality disorder, schizotypal personality disorder and avoidant personality disorder. I may be isolating myself due to unresolved trauma or performing what is known as 'ego-syntonic behaviour', which means I enact thoughts, wishes and impulses that pose no threat to my battered ego. Self-isolation is common in mental health disorders – we're protecting ourselves from more pain. But it can also be true that living and working in large towns and cities results in overstimulation for many of us, which itself can manifest as disorder. Most likely in my case, it is a combination of both ego-syntonic behaviour and overstimulation. For many people, living alone makes these problems worse; but for me, isolation in nature is proving to be a balm.

Over a hundred years before the development of attention restoration theory (ART) – which proposes that time spent in the natural world can positively affect our ability to concentrate and reflect – the morality fanatic, nature lover and revolutionary art critic John Ruskin advised artists to let go of themselves while in the natural world: 'They should go to nature in all singleness of heart, and walk with her laboriously and trustingly, having no other thought but how best to penetrate her meaning; rejecting nothing, selecting nothing, and scorning nothing.' There is comfort to be found in the knowledge that the natural world isn't asking us to think or feel a certain way; the natural world asks that we stop judging. It is what it is. It has been this way forever. Listen to that crow, isn't it as if you have been listening to it for a hundred years?

Studies such as one published by the *European Journal of Public Health* in 2010 suggest that health, including mental health, is on average better in rural areas, but most studies are quick to remind us that 'rural' has many definitions and that all definitions have their fair share of problems. Suicide rates in males living in rural areas still remain higher than for their urban counterparts, partly because they are the group least likely to seek support. There are numerous contributing factors to poor mental health in rural areas, such as lack of transport, high alcohol consumption, a difficulty accessing refuges for those suffering domestic abuse, low employment rates, poor housing, a general stigma surrounding mental health issues, poor internet service, health providers in rural areas being less likely to recognise mental illnesses, fuel poverty, a breakdown of close-knit community support, and poor access to health-related services. Clearly, a walk in nature is not a panacea, but its effect on your state of mind shouldn't be overlooked either.

Intuitively, the act of walking gives me the sensation that I'm not bound to my problems – I'm not stuck, literally or metaphorically. The natural elements I walk through also engage my attention in an effortless manner ('soft fascination'), allowing my mind to rest what is known as its 'directed attention system' – attention that requires focus. A study approved by the Stanford University Human Subjects Committee found that time in nature had a positive effect on rumination, a common factor among those of us who suffer from anxiety or depression. But just because you live in a rural area does not necessarily mean you are going for long walks in the countryside. An equally important clarification is that if I have a problem, a fear or a worry that I am ruminating on prior to a walk, it doesn't disappear when I get home, but I might just feel a little more hopeful.

> 'I went out to the hazel wood
> Because a fire was in my head,'

> W. B. Yeats wrote.

On this walk, I find a ram's skull by the river, complete with big horns and a spinal cord not too far away, but further away than seems natural. I want to bring the skull back with me, but after staring at it for a while I decide I should return with a bag to collect it, for fear the farmer sees me and thinks I'm a bog witch. I wouldn't want to blow my cover.

Moving through this landscape full of bones, shaped by people it shrugged off hundreds of years ago, makes apparent the 'biophilia hypothesis', which posits something that we have long been in denial about: we humans are animals, and we have an innate tendency to seek out the natural world. We come from the earth and therefore, rather unsurprisingly, we have a connection to it. Denying that connection is akin to self-harm. We are interlinked with the environment, and to such a great extent that, without it, not only can our physical health suffer, our mental health can collapse too.

Our brains were wired in the millennia we spent in the forests, jungles, savannahs and mountains. We've only lived in cities in the numbers we do now for a few hundred years, and some of us just can't adjust. Yet so many of us are removed from nature, or it is forcibly removed from us. In many parts of towns and cities, nature is considered a luxury – statistically, the poorer the neighbourhood, the fewer the trees. So we find new ways of coping in order to adapt and survive. At night, we watch nature documentaries about Siberian flying squirrels, macaques and elephant shrews. Watching nature, or 'technological nature', is supposed to be as good for you as being in nature. Violent incidents among inmates of a maximum-security prison were found to decrease when they watched nature documentaries. The inmates otherwise had no access to nature save for looking at the sky. I watched a documentary about desert falconers the other night, and one man said, 'To feel safe, a falcon must have her face to the wind.' I know how she feels.

*

The wind clears a gloomy late morning and the sunlight seems brighter in the sky for the clouds that still populate it. The trees are roaring, and above them all a wood pigeon flies so much higher than the other birds, higher than the starlings that glance the fields, higher than the rooks that chase the resident buzzard from their roost. All the way up, shoulder to shoulder with the clouds, is the wood pigeon, rising and dipping in the air with an occasional clap of its wings. Spring is in the air it flies through, and the tan rump of a rabbit is shuffling into the undergrowth across from the stream. The hour is fast approaching for the arrival of its mythological lookalike, the March hare.

Very, very rarely have I seen hares. Only at dawn out of the window, and once coming out of the hedgerow at dusk to vanish in a gasp of tall, thick grass. It is with good reason that it is the elusive hare you must find in every scene in Kit Williams's *Masquerade*. Throughout Devon, in the churches you may find an image, like a secret code: three hares leaping after each other in a circular formation. They are known as the 'Tinners' Rabbits' (although they are generally believed to be hares), and are so named because of the Dartmoor tin miners who adopted the symbol as an emblem– it is supposed that the miners used the Tinners' Rabbits as a sign of their patronage of a church, although the roots of the three hares are much older. Tinners' Rabbits garnish Devonian medieval churches, but the symbol itself is pre-Christian and is thought to be a riff on the triskele, a solar symbol of Neolithic Celtic origin comprising three spirals. Pagan Celts believed that hares were divine, a symbol of immortality and resurrection, and that time was circular rather than linear: creation was without beginning or end. 'I am the beginning of eternity,' Jack Hare says in *Masquerade*. 'I follow you round and round / You follow me round and round.'

From the migrations of the geese that I've started to hear honking over the roof, to the lambs that are taking the place of sheep lost to the unforgiving winter, second chances appear as simple as the wind changing direction. When things started going wrong at home, like a lot of children I started running away. Never far – into the woods, down to the river, into the fields. I found out later that a man in the village often looked out onto his field and asked his wife, 'Who's that girl in the field?'

It's a fair question, and I get the feeling that people still wonder, but the question should have been: 'Why is that girl in the field?'

I was in the field because there it felt like all around me was a universe in a constant state of renewal, and emerging from the field back into the world at home there was always the promise that it could have changed while I was away.

In many respects I've run away again, and it does feel as if I'm experiencing either a regression or a recurrence, I can't decide; but reinstating this connection with the wild feels very important to some fundamental part of me. There are plenty of problems that I can't run away from, even if the one I ran away with has left. Exorcising these concerns in my journal helps to tether them to something tangible, if only the page, and playing on my mind at the moment is my employability, or unemployability. Partly out of fear of debt, partly unconvinced I had what it took to be a scientist, I have no undergraduate degree because I made the life-changing decision in a Tesco car park to drop out of my marine biology degree just before it began, and at twenty-nine I'm beginning to realise that I'm not actually qualified to do anything except producing, and I wonder how qualified I really am to do that. What if I lose this writing job, what will I do? Without a car I no longer even have the option of cleaning to support myself.

Leafing back through the pages of my journal, I'm noticing coincidences that at the time passed me by – or, over time, have emerged to become significant. There's a note I made a few months ago that I don't remember writing, which says, 'It's how you say goodbye, not when or why.' This has proven very significant. My dad has always encouraged me to observe synchronicity, meaningful coincidence, for no other reason than it's interesting. I found it strange that, in a place with so many opportunities for coincidence, synchronicity happened to me so rarely in London. But I realise now that my life there was without meaning, and therefore without meaningful coincidence, because I was no longer sensitive to what was going on around me.

If I died in my sleep, would I be glad of my life?

No.

When you have a panic attack, a flood of adrenaline makes you feel detached from your body, something that is known as 'derealisation'. They say panic attacks typically last between five and twenty minutes, but it's as if I have been experiencing derealisation for years. I practised detachment from reality for so long that I forgot there was an alternative. I was not here. I was not there. I chose both fight and flight. Feet on the ground, head in the clouds. So, to be fully present, even for one moment, feels like the achievement of a lifetime. It can be the achievement of many lifetimes.

Where the rush grass grows in the breastbone of the valley, there's a pool where a clear stream runs between the hill and the river, filled with the black eyes of frogspawn. The persistent frost will kill this first batch, but there'll be more. A noise comes from the trees on the brow of the hillock opposite, and there's a flash of green as a woodpecker flies away. I'd forgotten until now there was a woodpecker in my dream last night. That's weird, I think – what does it mean? I've recently given up religiously reading horoscopes because I felt like I was clinging on to their forecasts a little too tightly; however, I seem to be replacing horoscopes with a sort of wildlife equivalent. I google what woodpeckers are believed to signify. Apparently, in some ancient cultures, they symbolise prosperity, luck and spiritual healing. In other cultures the woodpecker represents hard work, perseverance, strength and determination. Neither sounds as ominous as the last horoscope I read. I take note:

– Heal spiritually
– Work hard

These kinds of coincidences seem to come when the mind is present but in a relaxed state of non-thought, and this is a mental state – one of soft fascination – that time spent in the natural world tends to cultivate. Like the dimpsy hours between night and day, or day and night, synchronicity makes the walls of reality feel as if they are at their thinnest. These intermediary times were when I would venture out on expeditions with my dad that evolved into something we called 'owl hunts', as we saw a lot of owls. On Saturdays, having driven down to Devon from London the night before, he would get up between 4 and 5 a.m., depending on the time of year, to wake me. He'd then make as much coffee as would fit in his thermos and we would climb into his ancient sky-blue Mercedes estate. If it was a frosty morning, he would boil a kettle and pour it over the windscreen while I watched from inside, as ice ferns melted into the trees of our garden and condensation from the hot water mixed with the early morning mist.

We would drive for miles and watch nocturnal animals in their last procession before camouflaging themselves from the day. Deer, hares, barn owls, tawny owls, rabbits, moths, pheasants, bats, foxes, quail. Sometimes we could even lure Mum from the warmth of her bed to join us.

To see these creatures there had to be no one else around; if someone had come before us, the animals would vanish. We had to be there at just the right moment: the right place at the right time. Owl hunts were also one of very few instances where money didn't factor; other than the petrol put in the car, the experience was free. There was never any tension on the owl hunts, because where we were demanded our attention; there was no opportunity for minds to be elsewhere, worrying. They reminded us to retain a sense of wonder in the midst of everything else that was going on.

We were never bored of where we lived. We were willing to get lost in the same place over and over again because it was always different. Now I'm willing to get lost in the same place over and over again because, alone out here, looking at the earth anew like I'm a visiting alien, I realise what a meaningful coincidence it all is.

In the woods I sit looking down onto the valley and the older, thicker woods opposite, the sun sinking in the sky, its light still holding on to winter. In the last few months, the sky has become a light show more impressive to me than anything even Metallica could orchestrate. I am stunned by sunrise, sunset and nightfall, when clouds as thick as vape smoke pass over the moon that shines down like a flashlight. I'm being investigated by heaven and the moon is counting my dues – I didn't realise there would be so many to pay. I have finally woken up to the fact that some choices are irrevocable; you don't get to go back sometimes. I've been forced out of denial and into the necessary realisation that you only get one life, so how will you spend it?

Like this. This will be fine.

Even if the reason I'm staying out here is because my ego is protecting itself from further damage, what's the harm in that? This is a good life. The tree I lean on does not mind that I have made mistakes; that I have been running with my eyes closed for years of my life. *Rest now*, it whispers. *Lie on the ground and let the grit seep in. Let your mind sink into the mud, let the wind offer promises no man can keep, let the sun fall on you. Let it all in.*

6.

Lambing Season

I can hear the sparrows in the extractor fan. The sheep baaing in the top field. It's a calm early evening through which great tits, starlings and blue tits cruise. The air smells of sun. Lambs have started arriving en masse; more appear in the field each morning, shadowing their mothers and springing towards each other, then springing back to the ewes and rowdily headbutting them and sucking their teats. Spring is bringing noise with it; lambing season's a busy time and I can hear the rumble of the tractors and quad bikes down on the farm before first light. I was awake long before them this morning. I feel like I've been awake for years; I should have moss in my hair but it's only mid-morning.

Only yesterday, it seems, there was frost and bare branches, and now everything around me has started up again. There's summer in the sun that's beating down on the ground. It arrived one moment unannounced, and its rays are sweetening the air with chlorophyll rising from the land; there's a shimmer between the green and the blue. The hedgerows have come to life with blackthorn flowers and hawthorn buds, stitchwort, buttercups, dandelions, wild garlic, and the purple flowers and liver-spotted leaves of lungwort. Bluebells of the English and Spanish varieties burst out in clusters under the trees. All around is sweet. Sweet like the smell of decay that has begun rising from the verges of expired shrews and wood pigeons. Sweet with life and sweet with death.

The rain that ran in rivulets down the narrow roads leading from the barn to the fields where the woods lie has dried up, leaving a darker shade of grey alongside the verge, as if the water has been fossilised. Things rustle beside me. Everything has its eyes wide open, like a collective alarm clock has gone off, alerting us to something we are yet to see. Compared to the clean lambs, the sheep now look impractical in their oily winter coats, shaggy as fistfuls of wool fall off when they rub on the stone walls, waiting to be shorn. Suddenly, the slow worm, newt and flea are kings of the grass. The second batch of frogspawn is now frogs. There is the odd eggshell and chick skeleton.

Spring brings with it a white light, like the light of dawn. The light of a lack of oxygen to the brain. A vibrancy that saturates all living things. Aphids glisten. Grasshoppers raise their legs to their lace wings. All is glitter and transparency, all is new in its body and yet to take on the solidity of age. Every mark on my skin is in a spotlight, every scar, bruise and stretch mark, every spot and line, is in high definition; there are more fine lines this year. All this transformation is reminding me that time is still passing, despite my dormant existence, and I'm not sure I want it to. I want to freeze this point in my life – for once, I don't want anything to change. Can't we just stop for a minute? Can't everything stop morphing into something else so I can catch my breath? *No, it can't, but thanks for asking, we value your question. Please press 'star' to return to main menu.*

The evening wears on, the wind picks up and a spring storm arrives in a flash. I hold my hand out of the window from the comfort of a fire-lit room. Less than an hour ago, the sun was on the fields in which a handful of flyblown violets kneel before the dandelion. But the sun has disappeared from view, and only a few wounds of blue remain uncovered by the huge dark clouds that have arrived and veil the early evening stars. The storm tonight has brought hail, and with it an urge to feel the ice hit my skin. I hold my hand out until it starts to sting and is mottled red and white. The monk who created champagne said on first taste that it was like drinking the stars. My hand fizzes as if I have touched them.

The women in my family have a history of remaining alone after the breakdown of a long-term relationship. My great-aunt lived most of her life alone, 'married to nursing' as my dad puts it. After my parents got divorced my mum refused to even consider being with anyone else ever again. Thirteen years later, still wearing her wedding ring to swerve the septuagenarians, she stands by that – 'I don't want to spend the last years of my life changing some old bloke's nappy!' I assume my life is taking the same course, albeit a little earlier than anticipated. Being single seems to be in my DNA and I'm content in this state; I'm getting to know how to just *be* again without trying to please somebody else, anybody else. If I end up like Hope Bourne, then at least I'll know I've lived. I'd be very lucky to end up like Hope Bourne, I think. So I'm going to make the best of this. My Luddite tendencies mean I've never been on any dating apps, and now hardly seems like the time to sign up to Tinder and see who, if anyone, is within a three-, four- or even fifteen-mile radius to match with.

The power goes out. I light candles in the dark, listening to the pouring hail, and think how, if we all had less 'going on' in our lives, a storm like this would be a big event, and that maybe this is how dull life should be in order that we appreciate hail or rain on the roof enough to want to sleep under it. With very little else going on in my life, this storm *is* a big event – and I receive it like I would a romantic gesture. I look outside to see if the power is out all across the valley, and it is. But what I notice are the stars, thousands of them. Millions. The half-moon lights up the night and I can even see the silhouettes of the hills in front of me. The moon is vanished by a cloud. I leave the window open and lie back on the sagging floral sofa that swallows me in its ancient springs, cover myself in a blanket and fall asleep to the scattered sound of hail as it fades on the slate roof. I have started to sleep up here on the sofa every night, by the fire, under the beams. The bedroom feels modern and the light is cold. This room was where it all began, and where the life of the place still vibrates. Every day, from the sofa, I wander bleary-eyed early in the morning and start work at the kitchen table. It might be a little weird, but I like it. Living alone, spending any time over a couple of weeks alone, is very different to having a weekend away from everything on your own, or even a week – some wouldn't want to do that. I have developed a love of solitude in the long term.

The newfound silence of my life is broken by a car arriving. It hadn't occurred to me that the way I was living was in any way extreme until a friend drives down from London to stay, and on arrival screeches, 'You can't live like this! You cannot live alone out here like this without a car!' She looks wildly around the barn, at my small figure in it, and then out to the wide fields. This seems to confirm matters for her, as she spins back round to me, shrieking, 'You just can't. You'll die! You have to come back to London. You're coming back with me.'

I don't want to go back to London. I feel like I've only just escaped it. She shakes her head as if listening to a lunatic and lists about twenty reasons why I have to go back with her. I won't remember any of them – except that I don't have a car, and that I am alone. The day fades into dusk, and then night drops on us like a cloak.

My friend watches me leaning out the window, blowing smoke into the black. 'Don't you get scared, at night? Alone?'

Nope. I've always found that it's people you should fear, not whatever else is *out there*. Walking around a woodland at dusk can be eerie, creepy even, but somewhere where there are no humans is never scary, and there are never any humans out there in the woods. At one point in time there might've been wolves, but now there is nothing. I appreciate that at first this can be as unsettling as the alternative.

The next morning, despite my warnings, my friend lets her dog off the leash. It lumbers straight out into one of the fields where there are still-pregnant sheep. The farmer comes out and shouts over the fence, threatening to shoot the dog. I'm afraid that, for me, this is an expected consequence. She, however, is horrified. I understand it from the farmer's side – the dog could easily kill both the ewes and the lambs they now carry, just by chasing them, and that's his livelihood.

My poor friend leaves completely traumatised by the whole experience and will not return. Which is to say, this kind of life is not for everyone. When she came to visit me here, she likely viewed it as a break, a retreat from her frenetic, everyday life. She would not want to live here – that would be crazy – but for her it is a getaway from the city, and in the time away from it my friend not only got an education in the country code but a new perspective on her life back home.

In Thomas Malory's *Le Morte d'Arthur*, a fifteenth-century

reworking of Arthurian legends, there exists both the hermit of religion and the hermit of the woods; both act as literal and spiritual guides – their distance from the civilised world gives them an objectivity on life it is otherwise hard to achieve. The hermits of legend are a shelter from the storm, guidance for the next step of the journey, purveyors of wisdom. I can hardly say my friend regards me as a purveyor of wisdom – but, living in what other people see as a bolthole, perhaps the provider of a little shelter. And for myself, states of both isolation and contact are required to find a healthy equilibrium. I have learned never to treat anything as dogma – not isolation, not anything. The tree that does not bend with wind will break.

As nourishing as it was to have my friend stay with me in the barn, I'm happy to be in my own company once more. Solitude has become a craving, one that extends to technology – I don't want to be alone yet also on the phone all the time. Tonight, I have turned my phone off. The laptop is shut. I'm logged out of everything. No one can get to me here. I've started turning my phone off with increasing regularity, for days, sometimes a week at a time. I say to others that it's to work and I do find it easier to concentrate, but I also feel safe within the membrane of the present moment. I no longer need to stay in touch, and people's concern for me out here has decreased, as it always does; they check in at longer intervals and I make only sporadic attempts at communication. Now I can understand the temptation to get rid of it all – every app, every device. I am leaning hard into the temptation to go rogue.

In 1969, Michael Collins was given the title of 'the loneliest man in the universe'. Collins was one of the three astronauts who took part in the Apollo 11 mission that landed on the moon. Unlike Neil Armstrong and Buzz Aldrin, who would beam their infamous words back from the lunar Tranquility Base, Collins never walked on the moon. He never even set foot on it. Instead, he manned the command module that was orbiting the moon sixty miles above its surface, utterly alone. He was the reason they all made it back. While in front of the moon he could remain in contact with Mission Control down in Houston, but when he travelled behind it, he was completely cut off from humanity, unable to communicate with the Earth or his colleagues. But the label of 'loneliness' was thrust upon him. Interviewed by NPR in 2016, Collins said, 'The fact that I was . . . out of communications, rather than that being a fear, that was a joy because I got Mission Control to shut up for a little while. Every once in a while.'

Collins was alone in the command module for a relatively short period of time, just under twenty-two hours. Although his experience of being incommunicado is very different from what most of us will encounter in our lives, you can't get much more out of touch than Collins was, and he found it was nothing to fear.

The signal and the internet might be bad here – and frequently non-existent – but I'm in North Devon, not the dark side of the moon, and the ability to communicate is never far away. I still exist in a society where we are increasingly present without ever really being there. Connection pulses through our night skies in an organised queue of luminous orbs called Starlink. Even in cities, when only Sirius or Mars might be visible through the haze and the light pollution, Starlink's procession of more than 2,700 glowing satellites is visible. Starlink was launched by Elon Musk's SpaceX project as a new, all-encompassing internet service. Soon, this constellation will have many thousands more false stars, like a glittering necklace around the earth, or connection as a stranglehold.

One of the major transformations I've noticed here in Devon is that I have much more energy when I do finally see people in real life. And so, to conserve that energy, I don't want to be contactable every hour of the day. I don't want to be expected to reply to a message within a certain timeframe, but neither do I want to lose the people I love. I am aware that there is a bare minimum I must do in order to tend to the relationships that mean something to me, so I aim for just above that.

Author and silence seeker Sara Maitland built a hermitage on the moors of Galloway in Scotland in her quest to live in silence, and she has lived there for fifteen years. When I talk to Sara about the conflict of balancing the desire to be alone and maintaining important relationships she tells me, 'It is *always* complicated, and it always depends on both sides of the relationship . . . I have obligations of love.' She has spent decades in almost total silence, but with some of her family now living in America, in order to be a grandmother at that distance Sara recently made a compromise in her quest and decided to get a phone with WhatsApp capabilities. 'It's absolutely wonderful because my grandchild now kisses me when she sees me on the screen.'

Aloneness has changed completely because of modern technology and cars. But sometimes, even now, things happen that serve as a reminder of how remote living would have been without communication at such easy reach. When Sara and I were first going to speak, we couldn't because the phone line outside her house had broken. 'I suddenly realised I am more than a mile from my next-door neighbour,' she says. 'It's too much when you're over seventy.' Sadly, Sara will soon have to leave her beloved hermitage due to deteriorating health conditions. Without a car, I have realised how far a mile really is. Routine journeys that might take half an hour in a car are pretty much unthinkable on foot.

On my own and using my phone less, I am learning to trust my own judgement a little more. Most of the time this involves encouraging myself to believe that I have a shot at a good life now. 'I think you learn a certain kind of emotional discipline alone,' Sara tells me. 'But it suits some people better than it suits others. My sister said if she had to live a week in my house she'd kill herself – not quite literally, but she's never been alone for more than three or four hours in her whole life.'

Contrary to what we might assume, communication and connection have always been important facets of being a hermit. The hermit's hospitality, the lending of their ear, was meant to be unconditional for travellers, pilgrims and knight-errants. The hermit rejected society, not the individual.

Surely no two hermits communicated with one another as fervently as Herbert of Derwentwater and Cuthbert of Lindisfarne. Herbert lived on an island – now named after him – in Derwentwater lake in Cumbria. He was a priest, confessor and possibly not the greatest laugh on the planet, his main aim being 'to avoid the intercourse of man, and that nothing might withdraw his attention from unceasing mortification and prayer'.

However, he did not avoid the intercourse of all men entirely. The contemporaneous account of the Venerable Bede tells us that, every year, Herbert would visit his best friend Cuthbert, with whom he had 'a long time been in union . . . in the bond of spiritual love and friendship'. Bede describes one of their meetings in the historical northern town of Lugublia, where Cuthbert foretold his own death, saying, 'Remember, brother, Herberte, that whatsoever ye have to say and ask of me, you do it now, for after we depart hence, we shall not meet again, and see one another corporally in this world; for I know well the time of my dissolution is at hand, and the laying aside of this earthly tabernacle draweth on apace.'

Herbert was heartbroken. He fell down on his knees in front of Cuthbert and beseeched God to let him die on the same day as his friend. After much praying and beseeching, so the story goes, their souls did depart the earth on the same day. A mobile phone seems rather pitiful compared to a direct line to God.

After a period of silence, we are more attentive to what people are actually saying; we are more invested. Without feeling constantly bombarded, we have the time and space to be interested. And when we talk (or type) less, we are more mindful of the words we use. But with modern technology and the constant background hum of our digital connection with one another, is it even possible to be a hermit in the twenty-first century when we're never *really* alone?

There is now a wikiHow on how to become a hermit. *Hey, guys! Follow these simple steps to achieve spiritual emancipation . . .* The listicle suggests that you should welcome human contact as a hermit but that you must immediately delete all social media accounts. This is because we still imagine that hermits are a thing of the past, or that you must pretend that you are a thing of the past in order to become one – and for some that's part of the appeal.

Mauro Morandi obviously didn't get the memo. He was dubbed 'Italy's Robinson Crusoe' after washing up on an uninhabited

Italian island of pink sand called Budelli, off the coast of Sicily. He continued to live there as caretaker of the island for thirty-two years and built up a large social media following – particularly on Instagram where, in his eighties, he had almost 80,000 followers with whom he shared vignettes of his solitary life.

Technology is an expression of humanity, and a tool through which humanity expresses itself. Despite its dark side and the trolls that lurk there, to turn one's back on the digital world completely seems like a failure to understand society as it is now – as appealing as I admit that might be a lot of the time. Although connection in general is associated with increased mental well-being, studies show, almost consistently, that the more online we are, the more unbalanced we become in real life. Picking and choosing what, and how much, works for the individual is a modern-day art form, but do you think that if Herbert could have WhatsApped Cuthbert he wouldn't have, because he was a hermit? I doubt it. Whether Cuthbert would have wanted to receive the communication is another matter.

The day has been mild but the mist sinks into the valley as night draws in. Above the high hedges and the mist, some-times all you can make out is the tips of the wind turbines whirling like the legs of synchronised swimmers. It is at this time of day that the woodland is at its best, when the crooked branches are duplicated by their long shadows on the ground and the woods take on an eeriness that makes my skin crawl in the most pleasurable way. The stillness always catches me off guard and I will never tire of turning, in a moment of fear, to find nothing but tree and stone behind me. The oak and the ash have new leaves, waving next to buds curled tight as a fist. Dew collects on the mint-ice-cream-green oakmoss. The river runs cool and black. Tall, thick grass sags pearlescent in the evening's moisture. I have been drawn here since the day I arrived: into the woods, always into the woods. These trees have been my guardians, my night watchmen, my stewards, shepherding me safely to the next step of my journey. I've realised that we don't spend enough time with ancient trees. They offer wisdom you have to turn your mind off to receive.

This is how I've liked it, seeing only the occasional car and the land that we live upon; the fields and the woods to the left and the right of the country lane are always empty, save for the sheep in the top field. I have never seen another person in them – I've only seen the farmer that time he shouted at my friend. It's almost as if I willed every human being within a ten-mile radius out of my experience. Here, somewhere north of Blackmoor Gate, is a very niche glitch in the matrix. Or maybe the matrix, like the super-fast broadband, never made it this far.

I get back to the barn as the sun smashes like an orange squeezed across the dark hills behind. As the last of its light leaks from the sky, I walk up the stairs into the big kitchen-living room and turn on a light. I run the tap and put some water on to boil spaghetti; it's always spaghetti for dinner. While I wait for it to boil, I send a text. Just to let whoever know that, in my world, they are still a force in its rotation. I am lighting a beacon on the hills. This is the best I can do with artificial light.

I'll be leaving these hills soon. I don't want to leave, I could stare out of the kitchen window forever, but I can't afford the increased rent on my own and it will increase every year.

Everything is signalling that the end of my stay here has come. The clock has stopped telling the time. Two of the lamps have broken. And yesterday, the houseplants started to wilt. For now it seems my fears about both my phone and my home being invaded are unfounded; the ghost in the machine breathes only to send a two-line text instructing me to pack up his stuff and his dad will come and pick it up. One friend says I should burn his stuff. Another tells me not to pack it up, to leave it to him. But I do pack it all up because I don't want any more bad blood between us. We have enough for a lifetime already, and it did us no good. I must not think or act or speak out of fear any more, but equally there are some things I just don't need to put myself through. I will go out for a very, very long walk the day his dad comes to pick up his stuff.

Leaving houses is second nature for anyone who's lived in London; it certainly has been for me, I've been leaving houses for as long as I can remember. It's best not to allow myself to become too connected to a place for this reason, but my connection to the barn runs deeper than the building, the connection I am feeling is to the land that surrounds it and there is plenty of that for miles around. Leaving was always inevitable; good things don't last but, instead, different things begin. Leaving is also encouraging a realisation that, in many ways, being left here has been the greatest gift anyone's ever given me, or that I've accepted it as such. Either way, I'm grateful. He did the right thing in the end, and I feel lucky for the first time in a long time, so I accept my imminent departure with a shrug. The old, salty wind that blasts the drystone walls is calling; my attention is moving west, out towards the sea. I am heading where all storms begin.

Croyde

7.

The Witching Hour

It's a quiet dusk on the beach; the air is unusually still and the waves break gently, cautiously, on the horizon, as if they know something is coming and do not want to anger it. The tide is way out, a mile out, and rip currents have left the sand snakeskinned in patterns that wind their way up the beach until they reach the loose dry area near the dunes, where the marram grass grows. Cloud covers the setting sun, white as a moon. Over by the headland, bats pass through the half-light, catching midges and caddisflies in their dance to the death. There's no one else on the beach, which is particularly disorientating if you've ever seen it here in the summer, when it is crammed with bodies as close together as butterfly eggs on the underside of a leaf. There are no surfers out in the lulled waters.

The light changes from grey to purple as I walk out, way out to where the waves break, pianissimo. My boots splashing through pockets of sea water in the sand. A film of mist is forming, coming in off the sea; the stealthy waves like a reconnaissance team checking out the land that sits heavy and drowsy, off guard. I keep walking out. The sky is getting darker but I have nowhere else to be. No one is waiting for me to come home. I can stay out past when someone would start to worry, and play chicken with the waves, if only I could reach them.

I don't remember seeing the tide this far out here before. Perhaps a few miles up, at Putsborough, where we used to spend whole summers on the long beach, where I played with dead jellyfish when the tide was low, my mother sitting in front of the pink house with binoculars, 'keeping an eye out for paedophiles'. But I've not seen the sea this far out here, and soon there is nothing to see.

The mist that rolled in on the water has wrapped around me as a thick blanket of fog. Swaddling my limbs and my vision. The light is strange, un-invested in the land it should illuminate and unwilling to put up a fight against the fog. All around me I see nothing but the sand that radiates from my feet and the fog around my head. I can barely hear the waves, though I keep walking towards them. I should probably go home, and if there were someone waiting for me I probably would. But there isn't. The weather is my company, and I ask it to reveal the cause of its confusion. It lies somewhere out in deep ocean, between green water and grey skies.

I look back towards the dunes and see nothing. I look for a marker, some kind of identifier of where I am – the black rocks that flank the beach, the lime kiln, the cliffs, the smattering of houses, nothing. Nothing but sand and fog. I don't allow myself to become disorientated. I know the path; muscle memory has drawn a map on the soles of my feet. I know the way home.

Out here, like this, I could be vulnerable to attack, if anyone could find me, if anyone were out here, but they're not. When the weather's bad, people tend not to leave their cars or their houses if they don't need to for work or to walk the dog; they've seen it all before, and the tourists are yet to come. All I have to fear is what my mind can conjure, and right now it says only to stay and enjoy the thrill. Enjoy not being able to see my way home. Enjoy being a little scared. Enjoy the taste of the thick air on my tongue, sweet like honeysuckle mixed with nothing. Take me to the waves that break.

The tide is coming in now and I have reached the waves that roll so innocently over my boots, licking them with their salt-water tongue – they belie the rip currents that still kill people every year. An Olympic athlete whose holiday home I clean rescued a grandfather and grandson from drowning not long ago. Many more have died trying to rescue ones they love, and the loves of others. The tide comes in fast; I have to take a few steps back. The fog refuses to pass and the purple light begins to dwindle. Soon it will not matter that I cannot see further than this circle of sand, my protective barrier, drawn around me like a magic circle by the mist. The earth protects me from all advances. It draws boundary lines around me and no one who is not worthy will enter them again. Solitude does that to you; you suddenly find your self-worth in your back pocket, and once you've found it you wonder why the hell you let so many people in.

I head back through the fog, the light almost gone from a sky no longer purple but the deep dark grey of a storm cloud, though there is no rain, no thunder, just the muted air. My hair is wet. I can see nothing but travel with my mind's eye, trust myself and the instincts that have got me this far. I march blind through the loose sand until I hit the little stone bridge where the river runs that, as kids, we used to push each other into, saying it was raw sewage. (I'm now pretty sure it wasn't.) As I reach the grass, the fog dissipates almost immediately and a rabbit's white tail darts across the dark field. I walk towards the row of stunted cedar trees, still bent in supplication before the absent wind, their creaking black silhouettes from a land before time. It is the witching hour, and no one is around.

When I had to leave the barn, I was unable to find anywhere I could convince an estate agent I could afford on my own; despite rents being comparatively cheap down here and having never missed a rental payment in my life, my income is so low that they want a guarantor, and that's not an option. When the estate agents proved difficult, I thought of 'the hut'. The hut is a green hut on the headland above Croyde and Saunton, built by my great-grandfather so his family could spend time together there, and for his wife, Lucy, who was dying of cancer, so she could breathe clean air and take in the expansive views. The hut was a well-built but primitive construction in its day, made by the carpenters who worked at the Shapland and Petter furniture factory in Barnstaple and built on a gentlemen's agreement with the major landowners of the time, who are still the major landowners now.

In sepia photos of the hut my family beams from the past, full of hope and new prosperity in the 1920s, laughing in the wind, my grandmother, the youngest, always looking like she's up to something. It was a sanctuary for the family. When my great-grandfather died, things became slightly more complicated. While my grandmother was still alive, my parents went up and stayed at the hut a lot, as did family friends, but then she died when I was three and after a while a male cousin took control. Slowly, we were all shouldered out of it. But I'd heard stories about that place my whole life, I stared up at it from beaches in my earliest memories. I wasn't going to let go of what little we had quite so easily. When I was a teen I would go up there and sit outside on summer afternoons, skin cracked and red and salty after a day at the beach. One day I broke in and stayed there. The bed was covered in dead bluebottles and the warmth of a summer night.

I'm not as bold as I used to be. So when the cousin moved to Portugal, never visited and struggled with the ground rent, instead of breaking in again I set about trying to offer to pay it. To make use of the hut, to live there, to write there would have been a dream, primitive as the place is. I tried getting in touch with the landowning family but could never get further than their receptionist. My cousin was a brick wall. Things fell apart – quite literally in the case of the hut.

I now live about a hundred metres below the hut in a little seventeenth-century cottage in Croyde. It was somewhere I cleaned regularly when it was a holiday cottage. Somewhere I could never have afforded to live, were it not for the kindness of the woman who found me over her toilet bowl and was willing to accept what rent I could afford. 'You just need a platform,' she told me, as if she could see how far down the hole I was. 'Some basic stability and you'll be fine, my girl.'

Croyde in the summer is crammed with tourists, thousands upon thousands. There's a farmer we get veg from, he grows some of the best asparagus around because of the sandy ground on his farm. He doesn't live more than two miles from the sea, less than five from Croyde, and yet he hasn't been to the beach once in thirty years. 'Not worth it,' he shrugs.

In Croyde, the property prices are the same as in London, and in recent years a multitude of vibeless glass boxes have been granted planning permission in this seaside village that was once just bungalows and thatched cottages. The more people want a slice of it, the less desirable it becomes. But in the winter, the few hundred people who actually live here crawl out of the woodwork. The surge in second homes means fewer and fewer people live here all year round. In the winter, the small chocolate-box village rammed to the gunnels is a ghost town.

It's an early spring morning and the violence of new life looms in the air. The energy required by all the living things around me to create new leaves, new eggs, new nests, seems to have wiped me out. I wake up at five, open my eyes, roll over and go back to sleep.

It's after nine and the sun is up. The world has woken without me watching, which always makes me feel a little sad. But the curtains are open and they lift a little in the breeze, the lead-latticed window is ajar and I can see the neighbour's fig tree leaves creeping over the wall, large and splayed and looking for some shame to hide. There are two bedrooms in this cottage. The larger one with a double bed faces the tiny road that winds through the village, and that's more noise than I've been accustomed to recently, so I've moved into the single room overlooking the pea-size garden. There is the song of two blackbirds, sweet and bumpy like whortleberry jam. They are busy making a nest and I have been quietly observing them at it for a couple of weeks now. It seems like hard work. The female is backwards and forwards all day with sticks and moss. In and out of the shrub in the corner of the garden from dawn to dusk, to create a safe home for the two or three clutches of bright blue speckled eggs they will rear to fledglings this year. Occasionally they sit together, taking a breath on the garden bench I can see as I write.

The spring wind lifts the curtains higher as it blows in through the window, and I can hear someone mowing a lawn somewhere in the distance. It's a sunny day, the blue sky streaked with cirrus clouds. I'm missing the immediate views of the barn, but at the same time I know what is around the corner. A two-minute walk and I can see the beach. A five-minute walk and I am on it. Summer is coming over the hill – still a long way off but materialising slowly, like the leaves still curled in their buds under the rays of the sun.

This will be a very different form of isolation from the one I have just experienced. Here, there is a bus that runs twice a day. There are houses all around me. In the summer it will be bustling with people. I will cut myself off and, most days, hide. Unknown and unwanted, that's how I want to remain. Every day, I endeavour to remain the village secret. A local woman-iser who is friends with people I grew up with works in one of the ice cream shops in the village, and I frequently try so hard to pretend not to see him that I've tripped over the opposite pavement several times.

The cottage is by the gateway into the heart of the village, and I feel like I've transformed from hermit in the woods to a latter-day anchoress – a bad anchoress. In the thirteenth century, anchorites were all the rage at town and city gates. Unlike other solitaries, who were under no obligation to remain in the same spot and were free to adopt a life of rootless wandering if they chose to, anchorites and anchoresses – though usually placed under the umbrella term of 'hermit' – were men and women who withdrew from secular society to lead a strict ascetic, reclusive life of intense prayer while locked in a single cell, reliant on others for food and water and unable to leave. In London there were anchorite cells at Temple Bar, Aldgate, Cripplegate and Bishopsgate. These hermits would be confined to their cell sometimes for decades; no walks to the headland for a proper anchoress. Upon arrival in your cell as a novice recluse you were greeted with the sound of a choir singing the refrain 'In paradisum deducant te angeli', and also with such a thoughtful gift as a ready-dug grave, which you had to then clamber into and be sprinkled with earth. This ceremony was standard practice. Anchoresses outnumbered anchorites three-to-one in these cells. We don't know the reasons many of these women lived as anchoresses; some may have been forced into this life, but I imagine many gave themselves up willingly, just to retire and rest from it all, and for a chance to read and learn in peace. After all, this is what Julian of Norwich, perhaps the most famous anchoress, did.

Julian volunteered herself for a life of reclusion, and the revelations that followed she shared with the world. Most of these revelations were relatively hopeful. That she had a very progressive attitude towards sin, believing it to be 'behovely' or necessary, is an example of what the historian Janina Ramirez describes as Julian's 'cosmic' view of existence. But there is a sorry line that sticks out among her revelations: 'This place is pryson, and this lyfe is pennannce.' It's believed that, rather than referencing her cell, she is here talking about the earth as a prison and mortal life as penance, before the reward of death, and heaven.

Her famous line – 'All shall be well and all shall be well and all manner of thing shall be well' – I first saw on my sister's crockery. I thought it was the most beautiful thing I'd ever read and wondered who on earth this potter was. I discovered it was a quote from T. S. Eliot's *Four Quartets*. It was only much later, alone in a crowd at a reading of *Four Quartets* in Southwark Cathedral, that I found out that these words were, in fact, first written by Julian of Norwich, dictated to her by a vision of Jesus. Then I had a horrible thought: what if it was an incantation, something to repeat to oneself over and over as you rock in your cell? Despite the risk of bubonic plague that the outside world tended to carry, it still seems strange to believe in a god who would create all this, create you, and then ask you to hide away from it all. That's not my god. At night I walk out of my cell and into space. Above me, all around me in the cottage's tiny garden, is a carnival of blue-white stars in a blue-black sky, the galaxy spinning like a Catherine wheel as I smoke. I hear the palm trees next door rustling and see the black hands of the fig leaves bobbing in the breeze, and I wonder what more you could possibly expect from heaven.

That anchoresses consistently outnumbered anchorites is reflective of the choices society made available to women at the time. Although we have infinitely more freedom now, like any restrictive societal framework, gender norms can lead us to withdraw from society in order to live and conduct ourselves outside of certain expectations. However, once we've left, or withdrawn, our solitude is still viewed differently by the society we have departed, depending on our gender – particularly if we exist outside of religious frameworks.

Female solitude has been viewed throughout history as something transgressive, partly for our own safety – it has always been more dangerous for a woman to live alone than a man, because we are more vulnerable to what men, and supposedly the Devil, can do – but also because stigma has been one of the best ways of keeping tabs on us. Our state of mind in solitude is viewed differently based on gender: if a man is out seeking solitude, this is often thought to be the result of, or in the pursuit of, wisdom; if a woman is out seeking solitude she is probably crazy, or has been shunned by others for her (bad) behaviour.

As Coby Dowdell writes in the essay collection *Cultures of Solitude: Loneliness – Limitation – Liberation*: 'Crucially, while the male hermit's backstory invariably hinges on the hermit's critique of societal flaws, the female hermit's backstory consistently turns inward to judge the woman's behaviour against conventional gender norms.' This tends to be true of all solitary women in some form of isolation, of young women, of old women, of trans women, and indeed anyone who is considered by the outside world to have the appearance of being feminine (identifying as non-binary is a little more complicated in this instance; unless people are informed of our identity they will usually make their own judgements based on stereotypes and how they think we appear). Because the association has to do with what the feminine represents – temptation.

Historically, a woman either married and fell into an often-reclusive life of domesticity, or she did not, and instead eventually fell, through a series of morally corrupt incidents, into oblivion and died alone. Referencing the Marquise de Lambert's 1749 novella *The Fair Solitary; or, Female Hermit* (*La femme hermite*), Dowdell writes, 'As a fallen woman bereft of viable options for the future, the "fair solitary" is sentenced to physical banishment by a society governed by double standards of sexual propriety.' Not much has changed. This tends to be the assumed character arc – sin, then reclusion – that women who exist removed from society are to have experienced. This arc overlooks a life event universal to both sexes, something that has prompted many a man and woman to seek solitude: men tend to have 'moments of enlightenment', women tend to have 'breakdowns'. Whatever you want to call it, the results are typically the same: they opt out.

The idea that women go off to experience solitude in isolation in order to atone for their mortal sins and purify their shame is exemplified by one of the earliest female hermits, namely Mary of Egypt. Her *Vita*, written by Saint Sophronius, states that she was so full of carnal lust that she often refused the money offered for her sexual favours, as she was driven 'by an insatiable and an irrepressible passion'. To supplement this passion, she lived by begging and spinning flax. What we can surmise from Mary's biographer is that she was essentially a nymphomaniac. According to Sophronius, having had a good day's flax-spinning, Mary went on something akin to an anti-pilgrimage. She travelled to Jerusalem for a feast where, rather than enjoying some state-sanctioned worship and food, she went to find thousands of people to sleep with, and handily her journey there would be paid for by the pilgrims to whom she gave sexual favours along the way.

The deciding factor for Mary leaving the civilised world was an unseen force barring her from entering a church. She immediately realised this was because of her libidinous tendencies: the Virgin Mary was frowning upon her. She was being shunned. She prayed for forgiveness, promised to renounce the world and all its pleasures, and the Virgin Mary let her enter the church. Mary of Egypt then went off to the desert, taking with her only three loaves of bread, and she spent so much time out in the wild that, like Jesus, she learned to walk on water – which, in a desert, is a miracle unto itself. When she was eventually discovered by Zosimas, to whom she first recounted her tale, her whole body was covered in golden hair.

Obviously, the veracity of these reports is unknown. What is known is that Mary lived a life and then she left it. But hers has become the narrative with which women who leave society are often associated, however unconsciously, because, much like the stories told to children such as 'Rebecca, Who Slammed Doors for Fun and Perished Miserably', it has been of benefit to those in charge to find parallels with this cautionary tale. No matter how badly society treats us, leaving it has to look worse, because how do you keep civilisation ticking over if the women keep running from it? If the connotations of women and solitude go back to Mary of Egypt, they also go back even further – further than Mary Magdalene, living in a cave as a hermit three hundred years earlier; further back than the oldest king.

The sky has clouded over as the day has worn on. I put on my coat and my boots, leave the cottage and head out of the village. I'm out on the headland where white sea campion will be flowering soon. Opposite is the small bay of Croyde, with its marram grass dunes and the fields behind. Directly across from me is a formation of black rocks, and above those, when the tide is out, is the South West Coast Path. Up past pink thrift, dune pansies and water germander, where later in the year there will be evening primrose and sea stock. Past the big white houses, behind which are more rugged fields filled with Hebridean sheep and Red Ruby Devon cattle the colour of rusting saws. Up past the farm, up a little further to Baggy Point – a spit of land that swings into the sea, with sharp rocks rising from it like stalagmites – and then, out to freedom, where Lundy, the remote three-mile-long island, sits.

The weather changes quickly on the coast, and the cloud that had formed is burned through and blown away within half an hour of my being outside. Today, I am heading to a small pocket of coves, where the rocks are black and cracked like crocodile backs and the cliffs are small and nestle into one another. I call the place 'Crystal Bay' because down in the sand, in a shingle belt between the muddy cliff and the black rocks, are bits of quartz of varying quality – some perfect crystal, some more dirty-white formations. Croyde isn't far from the Sticklepath fault line that runs from Wales, through Lundy, and straight through North to South Devon, and these hydrothermal veins of rock crystal – often found in slate, shale and granite here – were likely created by the cooling of granitic magmas. Quartz is one of the hardest rocks; it is the clarity that remains when everything else has eroded away.

Bedfellows of the quartz will be blue mussel shells, cockles, limpets, flat periwinkles, the right arm of a Montagu's crab, and the otherworldly pink, gold, purple and opalescent white of baby oyster shells. There's a few wetsuited surfers in the water. A woman walks her dog on the sand, making the most of the time left before dogs are banned from the beach in May for the summer season. Otherwise, the place is empty.

Beachcombing is becoming my primary hobby. On the main beach will be mermaid's purses, kelp, bladderwrack, dog whelk and the odd herring gull feather. If it's been a stormy night, the sea throws back all our trash onto the shore – millions of little plastic beads, beer-can holders, netting, polystyrene takeaway containers, plastic toys. It's coming back to haunt us. I'm not going to the main beach today though, I'm staying at Crystal Bay. The sun dapples the water, implying a warmth I know the ocean does not yet have. I pocket the shining oyster shells and bits of quartz I've found, and walk over the black crocodile backs to where they meet the sea. There's a welt in one of them, smooth compared to its jagged back, and the tide is coming in. I touch the water with my fingers and then plunge my hand in, unable to resist prodding the beadlet anemone on the rocks. I can hear barnacles crackling like popping candy in the sun. I take off my big boots, take off my socks and dip my toes into the cool water. No part of me is anywhere else, my thoughts are all with my toes in the water. I am not trying to block anything out. I am here and only here. I momentarily forget all that has happened to me, and it is as if all that has happened forgets me too.

Over the years, I found that it didn't matter what I dismantled. Someone – be it a company or an individual – was always going to want to keep me down. That's how society functions, for the most part. The only way I was going to succeed was to succeed on my own terms, to not have someone in my business all the time, scrutinising and prematurely judging every move I made before the effect of that move had even been actualised.

I remember listening to the girls in my English class at college with plans for their lives – gap year, no gap year, university, become a teacher, married at twenty-five; maybe, in a tragic, spinster scenario, married at twenty-eight, also children at twenty-eight, preferably; children at thirty, worst-case scenario. To be fair, we were all under the impression that becoming a 'teen pregnancy' was so likely it would be a miracle if we were still childless by twenty, in which case the girls' plans were actually quite radical. But my mum didn't have me until she was forty. Maybe that's part of the reason why I sat there uncomfortably in my denim jacket, on the back of which I'd painted 'Fuck World War III' (I'm not entirely sure who I thought was pro World War III), saying maybe thirty, or maybe thirty-five, but not really meaning it because I didn't know what I wanted to do. As far as we'd been informed, you didn't study English to become a better writer, you studied English at university to become a teacher, and I didn't want to be a teacher, I'd hardly got on with very many of them.

I had no direction and no guidance during these years, and I resented the lack of those things when life in London was tough, because it was easier than holding myself accountable for the direction I, alone, had chosen. But that lack of direction led me here, and here I am glad of my life. Here, with my toes in the water, I find I have very little baggage, despite living a life that has gifted me some choice impedimenta. I will never have very much baggage, as long as there is no one carrying it around for me, telling me I forgot it, reminding me I should feel sad or bad about it all. No, thank you! Done that. Now I know what I want to do with my life, if that's only to enjoy living it. To the outside world, I am a broke nobody. But season after season, this nobody stays and watches the sun go down over the sea until the sky starts to blur into darkness, and then the bats come out and sweep the sandy cliffs.

8.

Evict the Goddess of the Deep

I come up here a lot, to sit by the hut on the jut of coastal farm-land behind where I'm renting now. The green hut is a landmark from beach-level. It's a little worse for wear now, although it's still standing after a hundred years when a lot of other things aren't. Despite my best efforts, I've made no progress with my cousin, who has ignored my offers to pay the arrears for the outstanding peppercorn ground rent – what I now pay a month for the cottage (which is very cheap) is what this place costs a year. It doesn't look as if I'll be living here anytime soon. Still, none of this stops me from enjoying sitting outside the hut where my family has sat for a century, and looking out into the afternoon. Out over what was rugged, isolated coastland and onto what is now rugged million-pound-property land. Beyond the land is the sea and beyond the sea is Lundy, the tiny island that I fix my eyes on whenever I am outside; it is the dot on the horizon where my attention always rests, distracting me even from the sun. I look out to the island today, but it's hiding behind a curtain of haze. Today, as is often the case, it does not exist.

It's a beautiful early summer's day and the hours loll out in front of me. I sit outside all evening as if I'm waiting for some-thing or someone to appear. The farmer did last time I was up here, but today nothing and no one does. All that happens is my love for the place deepens, which I'm not sure is what I want as it seems like the closer I get to the hut in reality, the further away it becomes in practice.

Tolstoy's short story 'How Much Land Does a Man Need?' is a parable about a man called Pakhom who greedily acquires more and more land, yet is never satisfied, even when he has more land than he could have dreamed of originally. Towards the end, a stranger offers as much land as Pakhom can stake out. He walks, marking out more and more and more territory, until he dies from exhaustion. 'That's a lot of land you've earned yourself,' the Devil says, looking down at his corpse. The Devil was the stranger all along.

Rather than being a symbol of affluence and avarice, many believe a patch of land should be, and is, your due. A rooftop garden or an allotment at the least for those who live in flats – just because it's not practically possible at the moment doesn't mean that we, as a society, shouldn't be striving for that. There's nothing wrong with people wanting enough land to sustain themselves and their family or commune – land on which to live and grow fruit, vegetables, livestock – if that's what they want. That's what I want. It's a fundamental desire. The problem comes when we start treating nature as a mere backdrop to our lives; when we own much more land than we could ever use and more houses than we need.

The Devonians and the Cornish were once part of the Dumnonii tribe of Dumnonia (from Domnu, the name of the goddess of the deep). Devon and Cornwall were the same country, and for a long time they remained that way, if not by law, then in spirit. Today, we share a police force – and a lot of the same problems. Devon and Cornwall, like many rural regions, are deprived areas that rely heavily on the seasonal tourist economy. Devon workers are among the lowest-paid in the UK according to HMRC, and the wages in Cornwall are even lower. From Cornwall and Devon, all the way up the country to the Hebrides, there are thousands of people living in rural, remote and deprived areas who are being made homeless unnecessarily.

When Henry David Thoreau went to his friend Ralph Waldo Emerson's woods in Massachusetts with the ambition of living as a hermit and writing his memoir, *Walden*, he had plenty of money but chose to build a secluded cabin in nature. His situation came about from a well-meaning desire rather than desperation. But what of the people who do it out of financial and emotional necessity, because they feel it is their only option?

The ecologist, writer and self-professed 'part-time hermit' Anne LaBastille built a cabin near Twitchell Lake in the Adirondack Mountains, New York, in the mid-1960s after her divorce. Although her love of nature was a driving force, financial pressures also played a part in her decision-making in this lifelong adventure. 'I felt that the creation of a rustic cabin would be the solution to my homelessness,' she explained. Critics of LaBastille called her 'escapism' bourgeois and middle-class, but for around $500 she built a cabin and obtained all the required permits she needed to settle there, existing frugally and in harmony with the land around her. Taking inflation into account, it didn't cost her much more than it had cost Thoreau a hundred-odd years earlier – and unlike Thoreau, who didn't need permits, cut down the surrounding trees to make his cabin, and was supported by friends and family, LaBastille bought all the materials to make her cabin and was self-reliant.

In recent years, the opportunity for a hermit, recluse, or anyone who wants to live alone has shrunk dramatically. As rents and house prices have continued to rise in correlation with the staycation and second-home property boom in rural areas – where there is typically a shortage of social and afford-able housing, and incomes remain low – it becomes increas-ingly hard to find somewhere for which you can afford the rent or the mortgage, particularly if there's only one of you. Skint loners like myself certainly can't afford to live alone in the city, and now many can't afford to live alone in rural areas either – and the remote countryside was kind of our last hope. I need not live in this particular place; it could be anywhere rural. People like myself are just asking for a roof over our heads in places where hardly anyone wants to live for half the year. For millennia, this has been the basic life of those who don't ask for anything more. But now there are giants in the room.

Where small clifftop homes once stood there are now glass houses the size of community colleges, and these have changed how the area here is perceived. Squint and it could be Malibu. One particular multimillion-pound holiday home along the stretch of coastland between Saunton and Croyde reminds me of how Joan Didion described Ronald Reagan's unfinished California pad: 'a monument not to colossal ego but to a weird absence of ego, a case study in the architecture of limited possibilities . . . as devoid of personality or personal eccentricity as the lobby area in a Ramada Inn'. This glass house can be rented out for £1,000 per night, with a minimum stay of a week.

A few doors down there is the music executive's decade-long folly that was made famous on *Grand Designs*. At the time of writing, the construction panels are still up, meaning that should anyone who actually lives here walk or drive past hoping to see the wide expanse of the sea that has been their neighbour all their lives, they are instead confronted with white panels and cranes left standing at unimaginable expense for years. The property is currently for sale for £10 million. Proportionality has become an alien concept here. I wonder when the people who own these multimillion-pound houses and only spend a few days or weeks here last pressed their heads onto a cold rock and muttered a prayer for the land. Touched the bole of a tree and thanked it. Considered how they could help stop this careering train from going off the rails.

Devon thrives on tourism, it needs tourism; without it, the county would be even poorer. Even in the 1970s Hope Bourne was complaining of holiday homes in Devon in *Wild Harvest* – how she lived near one that sat empty for eleven months of the year. But the industry that is holiday homes is complex, and although Hope might not have liked to admit it, it is not without its benefits for the people who live here year-round – after all, I'm living in one. Many (though not all) of the people selling high and renting high in rural areas have been relatively poor for most of their lives, and now they're just making hay while the sun shines. While cleaning, I've also seen how people here rent their houses out in the summer and live in an annexe or a caravan up the field. It's a livelihood. Holiday cottages supply a livelihood to cleaners and income to local laundry services, pubs, shops and restaurants. However, the staff have to be able to afford to live in a house down here in order to provide the service. We have to start thinking more carefully about how our actions affect one another, and their repercussions for the landscape. To this end, we must find means of enjoying the natural world sustainably. Yet I am dubious as to whether 'ecotourism' is the answer.

Ecotourism has been happening for decades, but in recent years the fashion has accelerated at light speed, and no one epitomises the human cost of this more than Mauro Morandi. When Morandi washed up on the unpopulated island of Budelli after fishing in his catamaran, he became a hermit, in love with the place and living about as symbiotically with his environment as is humanly possible. He was the only person to live on the island – which people were prohibited from walking on except for a dedicated path – from 1989 up until 2021. In 2021 Morandi was evicted by the Italian government so that Budelli could become an ecotourist destination. Explaining why Morandi could not be allowed to live on the island, the president of the national park said, '[Morandi] symbolizes a man, enchanted by the elements, who decides to devote his life to contemplation and custody . . . No one ignores [his] role in representing the historical memory of the place . . . But it's hard to find a contractual arrangement for a person in his position.' Today, you can't just build a hut on the land, you can't simply wash up on an island, you have to sign a lot of paperwork first.

Ecotourism has also arrived in North Devon. Its county border sign states: 'World Class by Nature'. After most of the Venn Quarry was shut down last century, the site was flooded and has been enjoyed by generations of people who live here, largely from the communities of Bishop's Tawton and Landkey, communities that would have been employed at the quarry when it was active. In 2016 the local council granted planning permission for an 'eco-tourism development' with 158 lodges and a forty-bedroom hotel. Signs were swiftly erected stating that the site was now for the sole use of the 'holiday community'.

'Free to those who can afford it, very expensive to those
who can't.'

Withnail and I

Over the last century, financial pressures have been major factors in people becoming hermits in the cheapest places they can
find – people like Hope Bourne, Anne LaBastille and the hermit
of Hampstead, also known as Harry the Hermit.

Harry Hallowes was originally from Ireland. In the 1950s he
moved to London, but through a series of unfortunate events
he became homeless in 1986, which is when he found the woods
of Hampstead Heath more gentle than the streets. He made
himself a den and lived on a half-acre plot. By the time property developers tried to evict him in 2007, he was able to claim
squatter's rights and continue his life there until he died in
2016, aged either seventy-nine or eighty. By then, he had lived
as a hermit in the woods of Hampstead Heath for thirty years.

He became the subject of a rom-com starring Diane Keaton
as Emily Walters, who falls for the character Donald Horner
(inspired by Hallowes the hermit). Shortly before the film's
release and a year after Hallowes's death, the *Sun* – in charac-
teristically enlightened language – called 'tramp' Hallowes's
home 'the most expensive hovel in Britain'. Hallowes's slice of
land was sold at auction for £154,000, and the proceeds went
to the homeless charities Shelter and Centrepoint. Not a bad
legacy for a 'tramp'.

The hermits of old tended not to be born into lives of poverty.
They rarely went to live in the wild because that was the only
place that would admit them. Rather, hermits often first

relinquished their worldly possessions and gave up their riches to the poor in a great display of purification, like the Italian brother hermit-saints Severinus of Sanseverino (d. 550 CE) and Victorinus of Camerino (d. 543 CE), who, having given up their riches and gone into the wild, were partial to self-mortification and tying themselves up on nearby trees in as painful a fashion as possible. Then there was Saint Francis of Paola (1416–1507), who lived in a cave on his father's vast estate, and the female hermit Amma Syncletica of Alexandria (c.270–c.350 CE), known as the 'Desert Mother' after the Desert Fathers – early Christian hermits who lived an ascetic life in the Egyptian desert.

Amma came from a very wealthy background but gave her inheritance to the poor and left with her blind sister to live in a crypt in the desert. She nimbly attained the enlightenment she had been after since childhood through the living of this hermitic life, would go on to be highly influential in the writings of asceticism, and amassed a squad of devoted female followers. However, many of these followers, she decided, were not up to 'the rigorous discipline of poverty'.

What Amma may have overlooked is that it's one thing to voluntarily relinquish something you have, having enjoyed it. To have luxury and give it up does, in some ways, just feel like another display of wealth. Why do we revere those who have given up wealth and comfort, when very few people show respect to those who have always lived without? It's a very different thing to have had a choice.

I mistake a white fleck of a gull for the sickle moon. Over the way are the big grey waves. The sea remains fierce and will take this land, bit by bit. But for now a coral-pink sun is setting somewhere over Lundy, through a band of grey cloud, and the whole sky is pumped full of altocumulus. The odd brown moth flits between the yellow bird's-foot trefoil, and a lovely herring gull finds its way home, back to its roost of the cliffs and dunes where the rest of its family cries. A large ship is sailing towards the island. I watch it drift out of my field of vision and pick thistle flowers and throw them into the wind, thanking the sea for this year, for having somewhere like this to live.

Many who choose to live in remote locations do so not only because it is the only place that makes them feel alive but also because it is the only place they can afford to live. My biggest fear is that soon we won't be able to live in isolation unless we can pay a hefty price. That we will be denied the ability to live unchained on the earth that is our birthright. That the wild will be meted out in quotas, like everything else.

That's why I'm still fighting for the green hut. That's why I've hired an adventurous locksmith to drive his van with thousands of jangling keys over the clifftop fields and change the locks on the hut. When I look inside for the first time in years I see almost nothing's changed; it's just as it was when I stayed the night here all those years ago, except I notice an old newspaper that was on the kitchen table the last time I was here has gone and my cousin installed a bath before he left for Portugal, which is an interesting development as it seems there's no running water here.

It's a warm summer evening, like when I broke in all those years ago, and the sun has penetrated the years of dust, the old wood, the sun-bleached fabric of the curtains and bedding; as it all rises in the hot air to meet me I feel like I'm right where I should be. I camp out a while, until I get scared someone will come and tell me off. I shouldn't need permission to be here, it is still the family's after all, but when someone takes something away from you, it can feel as if it becomes theirs to give back, and no one has offered to return this to us, no matter how many times I ask. The hut remains in limbo, and I wonder, where's the Devil when you need him?

Listening, always listening.

9.

Blue Hermits

There's a noise coming from upstairs. There's rarely a noise coming from anywhere inside the house unless I'm making it. My guitar fell over once – the event of the week – but most of the time life here is very still. I creep up the short staircase so as to surprise whatever has invaded my home, and the sound becomes more discernible. I can hear air through feathers, the distinct sound of wings, and then a body on glass. I rarely get to touch a wild animal these days, seldom have an excuse to, and I can't help but feel excited. The flapping stops, and there, on my bedroom windowsill, next to a precariously full water jug of past-their-best-when-I-bought-them flowers and an unread copy of *The Goldfinch*, is a small bird with big black eyes. It's panting from the exertion and staring at me.

'It's okay,' I whisper. 'You're safe.' I had a rescue raven when I was eight (which I'd originally thought was a rook, and so named him Rookie) and, although I am obviously aware birds can't understand language, I do believe they understand tone, intention, vibrations – like all animals.

The bird flaps again, but this time it only flies the short distance to my single bed, and then back again to the latticed windows. I sit on the corner of the bed and try to discern the bird's species. I don't recognise it at all. It's brown with a creamy-gold breast, but far, far too small to be a thrush; it's definitely not a sparrow, and it's not a linnet. I reassure it as I move my cupped hands carefully towards it. Holding gently on to its wings so as not to hurt it, I look at the creature in my hands. Only now, up close, can I see it has the faintest hint of orange at the peak of its pale breast. It's a juvenile robin. It's not struggling in my hands, so I allow myself a few moments to study it as I sit on the edge of the bed. It already has the wide, turned-down, grumpy-looking beak of an adult robin. He stares at me with his black, reflective eyes lined with delicate white lids. Still except for the occasional blink, he watches me watching him. *Your move.*

I take the robin, a little reluctantly, down the stairs and walk out into the garden. I open my hands, and for few seconds the small bird just sits there. Then, the slightest, almost impercept-ible push of pressure with his talons, and he's gone, past the fig tree next door that hangs over the fence and out of sight. His brown plumage splintered with cream vanishes. I can hear the frog-like chirps of house martins above. Swifts are whistling, mingling with other little songbirds too indiscriminate against the bright sky to identify.

Inside, it feels empty. I feel claustrophobic for the first time in ages. It's still early and I have work I should be doing. Follow-ing the publication of a short story I wrote about a woman living an isolated existence (who knows where the inspiration came from), I've been commissioned by a publication to write another, which I should probably get started on . . . although I've sent off the piece of art news I still write each day, I've done the work I *need* to do, and actually I feel like I *need* to get out of the house as a matter of urgency. Having something wild come in has stirred up a new energy, and without the bird the air feels flat and still. I feel a little blue.

I look at my collection of quartz crystal from the bay, glittering on the kitchen windowsill beside a melodramatic Pre-Raphaelite postcard of scattered goddesses in various states of lethargy, then at the pan and porridge bowl in the sink – that's one downside to living alone, it's only ever me who's going to wash up. I follow the trail of a spiderweb across the ceiling and wonder what it would be like if humans left a visible trail. Spiders have no secrets – what honourable creatures. I take a sip of cold coffee and listen as a family with a young child demanding something walks past, their voices fading as they head towards the beach. Here I am, on my own. I search for what it is, this thing I'm feeling, whether it's a twinge of loneliness, whether after all this time its metallic fingers have finally found a way in through my ribs. A friend called me for the first time in a long time last night, upset about her relationship. 'It's just so stupid,' she said. 'I should never have let myself get in this situation.'

'You can't blame yourself for getting into this situation,' I said, 'because situations change – this wasn't the situation at the start.'

I'd do well to remember this myself. I think of everything I thought I wanted – family, marriage, normality. The whole gamut seems so alien to me now, so not me, and I wonder how much I ever actually wanted it and how much I just wanted to see if I could have it, to prove something. Maybe it is the time alone, or maybe I have always felt like this and never had the balls to admit it, but if I share my life with someone then I want them to love me as an animal. What would I be if I were left in the wild with absolutely nothing to my name, if I existed completely out of context, and someone found me there and chose to make a life with me? That's what I want to be loved for – it's not loving me for who I am, because who I am is in a constant state of flux. I want to be loved for what I am, fundamentally. I want to be loved as a creature independent of my humanity and all the expectations that come with it. Maybe everyone else has already arrived at this understanding and I'm just late to the party, but, for me, this feels like something of an epiphany. This is all anyone can be truly loved for – what their soul amounts to when they have nothing. It's true we comprise the things we have seen and experienced, the things that have happened to us, that the body has a memory more powerful than the mind's. But that's only a layer of what we are. We are all states of energy and being and we should be loved as such, or it is better not to be loved at all.

This all seems pretty unrealistic, so I decide I am quite content not to be loved at all.

It isn't loneliness then, this feeling, because I've studied the fingerprints of loneliness in a London flat more times than I can count and they look like the eye of a storm. This is different. I'd have this feeling even if someone else were in the house with me. It's emptiness, and I need space in my mind and my lungs and my eyes. I need the empty expanse to fill me up.

I march quickly. Straight down the path, across the field, through the dunes, jumping over the black rocks, swinging from a rusty pole to keep my balance, up past the surf shack and the holiday rentals, up up up I march, breathing hard and deep. I walk the inland path where pink and white bramble flowers have unwrapped from their tight buds like crumpled tissue paper. It's mid-July and the beach is busy up where the sand is dry; there's a few figures in the sea and I can hear laughter echoing from the lime kiln below. A group of passing clouds loiter over the sea and sand; they're reflected as if in a mirror, and I am in just the right place to see the light bounce back up off the wet sand where the tide is going out. The sea is grey-green today and the waves are crested, white and fluffy like the clouds above them, rolling in over the mirror to the sky.

Solar flares of dandelions burst with energy in a moonrise palette of the last of the thrift on the headland, invaded now by tall muscle-pink thistle. I finally reach the top of the cliff and eat a homemade cheese and watercress sandwich and wonder why the robin affected me so much. The robin is a loner, this much I know. Maybe there is something to being content in your own company because you've never known it any other way. I watch the gulls flit with the swallows that have arrived, sweeping above and below me, black and white like ash on the wind. I'm tired and my mind is, for once, baggy without assistance. The island that comes and goes with sea mist is completely concealed by summer haze, and there is no land in front of me, the horizon is limitless.

I'm out for most of the day, and when I do finally come back inside I smoke furiously, dig out all the business cards I made a few years ago and never handed out, and one by one I cross out 'Producer' and scribble 'Writer'. A pile of about a hundred and fifty unused cards – I don't plan on using these amended cards either; this is nothing but a ritual. As if to convince myself that there is no turning back now. Not that there ever was. My past is a mirror to the sky; there are no limits any more.

If neuroscientists are correct and the distress we experience during periods of loneliness stems from a state of hypervigilance that our primate ancestors required to survive the threats of being alone 52 million years ago, am I missing a link? Admittedly, just because I say I am not lonely now does not mean I have never felt lonely. Maybe I lost the link. 'Loneliness', Maggie Nelson writes, 'is solitude with a problem.' Loneliness is universal. It is, we are agreed, an aspect of human nature that is undeniable and unavoidable at some points in our lives. But mere human presence is not an antidote to loneliness. Sometimes it can make it worse.

It's never pleasant for any duration, but it's only the protracted periods of loneliness that carry health risks. It can increase your mortality by up to a quarter. According to research performed by the psychologist Julianne Holt-Lunstad and her colleagues, loneliness and 'poor social connections' are as bad for you as smoking fifteen cigarettes a day. Older people feel lonelier than younger people, although some studies say teenagers and young adults are increasingly at risk. The Office of National Statistics states that women report feeling lonely more frequently than men, although other studies say men feel lonely more often. There is a sharp rise in loneliness when it comes to the disabled population – up to 50 per cent of people with disabilities will be lonely on any given day. A large-scale study of over 400,000 people in the UK found that loneliness also increased alongside population density, but that feelings of loneliness were found to decrease with proximity to green spaces. Some studies say more married people are lonely than those who are unmarried; others say the opposite. It is very common to feel lonely while living with someone else. Renters are more likely to feel lonely than homeowners are. Living with partners, family members or roommates who have substance abuse issues might make you feel isolated in your own home. That's the strangest loneliness – ironic loneliness, to be in the same room, or the same bed with someone, and feel utterly alone in the universe.

So, there's a lot of conflicting data, but all it can ever come down to is whether you have chosen to be alone, or whether someone, or a collective society, is making you feel isolated. Maybe you want meaningful connection but the sheer number of people means dissociating is the only means of staying sane. Those of us who are alone and don't experience loneliness have not been cut off from others but rather cut ourselves off – the choice is ours.

Between 1968 and 1970 at the National Institute of Mental Health, John Calhoun conducted the last in a series of experiments on rodents, officially titled 'Mortality-Inhibiting Environment for Mice' and otherwise known as 'Mouse Utopia'. The experiment observed the effect of reduced mortality and consequently overcrowding in caged rodents. Initially, the mice responded well to their seemingly benevolent universe; but despite living in a vast, comfortable cage known as 'Universe 25' and existing in otherwise utopic conditions – limitless source of food and water, no predation, abundance of nesting materials, controlled comfortable ambient temperature, and disease screening – serious behavioural problems evolved. With very few mice dying thanks to their idyllic environment, the population began to explode; being in too-close contact with hundreds, and eventually thousands, of other mice led to behaviours linked to overcrowding: aggression, violence and even depression.

In a paper published in the Proceedings of the Royal Society of Medicine titled *Death Squared*, Calhoun implied the end of any given species in conditions like these (his mouse population had ultimately dropped from its high of 2,200 to 0) and made the leap that 'For an animal so complex as man, there is no logical reason why a comparable sequence of events should not also lead to species extinction.' Despite the mice having an abundance of food, the experiment influenced extreme sci-fi cult classics such as *Soylent Green* (where people in over-crowded cities are mulched into wafers), and tapped into Cold War anxieties of food and water shortages and the downfall of the Western world. It was at this time that many began to feel disillusioned by their 'flower child' ideals and isolated from their fellow man, and by the end of the 1970s the use of the word 'lonely' in literature began its stratospheric rise – quickly surpassing the previous highs of the 1860s (an equally tumultuous period in human history) – and it is yet to see any sign of slowing.

More recently, Edmund Ramsden, a medical historian and critic of Calhoun's work, posited that the decline in perceived moral behaviours in the mice could have arisen 'not from density, but from excessive social interaction'. Rather than making the experiment redundant, in my mind the more recent interpretation reinforces the experiment's relevance.

In Mouse Utopia there were a few mice that chose to live in secluded areas, away from the rest of the population. Calhoun noted that these mice had typically been kicked out of the nest early or otherwise raised improperly and so lived in a state of arrested development; they failed to develop social bonds and other interactions associated with normal behaviours. The male mice in particular spent all day grooming, inspiring Calhoun to name these reclusive mice 'the beautiful ones'. When the population started suffering, the beautiful ones were spared both mental and physical stressors. However, this came at a cost. Calhoun believed they had experienced a 'spiritual death' and existed in a 'behavioural sink'.

The beautiful ones were regarded as having completely lost touch with normal social behaviours, including having sex and being good parents.

Whether I am lonely or alone, marooned or escaped, is down to freedom of choice and whether I want to be there or not; how I behave depends on this, and whether I am prepared to do away with normal social behaviours is the cost. As long as my spirit remains intact, it would appear that I am.

Unconcerned with normal social behaviours, Paul Burwell – poet, experimental performance artist, percussionist and general far-out phenomenon – took extraordinary measures to find out whether the presence of another solitary soul could remedy his loneliness, or keep his mind occupied long enough to distract from it. In the early 1990s, he contracted an ornamental hermit to occupy his garden shed at 147 Knapp Road in London, resurrecting a fashion that had died out over a hundred years prior.

The ornamental or garden hermit was a popular accessory in manicured gardens for any well-respected lord or landowner during the eighteenth century. There was an ornamental hermit at the Lulworth Estate in Dorset; at Hawkstone Park in Shropshire; at Painshill in Surrey; and many others in smaller, less notable grounds. The garden and estate architect Capability Brown had recently redirected the English garden towards a neo-classical style – its association with great Greek and Roman philosophers was something the idle rich hoped would rub off on them. Architectural design and landscaping was geared towards contemplation, or at least ornaments depicting contemplation. Grottos had already been made popular as a source of respite for the upper classes, presumably to distract from having to think about all that industrialisation that was going on.

The first recorded ornamental hermit is considered to be Francis of Paola, who lived on his father's estate in the fifteenth century. Around the same time, Pope Pius IV is also believed to have had an ornamental hermit in his gardens, as did the French cardinal Charles de Bourbon. But these men, and the men they employed, had spiritual and emotional inclinations towards eremitism. The men who served the aristocracy as ornamental hermits on estates in eighteenth-century England were doing it for the money. The men (and it was exclusively men) employed as hermits weren't men who had been found living a solitary life of contemplation and spiritual exploration; rather, they were usually local agricultural workers in need of a few quid and a chance to put their feet up.

Legitimate hermits considered these ornamental ones phonies. But the landowners only wanted the appearance of authenticity; to these ends, they encouraged, and usually forced, their hermit employees to dress as druids, in hessian sacks with twine belts; the hermits were not allowed to cut their toenails, fingernails, beards or hair. The ornamental hermits often had the same task as the hermits of Arthurian legend: to offer advice and counsel to the guests of the wealthy landowners who visited them. As well as being prepared to live as someone else demanded, you had to be a pretty good bullshit artist.

Rather than God, employers had dominion over their hermits, and so strict were their masters' demands – and so unsuitable were the men for this kind of pseudo-spiritual life – that their residencies as hermits tended not to last very long. The ornamental hermit at Painshill was under strict instruction to maintain appearances: not to go out and socialise, not to dress in normal clothes, not to drink. He was contracted for seven years but only served three weeks of that tenancy after being found at the local pub.

In *English Eccentrics: A Gallery of Weird and Wonderful Men*, Edith Sitwell retells the story of the unruly ornamental hermit at Ashby de la Zouch, who made a case for himself and his disobedient colleagues. People didn't like the hermit of Ashby because he didn't behave like one. He drank beer. He enjoyed food. He smoked a pipe. 'True hermits,' he said, 'throughout the ages, have been abettors of freedom.' They are nonconformists.

As the years went on, and as the employed hermits were often deemed a little too unruly for the job, the ornamental hermits faced the same problem many of us do now: their job started being taken over by robots. Automatons serving as ornamental hermits started to become popular in the late eighteenth century, but a few hardcore flesh-and-blood garden hermits remained. There was a hermit in the Pleasure Gardens in Vauxhall, London, until the 1850s. Then there was a very long gap until one appeared in the East End. In 1991, the performance artist Shaun Caton spent several months as an ornamental hermit in the garden shed owned by Paul Burwell.

Knapp Road is a small Victorian street and was 'quite grim, with murders, and a cemetery at the end of the road overrun with huge brown rats and burning motorcycles,' Shaun tells me. 147 Knapp Road had a long garden full of sheds and lean-tos that Paul had built with reclaimed wood. Some sheds were only big enough for one person; others had a bit more room. Paul had covered one of the sheds in shells and turned it into a grotto, and by this time Shaun was renting a studio from Paul.

One day, as Paul surveyed his city of shacks, he turned to Shaun and said, 'Something's missing.'

'What's that?' Shaun replied.

'An ornamental hermit.'

This would be the beginning of Shaun's longest, and possibly strangest, performance. He assumed the role of ornamental hermit and migrated from his studio to one of the garden sheds. Shaun's shed-hermitage was adorned with traditional and less traditional ornaments: skulls and books, shells and bones, and Barbie dolls. Paul, like the employers of ornamental hermits in the eighteenth century, instructed Shaun to grow out his hair and beard, and insisted that his ornamental hermit stay in his garden shed from dawn until after dark, often sleeping in there. Paul fed Shaun an assortment of rations during his hours in the shed – from antipasti and cicchetti to fish-head soup and worms cooked up with garlic and onions, and various other insects Paul deemed authentic hermit fodder.

Paul had a long beard and long fingernails himself – as Shaun says, it was Paul who initially had the appearance of an ornamental hermit. The concept of the hermit was something Paul had been interested in all his life and had read a lot about. Much like Edith Sitwell, he thought that the outsider was an intrinsic part of British culture, and he wanted to bring the archetype from the pages of history and storybooks to life. With Shaun being a performance artist, the two men told the who's who of who they knew and asked them to spread the word about the hot new performance: an ornamental hermit on Knapp Road. Paul charged an admission fee for guests to enter, which also got them a free drink that was usually embellished with something psychedelic. From inside the shed, Shaun would play music with the ornaments, people would watch and ask the odd question, sometimes Shaun would perform a birthing ritual with the Barbie dolls for the astonished crowd – and then the next guests would arrive.

Paul's very specific idea of what he wanted Shaun to look like as an ornamental hermit swiftly veered from the stereotypical to something less orthodox. After a month, Paul (who was apparently sober only very, very rarely) came back to the grotto with tins of paint in California blue. He proceeded to paint the sheds and then paint Shaun – and everything else around him – California blue. Paul had grown up on a boat and had spent years feeling isolated in the navy. He was a poet with a love of the water. When he wasn't on the river, he painted the world around him blue.

'I became the blue hermit of 147 Knapp Road!' Shaun tells me, still visibly excited by the madness of the experience.

Shaun's colouring was supposed to be 'the natural cobalt pigmentation of his skin' – that's what they told their guests, anyway. Shaun reports that even his 'very large' testicles were shaved and painted blue, like 'gyrating planets'. This proved to be an apt visual metaphor, as Paul didn't only have a say over how Shaun appeared as an ornamental hermit, but how he behaved. Shaun was instructed not to have sex with anyone, including himself, during his months as a hermit; if he did, it would ruin everything. 'It would break the spell,' Shaun says, 'the magic would vanish.' And so, he remained cobalt and celibate. Shaun is adamant he was always aware that his time as an ornamental hermit was a role, a performance, but in order to perform the role well, he had to inhabit it. He had to believe in the magic of it.

*

Eventually, even the window that people looked in through was painted blue, despite Shaun still being behind the glass. But by this time, Shaun had been an exhibit for months – he'd seen summer turn to autumn, and autumn was turning to winter – and he felt he had become 'a non-person, because I'd been scrutinised so much by so many people for so long, with so many people asking questions and looking at me through a window.' The life of an ornamental hermit is completely different from the life we usually associate with a hermit, sequestered from the world and all its questions and demands. It requires a disconnect from the part of the self that strives to remain hidden.

Shaun decided to stay behind the blue window until both he and Paul felt they had reached the end of whatever strange journey they were on together. 'I had to finish it for myself, and I had to finish it for Paul.' When the performance finally ended, everything that was covered in a thick coat of viscous California blue, the sheds and the lean-tos, was ceremonially burned.

'We lived it authentically, we didn't fuck about,' Shaun says. 'We did it to what we thought was true – to do all the rituals, the time frames, we thought we were trying to recreate an ancient archetypal image.' Maintaining this level of commitment meant Shaun felt displaced when he came out of the performance. It took him about a year to get back to normal and reintegrate and converse with people on the same level, and to stop thinking about being a hermit in 'a cosmic sense'. It was a comedown, to say the least.

'Why did you do it?' I ask him.

'We did it because we had to.'

*

For Paul Burwell, the ornamental hermit was not a status symbol, but a companion for an alchemical exploration, in search of a cure for the human condition. Similar to Buddhism, in alchemy there are numerous physical stages – birth, death and resurrection – as well as spiritual stages that must be transcended in order to achieve enlightenment or the emergence of the higher, perfect self. Paul and Shaun pushed the concept of an ornamental hermit living out different stages of transmutation to the limits of what was physically possible in a back garden – and, when Shaun started performing giving birth to Barbie dolls in his hermitage, to the very limits of sanity. Paul was getting Shaun to bring to life a fantasy he couldn't quite let himself live out, and the ornamental hermit was company for a fundamentally lonely man. A man who was trapped in his own aloneness without ever fully embracing it, perhaps knowing that if he did, it would crush him.

Having dinner one evening in the Spanish village my dad now lives in, I listened as he talked to a friend. Really, I was only half listening as I ate, but I had gathered that they were talking about the Buddhist monastery down the road. I heard my dad saying in Spanish that the Buddhist monks 'get up very early to collect egos'. How existential, I thought.

'How do they go about doing that?' I asked, imagining the Buddhists stopping passers-by and deconstructing their sense of self on the pavement before breakfast.

'By picking them up,' was the confused response.

'But . . . how?' After some more interrogation on my part, it turned out that *higos* are figs in Spanish, pronounced the same as 'egos'.

Over the course of the year, I have watched my neighbour's fig tree growing over the fence and into my garden and have welcomed it, and for months now I've been looking forward to some fruit. I don't know if the neighbours live here all the time, I never hear them – and I don't hear them cut back the side of the tree that was creeping into my garden, just as it is offering figs. I come back from a walk to find it like this and pick up the two fruit that fell on the ground during its pruning, thinking how it's funny that they let it grow wild until it bore fruit.

The figs have got me thinking of something I've been reading about the four stages of awakening that lead to enlightenment in Zen Buddhism. These stages are called 'fruit of action', from the Sanskrit word *phala* – relating to the fruit of one's actions and of one's chosen life path. The fruit aim to disentangle the individual from the material world through a life of contemplation (*Maha-phala*) and the fruition of each stage of following the Buddhist path (*Ariya-phala*). The latter begins by addressing the delusion of the thought that follows 'this is mine, this I am, this is myself'.

I'm sure the figs bear a lesson: there is something I am supposed to be learning here but I don't know what it is. Or maybe this time the lesson belongs to my neighbours. Either way, I cherish the two green figs I've collected and eat them on my porridge for the next two mornings. I sit outside, enjoying the novelty fruit on my oats, looking at the pollarded branches of the tree; it's peak summer. My neighbour will soon have a glut of ripe figs. I hope they like figs. I hope they know how to dry them, to turn them on a piece of cardboard in the sun. I hope they are ready for the seventy rebirths in human and heavenly realms that come with the fruit. I hope they learn to loosen their grip on it all as I am learning to loosen mine.

It's a cool morning, but the haze over the fields warns that the day will be hot. The blackbirds have left. I've been watching them sitting together on a bench the last few weeks – two generations. Having gone backwards and forwards making the nest, there was a brief period of quiet, then backwards and forwards again feeding the chicks, and then they were gone. They let go of their bond with each other, they let go of their bond with this place – they won't return to nest the next year.

This morning feels like the mornings of school summer holidays, when life seemed eternal and the concept of death was reserved for animals and grandparents. On mornings like this twenty years ago, I'd be put in the car and taken for the weekly shop. There were only a few parking spaces in the small town we shopped in, and whenever my parents had success in finding one of the few available in the square, they would proclaim, 'Zen and the art of parking.' Soon, it was 'Zen and the art of everything'. Zen and the art of mowing the lawn. Zen and the art of picking up the dog shit. Zen and the art of losing a home.

Although it was always said in jest, there was a kernel of truth: there is an art to letting go, not resisting and not forcing. It will come, or go, in time; it always does. Maybe I hold on to things so tightly because I fear losing them. Maybe it is the tightness with which I hold on to things that keeps forcing me to let go. Zen does not hold on to anything too tightly. It's a part of life that we keep losing things until we're left with nothing, until we get that this earth is all we ever had. Zen and the art of being alone in the universe.

IO.

Barrelling

Sometimes, when there's no one else here, as autumn turns to winter, when the winds are up and the waves reach thirty feet, I sit on a bench and eat fish and chips. I watch the surfers, my fingers tacky with grease and vinegar, hair wet from the drizzle, face covered in salty spray that rockets up from the white waves below, frothing at the bit. Blobs of spume fly up like dandelion seeds on the wind.

Today, the waves are good but not very big, and the sea is full of people. Croyde on a good day is one of the best places to surf in the UK, so I'm told – in 2022 North Devon will become the first place in the UK to be designated a World Surfing Reserve. Croyde's waves, dubbed the 'Oyster Falls', are famous for their barrels, the ones that curve like blue glass tubes – what big-wave chasers like best. Autumn is coming on and you can see it in the air and feel it on the wind. Vibrating within sunbeams are darker worlds. Woodfires and smoke across the orange hills, twilight from 4 p.m. The beach is emptying, slowly; the summer's blowing cold. Further out are the more experienced surfers, catching the bigger waves, pulled by invisible forces into the cold sea. One of my childhood friends is a surfer but I've never had much time for it. I didn't understand the mentality and I didn't like the 'beach girl look'. I was too busy thinking

137

I was a punk, and I thought punks don't get up at 5 a.m. and worship the sea like it's a god.

One day in 1986, the 'North Pond Hermit' – a man called Christopher Knight – went out and followed his calling. He didn't do what we might associate with 'calling'; he didn't go to Los Angeles and become an actor, he didn't start a business, he didn't save any lives, he named no planets or stars after himself. He walked off into the woods in Maine with a backpack on and set up camp. He lived there for twenty-seven years, subsisting on things stolen from the nearby cabins – insisting he only ever stole things he needed to survive (food and clothes) – until he was finally caught by police. In the end he had committed over a thousand robberies and left a lot of people feeling unsafe.

On his release, the world had a lot of questions for Knight, and his story was chronicled by Mike Finkel in *The Stranger in the Woods*. Knight insisted the wild was calling him. 'He said the tug to be alone was like this gravitational force, all his body was saying that he just felt more comfortable by himself. He was never lonely,' Finkel says in an interview. 'He said that he felt almost the opposite of that. He said he felt utterly and intricately connected to everything else in the world. It was difficult for him to tell where his body ended, and the woods began. He said he felt this utter communion with nature and with the outside world.'

That was his calling. That was it: to exist in total, unadulterated unity with the world.

Rewind a few years. It's Christmas morning and I'm working on the sofa bed of my mum's attic flat in Devon. I'm only twenty-four (nobody at the production company knows *quite* how young I am) and this will be one of the biggest jobs of my life – hundreds of thousands of pounds are in my hands, the project is late because the after-effects technician has barely communicated or done any work since the death of his grand-mother several weeks ago, and I haven't been able to bring myself to fire him. As freelancers, we are all expendable, and people have been getting angry that it has taken me this long to reach the conclusion that I will have to fire him. I am made aware, in no uncertain terms, that it is an emergency. My job is now also on the line. I spend the whole day trying to find someone to replace him and am barely present for this Christ-mas with my mum. Unlike the other freelancers, I am not on a day rate.

The advert I'm producing, a Russian panty-liner advert, is unimaginably bad despite the goat I thought it would be funny to suggest in a production meeting that has somehow ended up being written into the advert, along with its goat wran-gler and some lambs that it's my job to find. Soon the director will get so frustrated with the indecisive client that he punches his fist through the office wall. This is not what I want to be doing with my life. I'm exhausted. I feel as if every cell of my being is rebelling and has begun its astral projection onto some-thing else I might be good at, something that might even be worthwhile from time to time, something that will give me a sense of purpose rather than expendability.

We might not like to say it out loud too often, for fear of sounding like we're talking from a 'woo-woo' self-help book, but the majority of us would admit to ourselves that we feel we have a true self. One we deviate from when necessary in order to function within society, but there is always the notion that we must 'be true to ourselves', to 'speak our truth'. This is the self that makes us feel out of place when we are out of place. It's not the voice you have for others, it's the voice inside your head. The voice you hear that tells you to keep going; the voice that tells you to stop. That this isn't right, but maybe that is. It is said that, in silence, in meditation, you hone your powers of intuition – and intuition could be described as the guidance of our 'true self'. 'In silence you find an inner voice that is extraordinarily hard to define for those who have never heard it but very, very clear to those who have been lucky enough to experience it,' says Sara Maitland. 'I think usually people who are silent, whether they know it or not, are in pursuit of that experience, hearing this voice.'

Scientific analysis would tell us there is no true self. It's an illusion. That the notion of the true self has been formed by a sort of collective unconscious or 'folk intuition' and is, therefore, pseudoscience and immaterial. But you can't really argue with how you feel; and unless you are a Buddhist, this is how the majority of humans feel on a fundamental level. 'Everybody is original, if he tells the truth, if he speaks from himself. But it must be from his *true* self and not from the self he thinks he *should* be,' the writer, teacher and advocate of solitary idleness, Brenda Ueland, once wrote. We should strive to be our true selves if only because authenticity tends to have more interesting results, and not because we think it's noble – very often, it's not. I'm hardly advocating sword fights and murder, but it was through Caravaggio's experience of poverty, exile, violence and cruelty – inflicted both on him and by him – that he saw the world clearly; he saw how the light fell on both the beautiful and the damned.

*

Today, the light falls warm and low on the path in front of me, and even small stones have been given their own shadows. In theory, I have a fear of heights, yet I walk the South West Coast Path that trails high over the sea to the right of Croyde's beach almost every single day. I don't wear the gear most of the other walkers wear; I don't even own a pair of walking boots, and I've already worn out a trusty old pair of Converse since being here. It's dusty now, from the warmth of an Indian summer, and when I pass other people I always try to walk on the side of the path furthest from the sea – we all do, watching the dust from under our feet float out over it. If I haven't spoken to anyone for days, weeks, I will speak to someone here, if only to say 'hello', 'morning', 'yes, lovely day, isn't it?' A perfect amount of human interaction. I've never heard anyone shouting up here; everyone always seems pleased to be here regardless of whatever else is going on in their lives.

Walking up and down in summer and winter, in spring and autumn, watching the path and the sea change with the seasons, this barrier-less thread of sandstone between me and the rocks and the sea – this is my version of living with unadulterated intensity, being here on the edge of the world. The path here can shrink to between two and three feet wide, and just before Baggy Point it winds in tight to the headland, exposing a wide gully of nothing below. This bend is where the path is at its narrowest, its most lethal. It is a miracle people don't fall from it on a daily basis. There have been times when it's been windy and I've worried I might. When I've taken a breath and held it to look down below, and seen nothing but black rock and white foam crashing against each other, clapping.

A gust from the north hits my back and pushes me forwards and a little to the right, a little closer towards my maker – it whistles in my ear. But I trust each foot I put down, and must not put it down until I trust where it will land. And every time the land supports me, every time I make it past that bend to walk down to the beach again, to do this all over again, it makes me smile a little. This is what it's all about. This place and the things I've seen and heard here during the course of my life are the reason I write poetry that is (mercifully, in some cases) only published very rarely; it is the reason I write articles about local experience; it is the reason I've started writing a novel about a woman who isolates herself on the outskirts of a Devon village (again, where does the inspiration come from?). The reason to try – be the result deemed a success or a failure, whether it sees the light of day or not – is to write about *this*. Writing is how I connect to the experience of being here, it's how I express my gratitude for being here, and perhaps it's recompense for the lack of gratitude I expressed for so long. Having once wanted my life to be over, now one life does not seem like enough. I am so greedy for years these days, that when I hear of someone's death I'll ask, 'How old were they?'

'They were eighty-four.'

'Too young.'

In order to exercise as much agency as we can, many of us find that if we are to have a greater chance of succeeding in what we want to do with our lives, then we need to be where it's all 'happening', or where it's not. If I want to spend the majority of my time writing and not waitressing, I need to be here – it's freed me up financially, creatively, mentally, physically. It's gifted me a slower, more elemental existence that is conducive to my enjoyment of life and has inspired my work – they have become one and the same. Supplementing my writing with cleaning work, I can afford to dedicate the amount of time I feel I need to dedicate to my work. But if I'm not interested in making more money than I need to survive, what is the point of achieving anything? Why do I care if my work is rejected sometimes? Why does it discourage me if the concerned bystanders in my life tell me to return to producing, or at least get a qualification? Can't I just be satisfied being a cleaner and writing with no reward other than the act of writing?

I could.

When the sentence 'You don't come from the right sort of family to be a writer!' was shouted at me – and this happened several times – it was implicit that having nothing to fall back on meant I was only supposed to strive to earn lots of money; without financial capital, trying to turn my life into something that meant something to me was selfish and delusional.

Maybe it is. So what? It's my life.

As retirement stretches further and further away from my generation and the generations that follow, our working lives get longer and longer, so why should we not take a risk and allow ourselves a few years to do what we want, see if we can make it work? I accept that the cost of doing something that is important to me means that I have quite limited options when it comes to standard of living versus quality of life – inventiveness is required to get the best of both. I have to make the most of whatever comes along, and being alone means that the sacrifices I make along the way are my problem and my problem only. As long as we aren't hurting anyone else, as long as we pay our bills – and, really, even if we don't – we don't have to justify our lives to anyone.

The ocean that I look down onto from the path draws people to it all the time. The big-wave surfer Kai Lenny has talked about being on his own out in the waves, the biggest waves that exist on this planet. 'In my heart of hearts it is who I am,' he says. Under the big waves, in the barrel, 'it's the only time we can breathe underwater'.

When we dedicate our lives to doing something we feel is our reason for being, then it is almost inevitable that we will conflate what we do with who we are, and depending on the size of the ego involved, delusions of grandeur can be an occupational hazard. But rather than being something transactional, a calling is the desire to become one with something, a unifying experience where there is no mental distinction between you and what you do: 'It was difficult for him to tell where his body ended, and the woods began.' This tends to result in intense highs and intense lows. It is an all-consuming way to live.

Surfing these waves, chasing them and training to ride them to the shore, is something surfers dedicate their lives to. It's the reason for being alive and worth risking it for. Forget Croyde, Nazaré in Portugal is where you find the world's biggest waves. After receiving debilitating wipeout injuries that almost killed her, in 2020 Maya Gabeira returned to the water of Nazaré to surf the biggest wave of the year, a 73.5-foot wave, breaking the world record for both men and women (Kai Lenny came in with a 70-foot wave). Gabeira has complained previously that as a society we have a hard time rewarding women for courage, specifically if it's demonstrated in a physical way. If you look her up, so much of what is focused on is her injury, the time she wasn't surfing. But during that time she was still dedicating her life to the waves. She moved to Portugal from Brazil, she stayed in the water, she joined the rescue teams helping other surfers who were wiped out. She got to know that specific bit of ocean, the behaviour of the waves there. Her perceived failure, and how she responded to it, was key to her success. And more than that, her 'fascination with that energy, power, force and bravery' meant the sea was something she couldn't live without – it pulled her like a gravitational force.

I pick a blackberry. It's not ready yet but I'm impatient and hungry. The berry is deep purple crowned with red. It's tart and hard. A dead bramble leaf flies into my hair as I chew, and all of a sudden I'm high on perception. Everything's so vivid it's buzzing. I'm buzzing. The September sea is quieter than the summer one; it promises it has relinquished its bone-tingling quality and remains only chilly and glittering. I walk in, grimacing, trying not to squeak as a cold wave hits my midriff. I fall in and swim for a few strokes out into the sea, then turn onto my back. The rip current on my left is pulling me towards it but I'm far enough away for it not to have a hold on me stronger than I can swim. This is the first time I've swum since living here, and I lie in the iridescent water as far away from others as the cove will allow and laugh until I cry.

This was unthinkable a couple of years ago. To be living a life of my choosing. I don't know how it changed all of a sudden after so many years of the same. In a moment that had been barrel-ling, building, churning with pressure underneath every other moment I was living, it was coming, this moment like a tsunami that broke like a raindrop. I can't help but feel euphoric. If this is the only pay-off, fuck it, I'll take it. In moments like this when I just stop trying, stop striving, stop hauling myself out of the hole and instead look at where I am, I see I left the hole a long time ago. Now, I get up at dawn to watch the sea and worship it like a god.

II.

Hello, Stranger

Crystal Bay was never exactly busy in the summer compared to the throngs on the main beach, but now it's completely empty. I can return to my quartz hunting without feeling self-conscious. I inspect lumps of impure grainy quartz, marvelling at the jagged cavelets that run through the stones, only to drop them disdainfully back onto the ground. I turn over rocks, shift sand, to see what's hidden beneath, always looking for a perfect, crystal-clear quartz to match one I found and lost on an ill-fated trip to the Mojave Desert. I've spent weeks, months of my life trying to find something that even comes close to matching it. I think I might have every time something catches the light. But today I turn over a rock and a dark mark catches my eye. I can't quite believe it at first but there it is. A tiny fossil, or rather the impression of a fossil on a piece of slate – dark and grey and slightly rusty-looking around the sides from the iron-rich soil that leaches down from the headland in the rain – and there, on the edge, is the impression of an ammonite. The creature that made this mark is from millennia ago – its species no longer exists, but here it is, this impression.

During the summer, I was cleaning holiday cottages here every weekend. The dad of one of the other cleaners, a man called John E. Lewis, grew up in Croyde in the 1930s and '40s and wrote a book about life then. In *Croyde in My Lifetime* there are sepia photos of the village and the surrounding area, and when I looked at them I was struck by how agricultural and how insulated, isolated, it once was, all year round – even in the summer. There was a toll road into the village where gates could be closed and locked; white carthorses were loaded up with seaweed for fertiliser; men and women cut oats in the surrounding fields. John's dad would get in a boat and sail to Lundy Island to catch the wild ponies and bring them back to sell on the market in Barnstaple. Not so long ago, Croyde was a world unto itself, and it was likely a much harder life than the photos make it look. The compensation was a life infinitely more connected to the *genius loci* than the one most of us live now, even those of us who strive for something similar, something gentler. To not leave a mark any deeper than a faint impression of our existence on this rock, but to have lived in such a way that we made one.

Everything slows down by mid-October, it always has. The harvests are done and the holidaymakers are gone. There are tens of thousands fewer cars on the roads and it feels like the hedgerows have opened again, the country lanes have been unzipped and the belly of the land spills and rolls out for miles. The sun rises later and later in the hazy yellow sky. I wake up with condensation on the latticed windows. Thick clouds usually arrive by lunchtime and the village is quiet save for a few souls. It smells of woodsmoke from fires I can't see, and the jackdaws sit like gargoyles on the roofs, studying me with the same critical eye as the old men and women who sit out on plastic chairs in the hot village streets in southern Spain. But that's all that's here now; anyone who lives here is indoors, the lights are on early in a few of the occupied houses and the pubs. One moment I have the wooden blinds drawn every day as I work on the computer, my back to the passers-by on the street, the next I turn around and the village is deserted. It's the new rhythm of the seasons, the Anthropocene beat: the coming and going of people in accordance with the time of year. Now, the village draws in on itself, sucks itself in like an anemone.

Hikikomori means 'pulling inwards' in Japanese. It's a word used to describe a particular cultural phenomenon in Japan of people who are like secular anchorites. Hikikomori lock themselves in a single room, usually their bedroom. They are, generally speaking but not always, individuals from the younger generation who opt out of the high pressure and long hours of success-driven culture, as well as the pressure to conform to traditional expectations such as settling down and starting a family, and the shame that can surround unemployment and the benefits culture in Japan. The average age of hikikomori is thirty-one, but many are teens and some are now in their forties, or even older.

The phenomenon of the hikikomori recluse was first observed among Japanese youth in the 1970s, and by the mid-to-late 1990s it was highlighted as a social condition that was recognised by the World Health Organization in 2002. Previously, the word had been used in Japan to describe anyone who withdrew from relationships with others, and as a psychiatric term for symptoms of withdrawal in autistic, depressive, schizophrenic and aged patients. Now, hikikomori recluses are estimated to make up 1.5 per cent of the country's population, but the real figure could be much higher. They are Japan's modern-day hermits – or, as the writer and filmmaker Flavio Rizzo has described them, 'post-modern hermits'. He claims that their desire for solitude stems from ancestral desires for withdrawal.

There is a varied history of solitude in Japan: the culture of the solitary Yama-bito, or mountain people, from the eighth and ninth centuries; and the wandering Taoist and Zen monks such as the penniless monk, hermit and poet Ryōkan. But hikikomori are largely seen as suffering from a disorder. Many won't leave the house for weeks, months, sometimes years at a time. My sister (technically my half-sister's half-sister) Radha, who is half-Japanese and lives in Japan, says that most people in Japan think of hikikomori as social outcasts who have fallen through the net. It is, she says, 'considered a real shame, so people don't speak out about such problems at home'.

In 2011 the Japanese government estimated that 1.55 million people were close to becoming hikikomori; a 2015 Cabinet Office survey confirmed there were at least 541,000 people living in Japan as recluses. But this is no longer a Japanese phenomenon. People described as hikikomori exist in their thousands in South Korea, Spain, Italy, India, the US, France and the UK – many of these cases have been identified through studies from mental health centres, hospitals and psychiatrists where participants are referred to as hikikomori in both individual and group therapy. The term was originally attributed to young men, but it has repeatedly been pointed out that many women pull inwards without being noticed.

The hikikomori tends to withdraw while being completely reliant on technology, connected to others and the other world – the online world. Some are addicted to the internet, locking themselves in rooms in cities to play video and roleplay games. But it is not unheard of for the hikikomori experience to be positive. In taking a break from the online and offline uniformity and instead turning inwards with the aim of self-determination, some find their experience as a hikikomori helps their creativity. Others dabble in hikikomori as a finite period of time in which to take some weight off, no longer under pressure to do what is expected. One former hikikomori, the artist Nito Souji, explains that he wanted to do 'only things that were worthwhile'. He spent ten years as a recluse, which he says helped him develop his creative practice and resulted in a video game that explores the hikikomori experience.

Through self-development and introspection, the hikikomori often restores the energy they require in order to return to society – albeit transformed and interacting in a very different way. As when we remove ourselves from social media for a prolonged period, having successfully removed oneself from normal society, it doesn't have quite the same hold over us on our return, because we know that if it gets too much again we can always leave. Living in a state of partial detachment seems like a much healthier way to exist in the modern world, and I do sympathise with the triggers that cause many to become hikikomori. But I couldn't describe myself as hikikomori because so much of that existence (swapping the outdoors for the online, expecting the service of others, and not contributing to the chores of a family home) centres around living in a way that doesn't sit right with me, though I do sympathise. One of Japan's most famous internet entrepreneurs and a former hikikomori, Kazumi Ieiri, wrote that hikikomori is 'a situation where the knot is untied between you and society. No need to hurry; you can tie small knots, little by little.'

It would be unwise to romanticise large groups of people withdrawing from society as following an ancestral instinct – most hikikomori lock themselves in a room in a family home and rely on their parents for food and accommodation like a postmodern Peter Pan, which many don't have the privilege of doing. Radha has a friend from university whose older brother in his forties is a hikikomori. The brother hides from the parents, so meals are put on a tray outside his door and he uses the bathroom in the hours his parents are not around. Her friend wonders how he will survive when their parents pass away. As happens with many hikikomori, the danger comes when you don't re-emerge, when the damage done by the outside world, whatever that may have been, proves irreversible. Society as we know it is difficult for most and painful, even fatal, for many. It can be a difficult thing to live within a society we don't trust and feel powerless to change and, sometimes, some of us need a break from trying, if only to come back stronger. Or not.

Bernard Wheatley was a Black physician from the Virgin Islands. Studying and working in 1940s America, he experienced discrimination in his career and was often passed over for opportunities despite being the best in his class. Disillusioned, he left America for Sweden and, having worked harder than his white counterparts, achieved his ambitions of succeeding as a physician. Then he had a heart attack. The experience changed how he viewed civilisation and led him to believe that it was a danger to life – that the stress of working within this system had almost killed him – so he decided 'man could overcome death and control his health by living a life of love'.

Wheatley sold his worldly possessions and left his profession in the late 1950s to live in Hawaii. There, he initially worked in bars and ran up large hotel bills, and one such bill resulted in a court appearance. The court appearance and cardiac event are believed to have encouraged the final separation between himself and a system that revolved around the 'commercial society he loathes', explains a contemporaneous profile in *Ebony* magazine. He questioned the meaning of life with such intensity that he decided to seek a 'secluded place where he could earnestly seek truth without distraction', and he soon dropped out of the system altogether to live as a hermit in the wilderness of the Kalalau Valley.

In *Dark Days* James Baldwin wrote, 'Every human being born begins to be civilized the moment he or she is born. Since we all arrive here absolutely helpless . . . there is no way around that. But this is civilization with a small c. Civilization with a large C is something else again . . . Whatever it is that white Americans want, it is not freedom – neither for themselves nor for others.' It's not Americans. It's Civilisation.

We might argue that the desire to live in solitude and isolation for prolonged periods depends on triggers and traumas within an individual's life experience. But I can't help but wonder, or instinctively feel, that perhaps there is something in our nature rather than our nurture that yearns for solitude, and circumstances just peel back layers that already exist. So far, relevant research aimed at quantifying or isolating what that drive might relate to is close to nil. Clinical trials of inmates in solitary confinement are relatively widespread; those on the solitary public are less so. 'While there are numerous studies showing the harmful effects of solitary confinement on prisoners, studies of the general public are rarer because of the ethical concerns around subjecting someone to prolonged isolation for the purpose of a clinical trial,' the author and hermit chaser Paul Willis writes.

Mistrusting 'the system' is a common trope among hermits and recluses – not always in a tinfoil-hat kind of way, but sometimes. It can mean leaving the secular system for one of isolated religion; or, in other cases, leaving bureaucratic systems and societal hierarchies for something more natural – there are exceptions in what the earth produces, mutations, that there tend not to be in systems of governance and the daily administrative procedures that encapsulate our modern lives (the 'commercial society he loathes'). We choose a life of isolation because we feel unable to change a system we do not agree with, and instead of choosing impotent rage, we opt out of it. As the philosopher Jiddu Krishnamurti said, 'It is no measure of health to be well-adjusted to a profoundly sick society.'

Christmas came and went, and spring is on the horizon. A young woman is pushing her pram through the village; there's thin light coming from the sky, filtered through a pall of cloud. She's heading towards the path filled with puddles that leads down to the dune-fringed beach and the restless Atlantic. I walk quickly to lose her.

'Jade!'

I don't have my glasses on, so spin around and wait for her to approach before reacting. As she approaches, smiling, I realise it's a nice girl from the year below me who I have a habit of bumping into every few years in the most random places. The last time it was at the top of a hill. Today, I look feral. No make-up, hair unbrushed, big old baggy clothes and a huge sheepskin coat of my mother's that I used to call 'the creep coat'. I am different from who I once was, not only in appearance but in conduct. I'm self-conscious when I talk to other people now – even cursory pleasantries to people in shops. This began during the doomed relationship, where I would self-censor before talking to try to avoid saying the wrong thing, but the self-censoring of how I phrase things and what I say, and don't say, out loud has increased in my time alone, to the point where I don't say anything out loud without thinking about it. This constant self-analysis has warped into self-criticism and I only feel comfortable talking to a couple of people these days – they happen to be people I have argued with in the past, but we have chosen to forgive each other. The nice girl is the same as I remember her and is lovely to me as always, regardless of how bizarre I might look and behave. I admire her baby in the way only people who aren't very into babies can.

'Oh! Look at her. Is it a her?'

'Yeah, yeah.'

'Ahh, cute.'

We walk down the path together and I wonder if I am going to be duty-bound to spend the rest of my walk with her. I wanted to be alone. I always want to be alone these days. We talk about when she had the baby a few months ago while half my mind strays to the headland I'm planning on walking to, wondering if she'll be able to get a pram up there, and then she says, 'It's been a weird year this year, though,' looking to me for some sort of agreement. I have no idea what she means.

'With the baby,' she explains, 'and . . . Rachel dying.'

'Rachel?'

'You didn't hear?'

'Rachel from school?'

'Yeah.'

'No,' I say, shaking my head and looking over the hedge into the field, as if expecting to find an explanation in the grass. 'No one said anything.'

'Ah . . . yeah,' she sighs, 'Rachel died in February.'

Rachel was a girl from my year, someone I grew up with – not someone I was close to but someone I imagined would have a long life. She was an ardent Christian, which had always made her seem rather untouchable. It turns out that she had a rare lung disease, LAM (lymphangioleiomyomatosis), in which the abnormal growth of smooth muscle cells in the lungs results in holes or cysts, which block the airways and prevent the lungs from getting oxygen to the rest of the body. It 'tends to affect women of childbearing age'. On diagnosis, she had a transplant and was given two new lungs. All looked well, for a while. But then her body rejected the new lungs. Everything shut down.

I don't know what to say. It's completely thrown me. *Why did no one tell me?* I keep asking myself, while we walk and talk and agree how sad it all is, how lucky we are to be here, walking down the path, with her baby jiggling over the pebbles. I tell her how I thought I saw Rachel's first boyfriend, who committed suicide when he was about fourteen, in a car once, leaving Tesco, years after he died.

'They think it was the acne medication that made him suicidal,' she says matter-of-factly, but not without care. That's just the way it is. God moves in mysterious ways. She shrugs and smiles goodbye, continuing her walk down towards the sea that's so far out, leaving the beach bereft and flat. I am relieved she is off for a walk with her baby and not me. I'm still absorbing all the information and have nothing to say. I keep shaking my head. I walk over the rocks towards the promontory I like to sit on, about a quarter of the way up the coastal path. I don't make it to the headland today. Rachel is in the ground. This girl, who you could see in middle age when she was a teenager, didn't even get to see thirty. The sun is beaming a white line over the sea; there is the deep rumble of the waves. Nothing makes any sense.

None of my friends told me. When I ask, apparently everyone else saw it on Facebook, and having a pseudonymous, very limited account these days, I'm only friends with a few close schoolfriends on there. The end of her existence passed me by. Maybe I've cut myself off too successfully. Maybe I've made myself appear unapproachable. I certainly don't have the online connection a hikikomori might. No one thought to tell me – maybe no one thought to tell me because they thought I wouldn't care, or maybe they didn't. I write a card to her parents and worry I've said the wrong thing, but I have to say something.

Not being informed about something as important as someone's death, and life having carried on without missing a beat, continues to play on my mind for weeks – the whole thing's weirded me out, and it gets me wondering if maybe I have lost touch with normal social behaviours, like Calhoun's mice. I've shot off the earth and spun out of orbit and am now circling another, uninhabited planet. I've been reading a lot of Terence McKenna and have been ordering magic mushrooms off the internet, taking them to see what else is out there, what else I can see or experience or realise. Is there more to reality than meets the eye? Can I cure myself of my persisting fear of my ex? Can I have a breakthrough? McKenna suggests that the accidental foraging of magic mushrooms was fundamental in the creation of the imagination of our ancient ancestors. Could I ever reconcile all this beauty with the suffering that comes with it? From time to time, with a little imagination.

I first took magic mushrooms when they were still legal and

being sold at a stall at Reading Festival, and then didn't take them again for many years. There have been endless studies published and trials performed (most notably by Imperial College London) praising psilocybin's effects on depression, PTSD and anxiety. Silicon Valley is microdosing it at their desks to enhance creativity. Every national and international paper has been writing about psilocybin's positive effects. In my mind, this magic plant is positively mainstream, so much so that it's almost passé. But the mushrooms prove to be another example of how my life inside this little cottage has become one vast echo chamber.

The first packet I ordered was accidentally delivered to the holiday cottage opposite, and the people staying there for the weekend opened the package that was not addressed to them and complained about its contents to my landlady (maybe they had a bad trip). Her husband wanted me out. He's wanted me out from the start; he doesn't like how cheaply she's renting it to me. She's ignored him and let me stay because she gives more chances than most, and for some reason she always roots for the underdog. But the clock is ticking.

By the age of thirty, Julian of Norwich had received her visions. Then, she would lock herself away in a cell and study and write and commune with the divine, and then she would become a saint. I am fast approaching thirty-one and the only visions I've been receiving, profound as they may have seemed, have been supplied by psilocybin. Some trips are more constructive than others. For instance, I spend an evening besotted with a plum pie I've cooked. I cannot stop stroking its still-warm shell. I love the pie so much I could cry. It's just so . . . warm! Cherries are magnificent. Apple juice is about to change my life. I don't like cigarettes, though, it turns out.

When I eventually tear myself away from the kitchen area, I lie on the sofa and close my eyes. The room disappears and I go back to what feels like something, possibly The Mushroom, is telling me is a past life, and instead of a little cottage in a beachside village I'm in a sixteenth-century French palace, with high, gilded ceilings; everyone, including me, is in Renaissance dress. I'm being escorted to someone I am about to marry and am surprised by how good my French is. I wonder with all this talk of past life connections whether I can't put into perspective my present life connections, and in a way, I do. In the next vision, I see everyone I love transformed back into a child. I start seeing everyone like that from here on out: strangers, friends, family – I'll never be able to shake the image that we are all just children, pretending that we're not.

The overarching threat of being kicked out kind of puts an abrupt end to the whimsy of my magical mystery tours. It's all very well drifting, but what's the drifting for? The risk of eviction has given me a scare. I don't want to fall off this path; I want to get it right this time. If you aren't rich, you need credibility if you want to get by, and I'm not helping myself here in that regard – unlike Julian of Norwich, there aren't many who are going to want me canonised because of my visions. Backed into a corner, I decide I'll play the game, having learned a few short cuts. I will compromise with those who have been urging me to take a more conventional path. It turns out I think I agree with them: I want, feel like I need, a qualification if I am going to be able to make the solitary life of a writer work. Try as I might to ignore it, there's no two ways about it: I need more money. Admittedly, many would say applying to do a master's in writing without an undergraduate degree is as much of a folly as sitting at home tripping and hoping to understand the world better. I think it over for several months, but do, eventually, apply to do a master's degree – it seems pretty unlikely anyone will accept me, but with no undergraduate degree, I could get a student loan.

I begin preparing myself to move on, somewhere, and decide it's high time I tied up my loose ends. I mention this in passing to my sister Charlotte, and she volunteers to drive and collect a couple of my bags from my ex's parents. I steel myself and message him to arrange a day for my sister to pick up my things. He calls me from a pub – he's drinking, and I'm pretty sure he's drunk because he's saying nice things about me, that I'm a kind person, I'm unique, I'm a star. The flattery is making me feel uneasy. I can feel bad vibes under the niceties. I need to get off the phone. I tell him, as I always will, that I am sorry for how bad it got between us and that I hope he finds happiness. He tells me that I must be in a good place to say that. I say that I am. He tells me that he will slit the throat of any man who comes near me. I remember what it is like to talk to him. I could never understand how someone could go from being so charming to so scary within a sentence. I'd almost forgotten how quickly he can turn. I'd almost started to wonder if it was as bad as I remembered. Now I remember. I don't have to understand it. Just accept it and run. I make my excuses, hang up and drop the phone. This is how it always used to feel, like it was a fight to the death. I have not cured myself of my fear of him, and actually I don't think that would be a very good idea. I don't understand how I spent so long so close to someone I was so scared of. How did I get used to living in a state of peril every day where, whatever was being said, however nice, there was always a black full stop waiting to put an end to every sentence? It's amazing what a human being can get used to, and how quickly.

I'm grateful to my sister for collecting my stuff – the thought of having to do that gives me the fear, and anyway, I just want to stay here, floating through life. If it hadn't been made clear that time was running out on this cottage I doubt I would ever have applied for the master's. I would have stayed, content to mooch through the days seeing what I could see and being happy that I was here to see it. That would have been my choice if I'd had the freedom to make it. But I never seem to be able to get too comfortable for too long. I must make another leap, and this time, unlike every other time, I know what it is I want to do. With a master's degree I can earn enough money as a tutor to support a solitary life. The experience here and in the barn has been confirmation that solitude is my lodestone; it's how I get back to myself; it's how I think for myself; it's how I feel an affinity with nature, which is the most profound connection I've ever felt.

Without the help of others, it's still almost impossible for me to find anywhere to live, even down here, and I would really like to open up more possibilities for myself now. I have run out of favours and I am tired of having to ask for them. I need to stand on my own two feet and be responsible. Having published two whole short stories now, I test my luck and apply for a scholarship to do a creative writing master's at a prestigious university and am promptly rejected. I then apply to a different university for a master's in a breadth of writerly skill sets (without asking for a scholarship this time). As it happens, I've built up a decent portfolio over the years. It's decent enough to get me accepted onto a course in London.

On my last night in my home by the sea, I listen to the trees that rush like the waves. I stare at the stars and think how I'll miss them in the city. I'm still avoiding horoscopes, but I can't help but wonder if the planets really do have anything to do with the cycles of our lives; because sometimes it feels like everyone must complete a full circle of trials at some point. No telling when – that appears to be random – and yet it feels orchestrated. If you make it out the other side, you are emotionally evolved. If I have made it out the other side, I don't know where to begin. What do they say? That just when you think you have nothing left to learn, life shows you exactly how little you really know.

12.

Here, Again

However determined I might be in mind and spirit, it seems my body is rebelling at being returned to London – everywhere, it seems, holds memories I would really rather not be reminded of. I avoid East like the plague, but inevitably end up walking past his old flat, the alley where I stood with the police, the street where I was beaten up and mugged; then West London and the hotel where my drink was spiked; then South London, and the pub next to the house on the square where I was assaulted. Try as I might to avoid these places, sooner or later I end up going by. But I don't even flinch. I give my past the evil eye and walk on.

Then, out of nowhere, I start fainting – like the fainting goats when they get scared, I just start dropping. The first time it happens, I am cat-sitting in my sister's flat and faint in the kitchen and wake up in the kitty litter. It starts happening with such regularity that I learn to recognise the symptoms and get myself somewhere soft: dizziness, shortness of breath, cold sweat, hot flush, boom – like the start of panic attacks, which I am now beginning to get again. I cannot work out why they have started; there is rarely anything I am conscious of that has triggered them.

Maybe you have to be at a safe distance to see how dangerous life got, and now, as far as my body's concerned, I've put myself back in the danger zone. I read about what happens to the body during a panic attack to try to understand what it is I am experiencing. It turns out that the reasons and explanations for panic attacks (unfortunately) don't diminish the experience. All I surmise from the literature is that something powerful is happening to my body that my brain does not understand.

I'm convinced, as are others around me, that my constant fainting and weekly panic attacks have something to do with something isolatable, something for which I can take a tablet. There's a chance it could be exhaustion – I'm pushing myself as hard as I can, working harder than I ever have before because I don't want to fail, I can't. I'm trying to finish a novel that I just can't find a way to finish. I'm working as a secretary, a ghostwriter, copywriting, studying for a master's and volunteering with a charity that works with children in encouraging them to express themselves through storytelling and poetry. I love volunteering there, but my body puts an end to that, and indeed anything that is not essential.

As well as the fainting and the panic attacks, I start getting skin conditions associated with weakened immune systems – dermatitis and impetigo, all over my face. Weakened immune systems can result from long-term stress, which decreases the body's white blood cell count, I find out when I meet up with my old manager from the art news website that I've (rashly) left after three years as they wouldn't give me a pay rise. She says, 'Your body is attacking itself. You need to start paying attention to that. Slow down and look after yourself – really.' But I can't slow down; if I slow down then everything will fall apart. I have to keep up the momentum to keep my new world turning. Doctors can't seem to find anything wrong with me.

I have a full sweep of blood tests for vitamin and mineral deficiencies, for anaemia, for diabetes – nothing.

I'm staying at a friend's. It's the middle of the night and I go to the bathroom. The room starts spinning faster than my mind can calibrate, my ears are ringing and I can't make my eyes focus on anything, the cold sweat has arrived, I'm not quick enough to find somewhere soft, and I black out. When I wake up I find I've cracked my head on their bath, my nose is bleeding and I have a wound in the middle of my forehead that's also oozing blood. It is sporting this wound, which develops into a gnarly scab, that I will soon meet David, the man who will become my husband.

Like many master's students, I am studying part-time so I can keep working. It will take me almost two years to graduate and I will spend almost three years in London – I will need to ask for just a few more favours. This first year I am spending living out of a suitcase on the sofas of extremely patient friends and family members, while I save up money to rent somewhere. I'd say I'm travelling light, but there are standing stones smaller than my suitcase; its formidable size gives it an air of guardianship. I am lugging around my own personal heavy. My heavy holds everything: my clothes, my books, my passport, my mementos, my guitar, my candles; it contains the paraphernalia of a home. Saying that, I am missing home, Devon. Every time I go to Hampstead Heath and get a semblance of the wild, I miss it even more. As I watch the resident black cormorant on the lake raising its wings, triumphant as death, I think of the cormorants on the Taw estuary. The feeling that I want to escape has returned. I find myself in jammed Tube stations closing my eyes as hundreds of people shove past me.

I start searching for places outside London. I look, as I have before, at cheap, remote cottages in Wales and Yorkshire and wish I were there. Maybe I've chosen the wrong path, and if I have, at what point is it too late to turn off it? I don't want to end up down life's garbage chute again. But I've chosen to try and do the 'right' thing, and I've chosen to be here to do it, I remind myself. Don't overthink it. See it through, for once in your life, and then get out.

It's at a birthday of the friend I have being staying with that I meet the man who will become my husband. I meet him at 1.30 a.m., just as he is leaving, coat and backpack on; but he doesn't leave for another three hours. We are friends for a few months first, because we're both kind of wary – meeting some- one I like wasn't the plan, this could mess with my exit strategy, and it wasn't his plan either, he's content being single and has been for years – but we make each other laugh, and I could do with a laugh.

As we wander around the Middle Ages section of the National Gallery one afternoon, I tell him, almost as a warning, that I've basically been living as a hermit until very recently, and he laughs. There's no judgement, apparently he doesn't find this in the slightest bit weird or ridiculous, even though I'm pretty sure it is a little weird.

Maybe we'd have trundled on like this, sharing fragments of ourselves, for months, years, being cautious, taking things *very* slowly. Or maybe we would have taken it so slowly that we'd have stopped sharing things and drifted apart.

I'm visiting my mum in Devon. She is driving me through the early morning to catch the bus back to London when she has a heart failure on a dual carriageway. Mum's never liked back-seat drivers, so when I feel us veer over the rumble strip on the left-hand side of the road I stop myself from saying anything. She'll straighten up in a minute. But she doesn't. What happens next doesn't take more than fifteen, twenty seconds, but I can remember it moment to moment as if we inhabited those seconds individually for hours on end, studied and explored each of them before we moved on to the next.

We are driving along at about 50–60 mph and the bumping stops, not because these 'wake-up calls' have made Mum straighten up, but because the wheels are now on the other side and the rumble strip is underneath the car. We are veering further and further to the left. There is a lay-by coming up, and although I don't say a word, my brain staggers around for explanations as to what is happening. We are heading for the lay-by, but why? We are going much too fast to be heading for the lay-by. My brain lurches.

'Mum, what are you doing?'

No answer.

We fly into the lay-by's plastic bollard and over it, over the concrete island it rests upon. It is now evident we are not stopping here. We aren't stopping at all. It is now very evident we are going to crash somewhere. I just don't know where yet.

'Mum!' I shout. 'Brake!'

No answer.

I tear my eyes away from what's in front of us and to my mother. When my eyes finally pass the field, the lay-by, the trees, they reach her. Her grey-green eyes are wide open. Unblinking. Her hands are stiff on the wheel. It doesn't look like she is breathing. She is frozen.

I scream again. 'Brake! Mum!'

Nothing.

It's too late for me to do anything. My limbs feel disorganised and I'm too slow to pull up the handbrake or put my foot on the brake pedal. It's all happening too fast. I put my hand on the steering wheel to try to turn the car right a little, to stop us flying off the road and into the trees, but the other option is going back onto the dual carriageway and into a stream of fast-moving traffic. It's too late.

Mum's hands are still stuck on the wheel as I turn it a little, and then, I just let go. I stare at her, completely dumbfounded; I can't comprehend the nightmare in front of me. My mother is dying, or dead, I think, and I am dying, or dead. I turn my head to the fast-approaching green. The trees we're heading for. I look back at her, frozen, and at the leaves at our side. As we fly off the road and into the air, I don't feel as I had imagined I would, facing death. I don't feel scared. I feel profoundly sad. Profoundly powerless. Overcome by an all-consuming, gut-wrenching melancholia. Before a tree further down the bank stops our flight, just before I think, *So this is how it happens*, I remember David and experience a wave of deepest regret. I only just met him.

Impact.

I can't be sure for a second, but it seems we're alive. I'm struggling to breathe but my arms and legs seem to be okay. It seems that hitting the tree at such force has roused Mum back into semi-consciousness. The car is folded in on itself, smoke is coming from under the bonnet. None of the electric windows or front doors will open, my side is smashed shut, so I drag my still semi-conscious mum out of the back passenger door, worried the car's going to explode. It doesn't. A couple who were driving behind us, watching the whole thing in bewilderment, have already called an ambulance. In the back of the ambulance on the way to the hospital, the ambulance crew tell us something I already know as I sit watching them rip open Mum's clothes, apply heart monitors and inject her with morphine while I refuse it, for once determined to stay lucid: we are lucky to be alive. We're beyond lucky, as far as injuries go. I've got a cut that will become a scar on my knee and some bruised bones, but am otherwise, miraculously, fine – as is my mum, except for the fact we now know something is very wrong with her heart.

I was grateful for my life before the crash; now I am terrified of losing it. Everything is a threat to life: I don't like flying, I don't like people sitting behind me, I don't like being in the passenger seat of anything because I know that the Bad Times are coming to get me, I was never going to escape them for long, I knew I couldn't just have a nice life. But during the weeks after the crash, David tries to show me otherwise. He brings me food and cooks for me while I recover. I start getting nightmares, screaming nightmares about the crash. He is gentle with me, wakes me up from them and tells me I'm okay, I'm safe now. His gentleness and patience become the hallmarks of this period for me. Slowly, the dreams fade, and with their disappearance I find the panic attacks also start to dwindle; they don't go away completely, but they happen more rarely. I stop fainting, for the most part. He makes me feel safe, and I tell him this.

He has plenty of friends but considers himself a loner too – I smile to myself when I hear one of his closest friends call him that – so we give each other space, naturally, trustingly. I await some sort of backlash whenever I'm alone for periods of time but it never comes. He respects that I will always need time alone, and when I go to a finca in the mountains in Spain near where my dad lives and turn off my phone for a few days to rest, he trusts that I am on my own, doesn't even question it. Compared to what I've been used to, this is like night and day. But as soon as I realise things are starting to get serious, and they do very quickly after the crash, I start freaking out.

If he gets to know me, who I really am, he will realise that I'm no good. I feel like I've tricked him into liking me – I must've done, he seems to think I'm 'graceful'. I tell him everything I know is unlikeable about me to balance the books. It doesn't put him off. But, I tell him, I think I'm destined to be broke for my entire life. 'We don't need much,' is his reply. I have a panic attack in front of him in a bar before meeting his friends; he breathes with me and helps bring me back down. He gives me an antique ring for Christmas from Portobello Market with tiny little South Sea pearls; when one of them falls out, I spend half an hour in the toilets of the Odeon Cinema on Holloway Road trying to find it. I can't, and I come out of the toilets crying, insisting that this is a sign, it marks the beginning of the end – this is a message from the Bad Times, an omen, everything will fall apart now. He assures me, quietly, in the cinema corridor, that it means nothing. We'll replace the pearl next week. *Sure we will*, I think, convinced the evil little pearl is now free to ruin our lives. I question what I am doing and why I am doing it over and over again in my journal, because it's not easy giving yourself up after you've spent years putting the pieces back together, particularly if you've found you're quite happy with the result.

I've told him almost nothing of my last relationship, only that it was not good, specifically so that I don't have any excuse for behaving in a way he does not deserve (that he has put up with my erratic behaviour knowing so little is testament to his nature). Neither of us talks much about one another's past. We both want to get to know each other as the people we are now, out of context. I'm noticing that I'm harder than I used to be – I can cut myself off, shut down my emotions at the slightest hint of someone causing me emotional pain. Yet, somehow, I'm more vulnerable, more sensitive to everything and everyone around me. I'm finding I don't trust a comfortable life. I look for problems, warning signs. I think I am pre-empting disasters but am reminded time and time again that they have already taken place. David is patient with me, tells me I have to stop being so afraid of anyone and everyone getting angry with me, asks why I'm so jumpy at loud noises – 'I don't know.' Having finally saved up some money, when we move in together I find myself spiralling, nice and quietly, all inside my own head. I don't like having something to lose – this isn't what I'd planned, but now that I have it, I'm scared of losing it.

Then, as if by magic, my phone starts ringing and it doesn't stop. He's back.

At first, I ignore it – ten, twenty missed calls a day – but I worry I'm going to make him angry and that's always ended badly for me. The next time he calls, I pick up. He doesn't ask how I am, what I've been doing for the last three years, just tells me he misses me, what he's doing, where he's working, asks me to meet up with him, says that he still has photos of me. 'Not *those* kinds of photos,' he says, 'the other kind.' He says it so casually, why does it sound like a threat? I tell him, as nicely as I can so he doesn't get angry, as I will tell him every time he emails, WhatsApps, messages, that I can't see him again, that I just want him to move on and be happy. 'My new girlfriend's a millionaire,' he tells me. That's great. I seem to remember the one before me had a castle, so a natural balance has been restored. I'm happy for you. I hope life is good to you. I hope you use your talents well. Please leave me alone. But the calls don't stop. I don't want to burden my boyfriend with this, so I confide in a friend and he warns me that this is essentially stalking. Endless messages, pleading with me to pick up. He's dying, again.

One morning David asks what's wrong with me, because I'm shaking over my phone, texting, begging to be left alone, and I decide to tell him.

'Just ignore him,' David says, simply.

'It's not that simple, I can't ignore him, he'll get angry.'

'Does he know where we live?'

'No.'

'Then who cares if he gets angry? Just ignore him.'

This is what people were telling me to do for years and I ignored their advice because I thought I knew best – they didn't know what he was like, I did, and I had to make sure he was never angry with me or else there'd be consequences. But the advice sounds different when I hear it this time. I send a final message wishing him well and then I block him on every single medium, half expecting the world to explode, but there's silence, for a little while.

He sets up multiple new Instagram accounts to follow and message me on. At first it terrifies me, I feel harassed, as if my phone has been invaded and is no longer safe to use. Then I feel myself starting to pity him a little, the way he's behaving is pathetic – but that's how he gets you: the wounded-animal routine. Beware: it bites. Block. Block. Block. Every time I block one account a new one appears. 'Haha, I have hundreds of these,' he writes. I'm glad someone is finding this amusing, because the nightmares of him trying to force his way into my home have returned. I'm trapped in a car with him, trying desperately not to make him angry. Block. Block. Block. Every time I get an email notification alerting me that someone is trying to get into my account, which happens with surprising regularity, I wonder if it is him. Slowly, though, things do quieten down. I deleted my original Facebook account when we broke up and have set my other accounts to private, but as the Instagram messages from his pseudonymous accounts diminish, I decide it's time to stop being afraid. He's not a bad person, just someone who doesn't know how to deal with his pain and acts as if inflicting suffering on someone else will somehow lessen his. I dare myself to believe it's safe to start seeing his threats for what they were: just words, the words of someone lashing out at the thing that always responds. That can't be me any more. I open my accounts up to 'public', ignore the occasional message he sends, and wake up one morning finding I have the semblance of a 'normal' life. This comes with challenges of its own. It takes a couple of months before I admit to my boyfriend that I feel desperately insecure in all this stability – this is completely new territory and I am unsure of my footing, I don't know how to do a nice, normal life, living together nicely like people do. But then, neither does he. We'll make it up as we go along.

David's a city boy – born in Cardiff, he moved straight to London, and I know that it's more than likely he won't want a remote and wild existence. At the same time, I know all I can do is say that's what I want quite early on, like someone else might bring up children, or marriage. Monks in Greece are made to go back to the city before committing to an isolated existence as hermits or monks on their island retreats, to make sure that they know what they are leaving, so that having left it they never long for it. I love the galleries and charity shops, and many of my friends and family, the people who are the pillars of my life, are still here, but I have to get back to the green. Living in London again is only strengthening that desire – it's more than a desire, I can't live any other way now. Having been all I wanted at one point, now I fear being trapped in a conventional life. I grew up wild and I am now realising that's how I like it, so I float the idea of living in a caravan in a field. He's not thrilled by it.

As it turns out, though, he is up for a change, and while we plan how and when we will leave London for Devon, the whole world changes. The pandemic hits. I lose a lot of work at first, am sick with worry about my family, and there's the general fog of doom hanging over the city, but I find I quite like London during lockdown. With an engagement ring on my finger (not a pearl in sight), we walk to the parks at 4 a.m. with a hip flask full of rum when I can't sleep. Dust covers the cars parked on the road. The city has emptied like it does at Christmas. We walk whole lengths of London, looking at it with the eyes of time travellers. I sit in an almost deserted Trafalgar Square and wish only that the galleries would open. It's a strange goodbye to the city.

Stranger still, I'll be leaving the city married. Once we're engaged, I envisage myself drinking weak tea, trying to make conversation with women I have nothing in common with except being a wife, while the men drink and smoke and have interesting debates in the drawing room. It scares the hell out of me until I remind myself that Nancy Mitford lived a long time ago now, and being a wife has changed considerably since she helped formulate my idea of wedded bliss in the novels my mum gave me when I was younger. When I get my head back into reality, I remind myself that I can trust my instincts about people now. I have also learned not to turn my back on a good thing, no matter how different it is from whatever I had in mind for myself, because you can wait a whole lifetime for a good thing. When I was alone, waiting for a sign as to which path to take next, I promised myself I would recognise the good things in life and embrace them in whatever form they came, if they came at all. I reassure myself that I don't have to change to be a wife, don't have to lessen myself to fit into a marriage – David certainly doesn't expect this of me, so maybe I can still be me, independent of will but part of a team. Maybe it could even be fun. Expecting some resistance, I inform David that I won't be taking his name, because I couldn't be anybody else now. 'That's fine – it makes no difference to me,' he says. 'I just want you.'

Our attention consumed by the stress of trying to plan even a very small wedding during a pandemic, we know only that we will leave London, not where we will live – something will come up, I keep saying, without really looking into it, because I have been quietly ruminating on an idea for some time. I don't know if it's in reaction to being back somewhere so populated, but I want *space*. I want to experience somewhere far removed from this, more remote than ever before, isolated to the nth degree, somewhere where there is no nothing. I am craving isolation like salt. Remote places flash across my computer screen, week after week: the Highlands, North-West Wales, the West of Ireland, Spain . . . but is there not anywhere in the county I call home?

It's early summer and it's scorching. I am wearing all white but still struggling in the heat. I move with the boughs of the trees in the hot breeze to stay under their shade, while my eighty-year-old cousins (the cousins I am close to) seem completely oblivious to the thirty-five degrees of white heat piercing our skin as we drink boiling hot tea in their garden. We're talking about Croyde, about the green hut, and then they get to telling us a story about some ancient piracy on Lundy Island.

Lundy.

It's as if I had stared at it for so long I had stopped seeing it. I considered Lundy a distant, mystical land; I didn't even really consider it, it was just some place far out to sea that came and went with the sea mist. It was a place in abstract: somewhere other people went on day trips to see the puffins. How had it never occurred to me to try and live there before? Why had I never tried to get a job there? It was right in front of me for years, decades. I say to them that that's where I want to go, that's the place I have been looking for and it was there all along. They smile and say, as everyone will, that it's a nice idea and they wish me luck, but no one really thinks we'll do it. David hopes we won't. But I can't explain this feeling, how powerful it is. It's like all of those years of staring at the island are barrelling into a flash decision: I have to go there. I'll do anything to make it happen.

I don't weigh up the pros and cons as my soon-to-be husband sensibly does, I only focus my attention on getting there – I'll figure out the pros and cons when I arrive. After months of back and forth with the island managers, trying and sometimes seemingly failing to find a way in which we can make our living there benefit all parties, when I finally get the news that we've got the go-ahead, David seems reticent.

'What about the internet?' he says. 'I need to be able to work.'

'I know, me too.' (Although I don't have to do daily video calls.) 'The internet will be fine.'

'Everything I've read says the internet's terrible.'

I plead with him to take a chance and to come with me, but (rather unfairly) say I will be going with or without him – this is an experience of a lifetime and now I've found a way in, I can't turn away from it. There's just no way. I've missed too many experiences in my life, either through fear or because chaos hampered my efforts to see opportunities through, and I know this is the kind of opportunity that only comes around once. I want to experience as much as I can now. I want to really *live*. Doesn't he? Isn't this what we should all want, experience just for the sake of it? I do appreciate that the caravan in a field's starting to look rather tame now, but I keep encouraging him to take a leap. We're all still working from home, so let's make home somewhere like never before, if only for a while.

'All right.' He relents, smiling. 'Let's do it.'

Nine months after graduating with my master's, and ten days after getting married in the village where I grew up, we leave.

Lundy

13.

The Otherworld

It's a wet December morning and the wind is up. I've always said you have to have a death wish to want to fly in a helicopter, but it's the only way to get to Lundy in the winter. So here I am with my husband in a little heliport, consisting of what is essentially a munitions hut in a farmer's field at Hartland Point, where the windswept trees are stooped like crones. This is the furthest outcrop in the sea, and the closest knuckle of land to Lundy.

The helicopter runs twice a week to ferry visitors back and forth. This is also the only means of getting supplies to the island. When the weather is bad, the fog too thick (as is often the case), there is no helicopter. No visitors. No supplies. This all sounds very isolated to me, but it is nothing compared with what is to come.

At the heliport we watch a video from the early 2000s of elderly women in floaty skirts getting in and out of a helicopter, stuffing their chiffon scarves into their shirts so they don't get wound in and chopped up by the blades. We read posters on the wall about how Lundy is a place of scientific research, a conservation area on land and in water. All forms of life live here, some endemic to the island like the Lundy cabbage (which apparently tastes like Brussels sprouts – although, it being forbidden to pick anything living on the island, I couldn't tell you) and the Lundy flea that lives on it. There are also the endemic pygmy shrews that climb over you while you sleep, their tiny hearts beating so fast the slightest fright can kill them. Then there are the dolphins, minke whales, thresher sharks, puffins, Manx shearwaters, gannets, guillemots, skylarks, oil beetles, wheatears, peregrine falcons, merlins, Celtic sea slugs. The list is endless. I have my heart set on the dolphins.

After the flight talk, the vicar who – under normal circumstances – travels once a month to Lundy to give a service to the dwindling congregation of visitors, stands up in front of the small crowd and singles me out. 'Where's Jade?'

Hesitant, I raise my hand. This is the hand that found a crack in the fortress. Despite being told there was no way in, there was through the church. The vicar and the managers of the island have taken a leap of faith and let us rent the vestry in the island church. Neither the Landmark Trust nor the church rent properties on Lundy to the public in any long-term capacity, and the vestry has never been leased to the public previously; it's only used for the vicars to stay in when they give their services once a month. But the pandemic – and the cancellation of thousands of weddings – has financially impacted the Diocese of Exeter, as it impacted all churches in the UK, and the rent we are offering to pay for staying there will help recoup some of the massive losses of the last year. But what really turned the heads of the island managers was when I volunteered my cleaning services – you never know what skills might come in handy one day.

The journey over to the island takes around seven minutes by helicopter in the winter and just over two hours by boat in the summer. Seven minutes doesn't sound very long, but as we

leave the earth, the blades of the helicopter whomping furiously against the wet wind, the fragile plastic windows
rattling, the smell of petrol seeping into the cabin in which we
and four visitors wear face masks, and we feel the pressure lift
and the chopper rise and fall as we leave the land, the waves
crashing on the jagged cliffs below, then up, up over the lighthouse, out over the sea and . . . Nothing but water and air: it
feels like a long ride.

As we approach the island, the sun has found its way out of
a hulking cumulus above the island, showing the place and all
its crags in full illumination. Falcons sweep from their eyries.
Herring gulls plummet in a tailspin. Waves hit the rocks over
and over again, and you see how repeating patterns wear you
away. The island was once ten times the size it is now, and
emanates the distinct feeling that it is crumbling away a little
every winter. The sea bites at the shore and the paths; mud,
slate, granite and clumps of thrift tumble from the headland.
The ocean moves huge boulders around, changing the face of
the beach so that if you were on this island completely alone
and had no one to ask, you would think you were losing your
mind. At one point, a wide seam of yellow rock called lundyite
becomes visible, like a yellow brick road, and within a matter
of days it will have completely disappeared again.

The last glaciation gave Lundy its crags, large valleys, and
the gullies of Millcombe, a wooded, birded valley where a
Georgian mansion was built – its perfectly proportioned façade
seems out of place on this higgledy-piggledy rock, where the
only buildings that really fit in are the ruins – and the other
major valley of Gannets' Combe, so named because it's the
nesting spot for gannets, or 'Ganymede's birds' as they were
once called.

Up in the helicopter that now whomps above the church, you see how drastically the island's topography changes between its poles, partitioned into quarters by moss-covered drystone walls. The south end of the island is green and ver-dant, agricultural and shaped by the remnants of Bronze Age pattern farming. Streams flow from the fields down over the cliffs and out into the sea, the broad-leafed pondweed in these streams an almost luminous green. The further north you look, the more barren it becomes – by the quarter wall it has transformed, almost immediately, into moorland; an expanse of heather-smothered granite. The occasional bleed where the heather hasn't taken leaves a quartz-sheened moonscape and remnants of Mesolithic huts such as Widow's Tenement. Here, there are goats, Soay sheep, Lundy ponies, Sika deer and Highland cattle. Aside from the heather, as far as vegetation goes there is only the dried, red bracken; the golden molinia grass that moans in the wind; and dead gorse flowers that rattle in the shrub like a catacomb of loose skulls. The island is only three miles long, but as we rush back to the ground, it seems vast.

Back on land, I crouch low under the blades while people much taller than me manage to walk without fear of being decapitated. We are greeted by the islanders in their fire ser-vice gear – they work in the tavern, as cleaners, as wildlife wardens, as the emergency services, as maintenance; men who had never driven a tractor before arriving here ride one nimbly up and down the narrow cliff road. Out here, every-one is everything. There are so few people: twenty-four permanent residents now. When there was a working quarry, the population was three hundred. There is no island vet, optician, dentist or doctor. If you need a doctor, you're going to have to call the coastguard.

Ravens hobble along the ground with the crooked-legged sheep, and while my husband goes off to investigate the open-air gents, I am welcomed with, 'Ah, so you're the hermit,' by the island manager, Rob. I guess he's read the piece I wrote while in Croyde about being a modern-day hermit.

'Recovering hermit,' I joke, unthinkingly. Although it's not what I mean – that state is not something to recover from. What I mean is, hermit in spirit, but no longer hermit in practice.

Accompanied by the vicar, we make our way to the vestry. My husband and I will sleep in a single bed, which sounds romantic but is actually just very small. We'll cook on a single-ring hotplate with the only pot we could bring over with the fifteen-kilogram weight limit, and use the porch as a fridge. The lack of convenience is more than worth it to be here, and for everything it lacks there is something that makes up for it. The huge old church window that faces the writing desk. The font we will use as a fruit bowl, and the Wenlock stove. The skylight out of which I will see gulls, starlings, ravens and the moon. What I think is our utility cupboard door turns out, in fact, to open straight into the massive wood-beamed church. It's so unexpected I lose my footing a little, as if falling off the edge of the world into an entirely new one.

Lundy is known as both 'the otherworld' and Ynys Wair (meaning 'Gwair's Island' in Welsh). Legend has it that 'Gwair' is an alternative name for the wizard Gwydion, from the tales of the Mabinogion, who was imprisoned here. The otherworld of myth is a universe entirely unto itself; its reality is its own, separate from but running alongside our everyday reality.

Islands in Celtic myth have always been associated with liminal spaces, and to the Celts Lundy was one of the 'islands of the dead'. Much like the otherworld, the islands of the dead were akin to parallel worlds that exist alongside ours. Islands like Lundy were regarded as holy – as a gateway or a point of access to the gods. It was believed that such isolation brings us closer to the divine. And is likely why, later in time as religions and beliefs melted and fused, islands became a place of both pilgrimage and hermitage to early Christians. The island is a portal.

Like in Rome, the relics of Lundy's history are plainly visible as you walk over it. They are disintegrating like the melted metal remnants, still in situ, of the German bombers that crashed on the island in the Second World War, when the islanders were forced to take the Germans prisoner. You can spot the crash site near the half wall, because seventy-odd years later the vegetation still hasn't grown back.

Of the island's ever-eroding history there is still so much that has not yet been excavated. As far as we know, the island has been inhabited since Mesolithic times and, remote as it is, people have come here to live or to seek respite ever since. Populated in waves over thousands of years, in around 3500 BCE people from the mainland brought over agriculture and stone-working, pattern-farming and pottery. In 2000 BCE, people from southern England arrived with bronze and then iron. Then came the Celtic period, and eventually the Christian era, which would bring the island its first (now rubbled) chapel. The varied legends from the eras still spring from the island's rock like its clear water. The island's history is a distillation of chronicle, legend, folklore, superstition and religion. Strange findings and ancient burial grounds. Pirates and marauders. Giants and megalomaniacs. Kings and wizard kings. The Knights Templar and the Holy Grail. There is skulduggery afoot.

As the day draws to a close, I walk through the old stone village, and again I get the feeling I have fallen off the edge of the world and into another one, an older one, where time is neither linear nor circular, but static. This island contains all the habitats I am familiar with and it feels the same as the other rural, isolated environments I've known but . . . different. It's as if every living thing here knows a secret. We're due to stay here until the spring, but already I'm hoping we will stay longer, long enough to become part of the secret. Ever since the barn, I've realised that wild places give me the stimulation someone else might get from bungee jumping or driving too fast; it's the thrill of offering my life up without having to take a risk. In the barn, I had no idea how events would unfold, where I would go, who I would become. So much has changed. I have a writing career; I have a master's; and, most surprising to me, most surreal, I am married to a man who is supportive, a joy to be around. These things, and being here, are so far removed from where I was in my life all those years ago, and yet I haven't changed all that much. I still feel the same as I did then, on those first days alone. So blown away by it all, so grateful that I stuck around and saw it through. I can't imagine I'll ever feel any different now.

Within a few hours of being here on Lundy I appreciate how important the local pub was to the isolated village communities of the past – as dusk draws down, lights come on in the village and the few people here wander into its warm fire-lit main room: there's nowhere else to go. In the village there's also a little shop that's well stocked for a tiny island, and that's about it. The geese call out to the rising moon, and chickens quietly get on with their business of pecking in the allotments. Nothing changes over the centuries, only an exchange of the phantoms that live the experience.

I bump into one of the older contractors working here; he's from Devon and has been coming over for decades to work on bits and bobs on the island. 'You want to make sure you go and look at Old Light; they're doing restoration work at the moment, but you ask nicely and they'll let you up.' (Old Light is a disused and now converted lighthouse.)

'Cool, okay, I will.'

'I wouldn't go at night, though – I saw a ghost last time I was working up there.'

'Did you?'

He smiles, his eyes watering a little in the wind, and nods.

'Really?'

He smiles again and nods.

'What kind of ghost?'

'The figure of a man on the stairs.'

A shiver runs through me. 'I've always wanted to see a ghost,' I say. 'I'd never even dreamed of one until a few months ago.'

'Oh, there's plenty here,' he says, twinkling with excitement, 'down in Millcombe too – a whole family, supposedly. One guy working here woke up and found them all at the foot of his bed staring at him!'

As we talk in the half-light he appears almost translucent, and I feel a bit tripped out. Watching the occasional body come and go as we talk, I think about how humans have been coming and going in different forms on this rock for millennia. The fact that I am here means I must go. Like the sheep and the starlings, we've all taken one another's place and someone will take ours. Our impermanence, our transience, is all I can think about, looking into his yellow-green eyes, and it feels as if I have returned to the other side of a déjà vu. I am seeing ghosts as we speak. This island is both a sanctuary for birds on migration and for the transmigration of souls.

I walk up and out past the big black shed from which comes a cacophony of whistling and shrilling, the evensong of hundreds of starlings going to roost. Up past the silhouette of the rusting stone-crusher which is left from when the roads were built in the 1970s, a standing stone to bygone years and symbolic of what happens if you stay here too long. Up into the wide south-west field that rolls out into the ocean and the setting sun, in front of which stands a small herd of Sika deer, the antlers of an older male rising up like a black crown as he studies my progress through the fields. Before we came here, people told me the idea of living here was a bit far-fetched, it was a 'fantasy'. It certainly is. Maybe it's the emptiness here, how removed it feels from the collective consciousness of the mainland, but there is something transcendent about it all. It is completely mad and I absolutely love it. I continue exploring, following the path the old Land Rovers have made up the hill, past the graveyard where the bones of those whom we replace rest. Up past Old Light and down the centre of the island, marching over the last of the puff-ball mushrooms. I can see the other end of the island from where I stand, and now, as I head north, I have the moon and sun on opposite sides. The moon rising on the east, my right, and the sun setting on the west, my left, and in between them I stand like the scales, neither balanced nor unbalanced, but that which balances all that is put upon it – the weight of existence it is glad to hold.

*

Tonight, as the stars come out, the wind picks up, as it will do every night almost the minute the sun sets behind the sea, as if on a counterweight lever. It reaches its crescendo at around 4 a.m. and pushes and shoves the church, so hard it sounds like a solid force slamming against the walls. And then, over the roof, a stampede of horses. I thank the granite and the invisible hands that keep this church standing in 80-mph winds; it seems like an impossible feat, because I know this wind. This is the same wind that visited the barn. The wind that, accompanied by rain, made the house sound like it was going through a car wash. I feel closer to its source now. On this island, the old wind is at the height of its powers.

I wake up early, but have been asleep for a hundred years. I am covered in the dust and grit that has blown through little holes and cracks in the joinery of the wall. It's in my hair, on my face, on the pillow – it's everywhere. This constant assault of elements is also a reminder that it's time to wake up from the daydream of London life again; the world has my full attention once more. I wipe the grit off my face and lie in the rest of the dust, listening to the wind and the occasional tinkle of a falling piece of ceiling.

There will be winter mornings when the wind has tired itself out during the night and it is completely still and silent. In the moments of waking, only the cry of gulls will be a reminder that I'm not on particularly dry land. Then every single morning, as soon as I get up, I will open the red door of the vestry and look out past the escaped sheep grazing, the sheep shit that will have invariably arrived on our path in the night, out at the wall that leads down to the castle built by Henry III, out to the sea, to the sun that is rising, and out to where I used to be. When the fog is as thick as cheap duvet insulation, I will imagine where I am from the herring gull's eyes and it will take my breath away.

Compared with its tumultuous history, on the island these days there is a disappointing lack of wrecking, treachery, insubordination, treason and piracy, but the amount of rum consumed has remained consistent throughout the centuries. The twenty-four islanders who live here only have very loose ties to the mainland. They are mostly, but not exclusively, employed by the Trust as couples – to make the most of the available accommodation – and as there is no school, no young children live here. On arrival, we become known as 'the church people' and 'the church mice'. We know this because we are called the former in the pub by Ash, the bartender, who is suspicious of us because we live in the church, and seems worried we might christen him when he's got his back turned; and the latter by Sue, who runs the shop, and is not.

Living in the church means that the island's religion, its god, is at the forefront of my mind. It might be wishful thinking on my part, but with its holy associations and being considered a viewpoint to the gods, I would be very surprised if Lundy has not been home to at least one hermit in its existence. Now it can be home to another, and after an initiation with Walter Hicks Navy-proof rum, we are welcomed with (mostly) open arms. There are a few who don't think we're missionaries undercover. Instead, because a *Daily Mail* article about the 'virus-free island' came out just after we arrived, some seem to think that I'm an undercover journalist, here to do some scandalous exposé for the 'sidebar of shame'.

'I know what you're up to,' the Yorkshire chef says to me, holding his glass of Sauvignon blanc by the fire.

'I really don't think you do, though.'

It feels rude to say that I have far more interest in writing about the island than the islanders. But in the end I tell him exactly this. Although, to understand the island better, I do need to understand why other people want to come to it, and why so many people stay.

Everyone on the island, it is agreed, is looking for something else, something other than what we have experienced before – or, for some who have previously lived on islands such as Eigg, Tristan and Ascension Island, chasing more of the same. Some aren't looking for much other than to be left alone: they are simply antisocial, and being cut off like this suits them fine. Some are wilder than others. Some thrive on the sense of community being isolated like this gives – you are bonded by your geographical situation, if nothing else. The island's god is not one thing or another; it's the island's secret, and we have all come looking to get closer to it; everyone just finds it by different roads. Some see it through the wings of a gull and others through the green sea-glass. An islander by the fire in the tavern says something very similar to someone in Werner Herzog's *Encounters at the End of the World*: that everyone on Lundy was trying to jump off the margins of the map and ended up here.

Although religious myth is as rooted in the island as the gorse, as far as conventional, organised religion is concerned, the church on the island is rarely frequented – and only by a handful of visitors. 'I'm afraid I'll be struck down if I go in!' one of the islanders says. In the vestry, I open the unassuming cream door and am plunged into stained-glass windows – saints and boats and fish and doves with ecstatic light coming from their breasts – that shine when the sun sets to the west behind the church. Marble carvings and candles and an eagle lectern on which a big Bible rests, opened at the Gospel of John. 'In the beginning was the word,' it reads. This page has been open for God knows how long and even he's not sure. Or is this the beginning?

In the UK, almost all churches are built on an east–west axis, except for St Helen's, Lundy's church, which is built on a north-west–south-east axis. This was most likely to protect the church doors from the prevailing, battering, wet south-westerly winds, though some say it's to do with the Knights Templar whose crosses once adorned the church (what exactly it has to do with them seems to be unknown). The church here – as churches everywhere now tend to – has more uses than worship and prayer. In the nave are educational boards about the island's wildlife and its history. The church will stand completely unused in the months we are here unless I sit and work in there for some space, or come in to exhale and hear the wind, see the afternoon light fall through the windows. Otherwise it is a vital shelter for the materials used in the various conservation projects, and an equally vital tea and toast break room. The eaves and slats in the bell tower are a roost for ravens, which push out into the sky like belches of coal smoke. Starlings chatter and scratch. A church that wants to stay standing knows how to make itself useful to all things. The thing most responsive to change survives.

At dusk, seals pop their heads out of the glassy water down by Rat Island – a huge rock off the south end of the island – and a tiny fishing boat makes slow progress past the west side where, looking out, there is only water until Ireland. A sparrow perched on a rock sings out into the sea, a song for the land it has abandoned. Lundy, like many of the western Celtic communities, was heavily influenced by Irish Christianity. Cairns or burial mounds have been found all over the island. But the Welsh influence remains strong in the graveyard on Beacon Hill, next to Old Light, and it is the Welsh influence that illuminates the story behind my wishful thinking about the island's first hermit – a woman.

The medieval chapel in the graveyard was thought to have been dedicated to the daughter of a Welsh chieftain, Saint Elen, or Saint Helen of Caernarfon (not to be confused with the better-known and completely unrelated Saint Helena, whom the new church is named after). But there is a more likely candidate. Buried in a lengthy paragraph about the ruined chapel on Lundy, Historic England posits that the chapel may in fact be dedicated to Saint Endelienta, a Cornish saint born in 470 CE. She was the daughter of a Welsh king and the supposed goddaughter of King Arthur. Endelienta (in Welsh records she is called Cenheidlon) is known to have lived as a hermit in Trentinney, Cornwall. A few miles west of Trentinney is St Minver – where my great-grandfather was born – which is named after Endelienta's sanctified sibling Menefrida, and a few miles north is a place called Lundy Bay.

Endelienta was born in South Wales to King Brychan, who is best known for his numerous and much-sanctified progeny. From South Wales, Endelienta travelled across the Bristol Channel to join some of her twenty-four siblings in the job of converting the unruly people of North Devon and Cornwall to Christianity. On her journey, she came to rest on Lundy, and it's presumed the island had the same effect on her as it has had on many, as she decided to stay a while, and founded her chapel. From there, she moved to Hartland to join her brother, Saint

Nectan of Hartland. Nectan was a super-hermit who managed to carry his own head back to a holy well after it had been cut off by robbers. When he got to the well he promptly died, and the blood he spilled on the ground gave birth to foxgloves – or so the story goes.

Eventually, Endelienta settled in Trentinney, where she is believed to have been killed by Saxon pirates. But before her death, this female hermit would retreat to Lundy time and time again for meditation. That she kept returning to this island when no voyage back then was easy, and everything was more dangerous for women, is testament to the profound effect the island must have had on her, and to the strength of will she must have demonstrated to be permitted to come back. It seems surprising that her story with regard to Lundy has been so over-looked, as in Cornwall she is the patron saint of storytelling, and even has a book festival named after her.

Having completed ten days of quarantine on the island, I vol-unteer to help clean during some of the changeovers, as there are still a few visitors on the island. I'm told about all the para-phernalia left behind by the pleasure-seekers. The weed from the travellers, the coke from the divers and the climbers, all looking to maintain the buzz the island has given them – or to surrender themselves to it and experience a connection with the sublime. I'm instructed that magic mushrooms grow wherever there's sheep's piss (everywhere), and although it's a tempting prospect, I can't see that anyone would need halluci-nogens out here. In your blissed-out state, not only would you be liable to fall off a cliff or wander, giggling, into a ravine, it could all become too much, too vivid. Maybe my senses have been sharpened by shrooms of the past, but it already feels like

I'm experiencing too many lifetimes all at once and I've only had a coffee. I don't need to get any closer to God than this; I feel like we're nose to nose.

Although many good, God-fearing Christians and pre-Christian Celts came here looking to feel a connection with the divine, Lundy has also been home to a plethora of dubious characters. In the waxing and waning of the light, you see how this place could be believed to be closer to the gods – being removed from the land does somehow make you feel closer to the sky. And by staring out at the grey vacuum of the ocean, you understand how one might come to believe that there is no such thing as consequence here. The Templars owned the island in the twelfth and thirteenth centuries, granted to them officially by Henry II in 1160. The Templars may have legally possessed the island, but they hardly had control of it. At that time, and for centuries after, it was under the control of the rather un-Christian and unscrupulous marauding family of the de Mariscos, for whom the tavern is now named. (The family was also the namesake of a club in Woolacombe that held foam parties and had floors so filthy it's a miracle we didn't all get conjunctivitis.) The castle on the south end, behind which the sun rises, was built by a fatigued Henry III to try to keep them out once and for all. It didn't work.

It's Christmas Eve and all hell is breaking loose in the UK. Owing to the pandemic, this December there are fewer than a third of the guests the island normally sees at Christmas, and it is generally very quiet. On the radio we hear that hundreds of thousands of people are dying, and we worry about our families. In reality, being here on the island, doing my mother's weekly grocery shop online and not fussing and breathing on the people I love is best for everyone. I know this, but I can't help the feeling of frustration, of powerlessness.

We light candles and go into the church, sheltering our flames. It's after midnight and the electric's off. We sit and listen to the wind shake the doors. In the big church, our candles only light what is immediately around us; the brass of the candleholder shines golden and the oak eagle glows. We sit on the pews and say what a place this is to have ended up in on Christmas Eve. As the candles flicker and the death toll continues to rise, I put my head back to look at the dark ceiling and think, *Enough, now. Please.* But the Doomsday Clock keeps ticking. As my candle burns down, I think of everyone I love and pray they're going to make it through this.

I grew up in a household equidistant between being quietly religious and wildly heathen. Saint Jude, the patron saint of hopeless cases, has been called upon by my mother on my behalf so many times he has started to wear a disguise. I was baptised 'just in case'. We light candles for the people we love who are ill, or the people we want to remember, or someone who needs some good news. My mum has a Catholic hangover from the convent school she went to, yet tells me stories of Cambridge in the sixties – how she walked into King's College Chapel tripping on lysergic acid and it being one of the most profound experiences of her life. My dad is more of the spiritual ilk than religious, and when swallows flew into my parents' room when they were high, having only known each other a matter of weeks, he decided it was a sign they should get married – their marriage lasted thirty-two years. But other than a couple of New Agers, my friends are strictly secular, which is the status quo. Yet for lack of religion, many of us are still searching for something 'else' – only, we aren't entirely sure what that thing is. And maybe it's not just one thing. UFOs, social media, CCTV, therapy . . . now that we have no God we have found new ways of being watched over, and watching over others. New ways of being seen and having our existence validated by being perceived. Even conspiracy theories are a means of assigning 'intelligent' organisation to otherwise random events or beliefs. It's connecting dots where otherwise there is just empty space. So where does the heathen turn when there is nowhere else? Who – what – do we ask when we need a sign? We ask the empty sky, and when the sign comes we don't quite believe it.

Standing outside on a clear night, watching a cargo ship drift through the otherwise empty sea, I think about the book I've just been reading. Someone had been trying to make a life-changing decision and had gone out for a walk at night to think about it, and then, above them, flew a shooting star. I'm wondering if I'm on the right path, as I always do, having been on the wrong one for so long. The wind has been wreaking havoc with the internet here – which is not very good, it turns out – and my husband's had a frustrating day's work. I feel guilty. I know that ultimately I am responsible for that bad day at work. I'm wondering if it's fair to let my desire for wilder and wilder places change my husband's way of living so drastically. I have taken for granted what a drastic leap this is for him. Despite my belief that this experience here, the pros and the cons, will gift us what my friend calls 'psychological richness', I have been selfish in my desire to come here. I wasn't like this before – this self-serving nature is a recent addition to my character, since living alone – and I hope I am not tinkering with our future in any way other than to improve it. As I wonder if it's all for the best I think, *How nice it would be to have a sign as clear as a shooting star.* And then, to my complete disbelief, a shooting star dives across the sky. *No,* I laugh, doubting it. *That's just a coincidence.* And then again I wonder, *Am I on the right path?* Another!

Then . . . no more.

It might well be meteor season, but I choose to believe that there is no power higher than that which manifests through nature and the cosmos. And here, with everything but the natural world stripped away, I am as close to it as ever. Whatever my god is, it is here: somewhere between the layers of reality, curled up in a proton, in the beat between wings, somewhere there is the spark of the divine.

14.

Watercress Dreams

Standing on the corner of the road below the black wooden fisherman's cottage of Hanmers nestled into the headland, I watch a seal bobbing near the rocks by Rat Island, unsure whether to struggle above the surface for air or go beneath while the sea is churned. It's just before the start of shutdown, two weeks on the island when it closes completely to allow the islanders to get a break from the constant stream of human traffic, and essential maintenance work to be done. There will be no visitors, no helicopters, and only the twenty-four permanent residents remain. As I watch the seal, a coastguard helicopter performs a practice run over the South Light (the southern lighthouse), dangling a stretcher from a long rope. I look out at the late December sea and think, *What if they were looking for someone, what if this wasn't a drill?* It's a long way to a hospital from here. A few days later, I have my first wake-up call about the extent of the island's reliance on the mainland.

I've gone for a night walk where the sheep stand spooky in front of the full moonlit sea, and there's the gentle rushing of the waves sixty feet below. It's a novelty to walk somewhere – anywhere – alone at night and not feel like prey. But tonight it's too freezing to stay out for long, and I march back to the vestry where I get straight to lighting a fire. I'm fussing over some kindling when I hear the distant slicing of a helicopter. Opening the heavy red door, I walk out onto the path. A searchlight is beaming across the black sea and heading towards the island. It whomps over the church and lands in the field next door.

I return to the crisp night and stand watching the helicopter. There is a mountainous bank of ice-blue cumulus ringing the island. On the shore, the lights of Croyde, Woolacombe and Bude glow. I see that the helicopter is the coastguard, and this time it is not a drill. Its engine stays running and, as if the blades are blowing away cloud, the sky above the helicopter clears to reveal a dark night sky and stars. The moon is blooming in the droplets of mist above the church. An icy wind blows.

The roles the islanders have to perform include fire marshals and emergency crew. They are in their special hi-vis jackets, ready for the power that an emergency puts in their hands. But as not much is happening, everyone's hanging about smoking rollies while someone reverses the Land Rover, which is functioning as an ambulance, up to the tavern, which is functioning as an A&E ward. I watch from a distance as a stretcher is taken from the helicopter into the tavern, but fortunately the man the coastguard has been called for is able to walk. It's a twisted intestine, the poor bastard, something I thought only horses could get. He heads back to the mainland for treatment, and his family decide, rather than going back with him, to extend their stay a few days – that's the kind of power this island has over people.

Once the coastguard leaves, I lie by the fire, which has finally taken, and stare at my app that maps the constellations. I have Andromeda directly above me, behind the fire is Hercules, and there glow the first sparks of the Quadrantid meteor shower.

All around, the air tingles with a sense of vulnerability, as if sparks from the meteors are falling on us. When we think of self-sufficiency these days, the concept is often limited to sustenance. On Lundy, self-sufficiency must be many things, but on an island so small with so few people, its inhabitants can only stretch themselves so far.

It's New Year's Day. We're leaving tomorrow and going back to the mainland for two weeks while the island goes into shutdown. I'm stuffing socks into my backpack, looking forward to finally collecting some more warm, waterproof clothes, prescriptions, contact lenses and other things one might generally need to survive the six and a half months on a wind and rainswept island – things that weigh a lot more than the fifteen-kilogram weight allowance. The rest of what we packed for our time here is still in a big backpack in a storage unit back home, waiting for us, along with the rest of our life.

I absent-mindedly check my emails. There's one from the Landmark Trust manager, Derek. 'The situation's not looking good on the mainland,' he writes. Christmas is already having a knock-on effect. It seems that almost every family gathering has led to someone's exequy, and I'm thankful I didn't have the option of putting my family at risk. If we leave tomorrow on the last helicopter, who knows when, or if, we will be able to come back. The islanders have never let anyone who is not staff or a contractor stay here while the island shuts down. But, Derek says, extending a virtual hand: 'Would you like to stay?' The choice is instinctual. In trusting us to respect the dominion of shutdown, they are giving us an experience that is unlikely ever to be repeated.

'Shutdown here, and what happens, is sacrosanct to the island,' Derek says to me the next day, frowning a little as he talks. This hadn't been the plan. Letting outsiders in is a risky rite of passage, and as the fire burns behind him it does feel sacrosanct; it is as if we're being let in to a magic circle, and once we're in, he will have to draw an invisible line around us to seal it once more. Every island must have her secrets.

The next day we stand by the walls of the church and watch the last helicopter leave the island, and with it the final handful of visitors. This is the helicopter we were booked on, and we watch it fly back home, unsteady in the wind. There will not be any supplies now for two weeks and it feels like I've fallen backwards out of a plane. All the attention I had been putting on life back home, and being in a wider world, pours into my mind and dissolves, fizzing, in confusion before settling in: this is it, then. We are cut off and there is nothing but the island now. This isolation is more concrete than when I lived in the barn and would have to wait weeks at a time to buy food. I knew that if I kept walking for long enough I would eventually get to a shop. If I really needed it, someone could drive out and bring me food or take me shopping. This is different. All there is is what is here.

The staff have prepared for shutdown as they do every year, by stocking up their freezers and ordering a big veg box to last the next couple of weeks when there will be no supplies. We, however, are somewhat unprepared. The lack of a fridge or freezer in the vestry, and the fact we have spent the last week eating everything up before we were meant to leave, means we have to hit the little shop hard before it closes for the next two weeks and buy up what few vegetables we can.

The islanders have done this before and hit their stride, hands full of broccoli and chillies, but they only take a few paces before the rug – the whole floor – is pulled from under all of us two days later. A national lockdown is announced. It will last for the next four months. There is no going back for more supplies, more clothes, more contact lenses; no prescriptions, my guitar will stay on the other side of the sea (alas, I will not be learning 'Classical Gas' any time soon), and our bags that we packed ready to come back here with us will have to wait in the storage unit for months. Fortunately, despite the rickety internet, my husband and I feel the same about this turn of events: there is nowhere we'd rather be than on a near-deserted island.

It's not yet 4 p.m. but the sky caves in to the weight of darkness early these days. The silhouettes of wild horses up by the half wall slope gently in front of the iridescent sea and the sinking sun. The sun is bright orange as it sets, as if to make up for the lack of colour in the sky throughout the rest of the day. It lights up a cloud above the lighthouse, half pink, half grey, and this is mirrored in a puddle that turns pink and yellow and silver. For an hour we have technicolour, and there is just enough light left in the sky to complete my chore for the day.

I'm heading to the east side, down to the beach sheltered by the cliffs from the setting sun. Here the light is electric blue, save for a low mantle of light grey cloud that has the faintest hint of peach. The sea is choppy, white crests streaked across the waves; the vista light and fresh, and in the lulls, turquoise blue. Big black crags of rock rise up from the beach from which rock pipits *peep peep peep*. Hunched silver cliffs of slate border the winding, unguarded road down, and clods of grass have fallen from the headland. I never bother to look at the tide times and I often get it wrong, but not today. The tide is out and the pebble beach is rich with bladderwrack, oarweed and sugar kelp; there are all sorts of strange weeds from the deep sea with suckers like octopuses, wet and thick with kelp flies and seaweed flies when moved. There's also an empty six-pint bottle of semi-skimmed milk, an empty bottle of kitchen cleaner and a full tub of margarine – being a protected area of conservation does not protect the island from pollution washing up on its shores, particularly when there are easterly winds. But also there is what I have come here for: driftwood.

There are three hundred different types of seaweed found around Lundy's shores, and almost as many types of driftwood. Massive logs, tree trunks, bits of broken fences, floorboards, ripped branches and little sticks are all washed up by the sea. Sometimes the waves will have been so big overnight that I won't need to go on to the beach – they'll have been thrown onto the road. I stuff them all into my bag one after the other. Some sticks are too beautiful to burn; they have spent months, years, in the sea, and are bleached white by the sun and the salt, pocked with black marks that match my houndstooth coat. The larger wizard sticks I use as implements to help me back up the incredibly steep hill. Every time I walk up it, I think of a tragic story I was told about a man who had 'visiting Lundy' on his bucket list. He came over here on the boat and, moments after his arrival, as he walked up this mean hill from the jetty, he had a heart attack and died. I lean heavily on the large branches, just in case. Out here I become a wild old fishwife, hunched over gathering sticks, protected by a large hood from the salty wind – I am in my element. This bundle in my bag will last us a couple of fires, and then I will come back out and collect more: the sea keeps on giving us what the mainland keeps providing, shedding wood and rubbish like dead skin.

I walk back up the grass hill towards the red door of the vestry, behind which is the rusted stone-crusher that filters the very last of the yellow light of the sun through it; the tall stone mass of Old Light; the wind blowing over the black bales, over the fat sheep, hitting the walls of the church. Absorbing it all as the light fades, with a heavy bag full of wood, I feel a sense of accomplishment, something very simple yet very tangible and undeniable: what I have collected in this bag means we will be warm for another night. I have done something worthwhile today.

Sticks can only spark so much joy, particularly as we are now three and a half weeks in with no fresh supplies and the easterly wind is determined to stick around. The sky sags with fog. Every time we think the boat might come, the easterly proves us wrong: the boat can't dock even with a mild easterly and we're talking a minimum of 35 mph, often twice that. Each evening as the sun goes down and the wind picks up, we perform a ritual battening down of the hatches, stuffing blankets, fleece-lined waterproof trousers and coats in the spaces around the doors and the two-inch-wide gaps between floor and door as draught excluders. Our world has the uncanny feeling of being in a Tarkovsky film. Wandering through foggy, windswept barren-scapes, unable to hear our own voices, only our thoughts. We are in the Zone, walking into the wind with feet never touching the ground.

The wind is so strong at times that I can lean my entire weight into it. After a bottle of wine one night, when it picks up to 70 mph I go out and throw myself into it, over and over again, never quite believing the wind will push me back, but it does. I'm reminded that I can be recharged, re-energised by things other than food. This is good news, as I'm down to rationing one vegetable per meal. That vegetable is usually a potato. I curse the barren allotments. We are running out of onions, we've run out of garlic, we've run out of everything except lentils and rice. Even the spaghetti has run out. I have been squeezing lemons and boiling it up in our lentil soups for added vitamins, but they're finished now, too. We have half a butternut squash left that I've saved for our Valentine's Day meal tomorrow, and that is it. The boat must come in. We cannot wait another week. I am someone who is used to eating about three different vegetables a meal. I adore vegetables. They are cheap and they give me life. Without them my body is going into shock, I'm covered in spots, I feel tired and thirsty all the time. I have become obsessed with the nutrients that continue to ghost me. At night, I study the nutritional information of almost every bean on the planet – what I discover is that they're good for lots of things, but what they lack is vitamin C. In the back of a Land Rover after cleaning a property on the first day of shutdown, when we realised we hadn't got a veg box, I'd joked that I was going to start printing t-shirts that said 'I Went to Lundy and All I Got Was This Lousy Scurvy'. This now looks like a distinct possibility.

Self-sufficiency of varying degrees is not usually the purpose of those living in isolation, but rather a by-product. Not the kind of survivalist stockpiling we have witnessed in response to Brexit and Covid, or maybe on Netflix awaiting a looming Armageddon, but rather the ability to live in harmony with nature, to cultivate it, and to use an allotment or the land you live on to provide for yourself. Alone, in remote locations, you tend to have little option but to rely more on yourself and what you can produce, harvest and store. Having been forced into various degrees of isolation by the pandemic and the tumultuous times that have followed, self-sufficiency is on our minds more than ever. You can even employ 'survival consultants' who will 'help rewild your home and your life'. Although my mum and many her age are just old enough to remember rationing, for the first time in several generations we could not necessarily buy what we could afford, and it came as a shock. Many of us stood staring at desolate supermarket aisles, as unprepared as the island for a kink in the supply chain.

By 450 BCE, the Bristol Channel was part of an international trade route, and by 150 BCE Lundy was trading with Carthaginians in Algeria. It was hardly Zanzibar here, but for many centuries it was an important trading point. In many ways, the island has become more isolated over the centuries. In the winter weeks of Covid lockdown, there is little passing traffic other than vast oil tankers, car transporters and cargo ships not destined for here; no one stopping off and trading. It has become a tourist island, and so it has become increasingly reliant on the outside world we are now cut off from. That the island is not more self-sufficient with regard to sustenance surprised me – maybe this lockdown will inspire change in the future. But to be self-sufficient is hard work, such hard work that very few people manage to achieve it, which is one of the major reasons hermits are often deemed parasitic: they're rejecting society while still relying on it. But according to the Venerable Bede, our man Herbert of Derwentwater, lover of unceasing mortification, was entirely self-sufficient and – except on his yearly trips to see Cuthbert in Lindisfarne – sustained himself entirely on the fish he caught in the lakes surrounding his island and the vegetables he grew around his tiny cell.

With vegetables growing around her leaky caravan, 'Our Lady of Exmoor' Hope Bourne – the woman whose life I seem destined to envy a little for the rest of mine – lived entirely self-sufficiently save for porridge, tea, a weekly loaf of bread she bought from the village and whatever the local farmers gave her from time to time. Hope, looking as wild as you might hope, with hair pointing in the direction of whichever way the wind was blowing, would often be found out on the moors picking mushrooms, blackberries and nuts, collecting wood for her fire and water to drink from the spring.

Her book *Wild Harvest* is a detailed, extreme instruction manual/memoir about self-sufficiency in the 1970s – *The Good Life* with bullets. Bourne grew her own vegetables in the fertile soil next to her caravan. She would fish from the river that ran through the valley and shoot rabbit, hare, pigeon and some-times deer for her pot – not necessarily with all the right per-mits. The only thing she wasn't self-sufficient in was bathing, particularly in winter. John Mitchell recalls how in the summer months he'd have to check the coast was clear when he took his children swimming, as she would bathe naked in the deep pools of Sherdon Water. But more often than not she would walk over to his uncle's farm and take her weekly bath there. Living as she did, he says, meant it was unavoidable that she smelled and had fleas, and his aunt tired of having to put flea dust on the sofas and clean out the bath after her visits. If she hitched a ride with him, he'd have to fumigate the Land Rover. But they accepted that was just a part of who she was, and a con-sequence of how she lived: if you existed as she did – walking for miles, killing animals, living without a bath or running water – that's what you'd smell of.

There are gruesome realities if you want to be self-sufficient and eat meat, and Bourne covers these in exacting detail in a chapter about skinning, hanging, smoking and gutting. This part of her life I envy a lot less. Regarding the ethics of killing, she observes it all around her. 'Killing is part of nature's pattern. Living with nature is very different to looking at it in pictures.' Killing made her feel a part of the nature that she immersed herself in. She claims that we all have the hunter's instinct, and makes the case that, as on Lundy, without an apex predator, animals of one species must be culled as part of the preservation of all species and as part of conservation efforts.

To find out if anything needs to be culled, I join ten of the islanders on a 'stock take', which involves counting the entire populations of goat, deer and Soay (descendants of wild, hardy, primitive sheep from the Western Isles of Scotland) to check their numbers haven't climbed too high. We are spread across the width of the island with three islanders communicating with radios; the rest of us are to communicate using hand gestures and shouting – mostly shouting.

We wait until everyone's in position and then, avoiding the rare migratory pink-footed goose that has decided to pay a visit, start marching. Our job is to walk the length of the island and back and accurately count the number of livestock. Before the quarter wall we spot a couple of hinds running from us. One of them only has three legs. I call out to the others to let them know – they take the tally of numbers but are sure that the hind is just injured and holding its leg up. By the half wall, flocks of Soay and goat are counted, as are herds of over fifty deer that we find are spread across the width of the island and the only place for the deer to run is further north. I spot the hind again. This time she's close enough for us to all agree she only has three legs: the fourth is nothing but a bloody stump, the wound is fresh – she must have caught it on one of the fences. I half expect someone to try to catch her and look after her, clean the wound at least, but she's left to get on with it, whatever it will be. That's how things go here, and although I will never be able to rid myself of the urge to interfere, I will come to respect that there are good reasons not to. A few weeks later I will see the hind while I'm out on a walk. She looks like she's healed completely and runs with the others as if she has lost nothing.

When we finally reach the north end of the island, everyone comes from their far-flung locations to the middle of the island to eat lunch in a wind tunnel. As we get out our sandwiches, the huge herd of deer we've been pushing up the island finally has nowhere left to go and runs up past us. Less than a couple of metres from where we sit are fifty, sixty animals: hinds, stags and juveniles running up over the cliffs, jumping huge distances over rocks, hoof after hoof after hoof hitting the ground, wild black eyes absorbing our forms, mirroring them back to us, as the deer flee. I sit and watch, open-mouthed, forget to even reach for my phone. This marks the end of the stock take, which suggests that, for now, the numbers are sustainable. But when they get too high, the animals will be culled, the meat will be eaten, and the earth will continue to turn as if it lost nothing.

Hope Bourne lived in very extreme ways – eating food, usually meat, when it was mouldy and rotten; drinking unsterilised water; and leaving a broken leg to heal itself. And the

extremity which she lived was either a by-product of or conducive to some hard-line views, some of which I find difficult to
reconcile with a woman who loved the natural world and had
experienced poverty. One of these views was her romanticism
of the hunt, and she did also tend to bash the welfare state, a
stance that can be symptomatic of this kind of extreme self-
sufficiency. It's a remarkable achievement and testament to a
person's resilience to live a self-sufficient life, particularly on as
little money as Bourne did, but the pitfall is thinking that,
because it has been possible for you to live off next to nothing
through self-reliance, everyone should be able to, and that
everyone is capable of it – when in reality it's only achievable
for a rare few. But for those rare few it becomes their life, and
their reason for living is in exercising this fox-like agility at
keeping themselves alive.

When old age and illness forced Hope to move from her caravan into a sterile new-build in Withypool, she was unable to
exercise this fox-like agility and she began to decline. Though
she retained some of her maverick tendencies and moved all
her chickens into the new two-up two-down she'd been put in,
not only was she made to feel unwelcome in the village, she had
been removed from everything that had made her feel alive.
There was no magic, no surprises in her new life. Farmer John
says he would find her in the village sitting on the bridge, her
head bowed, staring at the river.

'How are you, Hope?' he'd ask.

She wouldn't even look up, just continue to stare at the river
and then shrug. 'Never mind.'

Hope's view that luxuries tend not to add anything meaningful to a life was shared by the early Christian desert hermits,

the Desert Fathers. However, most of the food Hope referenced, and seemed to delight in, they would have considered a luxury. The Desert Fathers renounced all indulgences, including most food, and incorporated limited diets and intermittent fasting into their spiritual experience – whether this was a means to an end or an end to a means is debatable because living in the desert, there wasn't much fare available. The Desert Fathers were 'free to feed on the word of God without distraction by appetite', as Sister Benedicta Ward wrote in her introduction to *The Lives of the Desert Fathers: The Historia Monachorum in Aegypto*.

The Desert Fathers' diet consisted mainly of bread and green herbs, sometimes lentils, cornmeal soup, and fresh bread if cooking facilities were available. If they weren't, the bread was paximathia – a small dry loaf to which salt could be added. It would be taken into the desert and could be stored for months at a time before being soaked and eaten. Dried fruit, nuts and olives were eaten if available, and the hermits might cultivate a small garden, but most vegetables produced were salted and preserved in brine and reserved for visitors. The desert hermit Macarius of Egypt spent seven years eating only pulses and raw herbs, and then spent the next three years consuming only a little bit of bread and oil. Wine does not seem to have been considered an indulgence, but the hermits' diets were so restricted that, according to Ward, they would fantasise about fresh fruit and milk. 'What they dream about is fresh, juicy fruit, and from such dreams one obtains a very clear if oblique light on the fasts of the hermits. What were their luxuries? Grapes, which would be passed from hand to hand in wonder; figs, sometimes monstrous figs that were held to be the real fruits of paradise.'

*

Whereas the hermits in the desert were often plagued with brackish water, Lundy is blessed. The island is entirely self-sufficient when it comes to water. Most of the water – drinking, bathing, flushing, cooking – comes from the sky, and the rest comes from the springs that burst through the granite. To help it through the summer months Lundy relies on the rain we are now being drenched with in the winter months – although this has been a *comparatively* dry winter, and from April on it's a dry spring here, too. Aside from a few storms, it will remain dry.

A Lundy Field Society pamphlet from 1989 reports that a water diviner was brought over to find water during a particularly dry spell, and she did. A new borehole was created and the island survives in part on the water this diviner discovered. But every spring and summer the land seems to just keep getting drier. There was a summer on Lundy a few years ago when it was so dry and the water levels fell so low that the islanders had to leave the island until the water level was restored. This year, this situation will become increasingly desperate over the warmer months – each day we are promised rain and each day the sky is blue and streaked with cirrus clouds; the grass is golden and the earth cracks beneath the rays of the sun; the linnets sing, coaxing the beams towards the drying grass seeds. We talk of rain dances but the rain clouds pass in minutes with the wind. This situation becomes so desperate, in fact, that to my delight there is again talk of water diviners.

The islanders are mindful of water usage all year round because of what summer tends to bring, and the water shortage we experience here is yet another reminder that we are all beholden to the elements. Out here, you can't help but respect the natural laws that govern us – ones that seem so translucent

and pliable, so bribable, in towns and cities. This is the end reality for all of us. Everything is enhanced on Lundy, as if we are
living our universal reality under a microscope: every problem,
every joy the natural world gifts us is magnified and there is no
option but to respect it and work with it. That should be our
default position: to manage our consumption with the rhythms
of the weather and the seasons of the earth – abundance all the
time is not a birthright, despite what some New Age podcasts
might tell us. Sometimes we should go without in order for
there to be something left.

One day, we will all have to come to the inevitable conclusion that, as much as renewable or green energy may help us,
if we want to retain some of the planet we will have to use and
consume less of everything. Here, we only shower once every
three days, but still the farmer-cum-chef, Tom, complains of
my water usage. 'In the Arctic, you had to turn the tap on, and
then turn it off again while you lather up,' he says. But we're
not in the Arctic and, I point out, nobody else on the island is
doing that.

The land here can't be cultivated to the extent it once was, in
order to retain its areas of conservation, and by the time we
arrive the larger allotments have been out of use for a couple
of years – some of them much longer – because the islanders
are kept so busy. Up until the late twentieth century, the gardens and allotments produced enough vegetables for the
island, in that respect, to be almost entirely self-sufficient.
Lundy and its marine life were unprotected until 1973, and it
became England's first marine conservation zone in 2010; previously, the people who lived here fished as much as they
wanted and generally played pretty fast and loose with the

wildlife. The eggs of falcons and gannets were pilfered, and the puffins were killed as food for the pigs and their skin melted down into candles. Until the mid-twentieth century, the island's lobsters were up for consumption and were a special at the tavern. You can still fish here if you bring a rod and line – limited to two – and you'll likely get either a sea bass or a mackerel for your troubles, but you won't see it on the tavern menu. Nor will you see any of what was once 2,000+ conies (rabbits) that were used for food and fur. At the time of writing, their numbers haven't recovered from a bout of myxomatosis a couple of years ago, and I'm told of gruesome scenes of 'zombie bunnies' crawling through the beer garden and little children running after rabbits whose eyeballs were falling out.

For a brief spell, Lundy was under the ownership of Augustus Christie (of the same family who own the land my family's hut is built on), who had the desire to own 'all the land he could see from his windows', which included Lundy. He had no particular interest in the island and rarely visited, but he did enact vital restorations before he sold it to Martin Harman, whose children were to be Lundy's last family before it was bought for the National Trust by Jack Hayward. Harman would become notorious for minting his own coins for the island complete with his own head on them. He called the currency the 'puffin', before being informed that this was highly illegal. Harman also introduced the now much-coveted Lundy stamps, which to this day are the official stamps used for mail being sent from the island.

Harman had his faults – he was a 'megalomaniac' in some people's eyes and 'turned the island into a petting zoo', as one person has said. He also planted so many invasive rhododendrons (which are of no benefit to most pollinators) that during this lockdown a whole day is set aside to hunt them down and root them out. But many grow in perilous spots and are instead marked out with white flags that wave in the wind, unwilling to surrender.

When Harman owned the island, corn, root crops and garden produce grew, as well as cattle, poultry, horses, pigs and sheep. The island was self-sufficient in dairy, meat and many vegetables. Most of the animals Harman introduced – Soay sheep, wild goats, Sika deer – remain in large numbers, as do the Lundy ponies. A hardy cross between several (native) breeds imported by Harman, they are particularly suited to withstanding the bitter winter winds. The partridges, fallow deer, hares, wallabies, squirrels, peacocks and variety of exotic birds do not. His misguided escapades aside, Harman had aspirations for the island and decent principles: he wanted it to be 'self-supporting and not to be turned into an island for the wealthy . . . to remain a remote, wild, and primitive island where wildlife predominated and all lived in peace and seclusion'. Those feel like pretty solid ideals, albeit the ideals of an idealist – but someone has to be.

Meadow pipits flee my path *peep peep peeping* as they rise and dip away below the cliffs. It's early and there's a metallic measure of light pouring from the corner of the grey, overcast sky above the grey, undercast sea. The wind is blowing from the south-west and is cooling my cheeks, which are hot from marching and a lack of sleep. It blows against me as I arrive at the boundary walls and stand by their crumbling stones below the castle, looking out over a sea lit silver by the pearl of the rising sun. Black forms of shags (a smaller species of cormorant) slide through the water with their long necks like Loch Ness monsters; with one raise of their wings, they lift their black bodies from the waves and fly low and determined over the sea, away from the boat chugging towards the island.

The *Oldenburg* is coming in, finally. With the boat arrive the first fresh supplies in a month. The *Oldenburg* is Lundy's ferry and usually only sails in the spring and summer season, but on 4 January everything changed – and without a helicopter the last few weeks have been a scrabble to get it out of its dry dock in Bristol, where it's been undergoing the yearly maintenance on its hull. It's been a month of thick sea fog, wind and rain; a bleak month that we were unprepared for on every level, and which, even my husband agrees, has been thrilling, if tiring. The arrival of the boat with fresh supplies and post is better than Christmas. Living on Lundy during lockdown is a little like living in an idyllic communist state: the shop is very well stocked, for a tiny shop, but there is only one kind of everything and not very much of anything, particularly if you only have a hotplate to cook on.

Since the visitors left, a lack of bureaucracy has followed, which has proved liberating in almost every aspect except for the grocers who supply the vegetable orders and seem to have us over a barrel. The grocers have final say with the veg boxes. There are no returns on any orders, even if it has been delivered the day before the ship sails and items still turn up rotten – this happens to our cabbages, our lemons, our oranges, so many things are ancient before they were even put on the boat, and then you might not get any more fruit or vegetables for two, three, four weeks. It's a talking point if things come in fresh. I haven't seen a garlic clove that isn't already growing a new bulb of garlic inside it for as long as I can remember. It's the little things you miss.

Like a Desert Father, I dream of the food I cannot have. I long for fresh greens, salads, avocados, croissants, fish, processed food, variety. The irony is that although this experience hasn't tempered my desire to grow my own, it has given me a new appreciation for the luxury of everyday variety that we have become so accustomed to on the mainland. I miss supermarkets, God forgive me.

The same day the boat finally comes in, I hear the first songbird fill the afternoon with the promise of sun after two weeks of the thickest fog. Its song is unfamiliar to me, but it tears through the grey air like a crack of sunlight. A skylark. The bird of wide fields, wildflowers and long grass that I've not heard very often, not even living just across the sea. The skylarks bring good weather and soon we have cool blue skies and a timid primrose-yellow sun exhaling on the brown, dead ground. Whenever I hear the birds I stand and watch, transfixed by the sounds. As they sing, the skylarks fly higher and higher into the blue, as if their elevation is powered by their song and they cannot rise above the ground without singing. High into the blue they levitate, so high that you blink in the sunlight and their form has disappeared, and only their song remains. Then it is as if the sky itself is singing.

15.

Tibbetts

If silence were an object, it would be a window – a space for illumination, a means of escape. In hindsight, it's understandable that I embraced solitude and silence after the barn. Why I keep seeking it out now, when I am the most content and secure I have been in living memory, is still a bit of a mystery to me. If I go away, or my husband does, we miss each other, but as I accept that he will always be drawn to the hustle and bustle, he accepts that wanting to be alone every now and then is just part of my design – a bit of both is good for us. And anyway, I don't think of it as 'being alone'; it is taking time to be tuned in to my surroundings, to be dunked head first into my immediate reality. Which is why, even here, on this remote, barely populated island during lockdown when it's as quiet as it could ever be, I seek the limits of silence that the island can offer me.

Up by the wall that marks three-quarters of the island, there is an old grey stone admiralty lookout: a square building surrounded by a circular granite wall, called Tibbetts. Tibbetts is ringed by churned-up mud from the Highland cattle and wild horses in the winter. It was built on a site called Gibbets, where islanders would hang pirates and marauders to rot in metal cages called 'gibbets' that were shaped like the human form – a warning to anyone else thinking of taking Lundy as their own. Tibbetts is completely removed from the rest of the island, which is practically empty now anyway. It has no electricity and no drinkable running water. It is as cut off as I could possibly get here, and as soon as I saw it on our first walk up the island in early December, I knew that was where I wanted to go. Surrounding Tibbetts there is only moorland wilderness; dead purple moor grass and russet-coloured bracken; thick shrubs of heather, granite and very little else. It is up where the big animals live.

It's the end of February and today is the first warm day of the year – it's the first warm day since we arrived three months ago and I've spent it in a wetsuit with my hands in the turquoise waters, studying strawberry anemones, Montagu's crabs, luminous green snakelocks anemone and brittle stars in the rock pools between Mermaid's Hole and Surf Point at the southern tip of the island. A lobster-pot boat sails back out to sea while an islander lying on the shore happens to be playing Enya's 'Orinoco Flow (Sail Away)' on her speaker with zero irony. In our wetsuits we sing to the fishermen across the empty bay, our voices and the boat's engine the only sounds echoing off the rocks. 'The people who stay at Tibbetts are either cool or weird,' Alice, one of the furloughed tavern staff, says to me. 'You're weird.'

After a hot shower, I pack several bags and set out for Tibbetts alone around sunset. Normally when people stay at Tibbetts there's a Land Rover to take you, your belongings and all the food and water you will need for your visit. I don't mind a trek, so I set off on foot as the sun is going down, with my travelling backpacks – full of the jumpers, food, litres of water and bundles of kindling I'll need for the next few days.

It's by the quarter wall where the magic happens. The path

is lined with puddles and the molinia grass that moans in the wind is white-gold like the streaks of cloud in the chalky-pink sky above it. I'm only wearing a jumper and the air is dry, but there is a breeze coming from the east and on it I smell the goats before I see them. Like something out of a children's folk tale, three billy goats with huge horns appear on the crest of a white-gold hill, a pink sky behind them. One is brown, one is black and white, and the other is as white-gold as the grass and the clouds in the sky.

It's in this half-light I see the Highland cattle, huge and immovable, and the wild horses in front of the calm orange lake of Pondsbury. The animals haven't had much interaction with humans this past year, and almost none for the last three months, and they're becoming a little wilder again; the deer have been letting me know who has the lay of the land as they watch me on my walks. As I pass the goats with their horns and the Highland cattle with their enormous prongs, I become aware of how vulnerable I am as a human, all brain power and soft edges. As the light continues to fade on the west side, the sky deepens to purple-blue and pink, and the silhouettes of the cattle become increasingly difficult to distinguish from the boulders that line the path.

In the distance I can see the shape of Tibbetts. Built on the east side about ten metres from the cliff edge, it stands grey and proud. It's an odd-looking building. The windows flash as it reflects the setting sun. Without backpacks it would take about half an hour to get there; with backpacks it takes about an hour, with a couple of breaks to rest, but I enjoy the effort, it makes me realise how disconnected the place is from the rest of the island. When I finally reach Tibbetts, the sitting room window still glows with the last of the light from the sun, but the sky above is lapis blue and a bright yellow moon hangs behind the building.

I step inside the wood-panelled living room and immediately decide that I won't be sleeping in the bedroom but in here, on the daybed opposite the fire – there is no other heating. In this room you can see the world turning. The sun has disappeared behind the sea on my right, leaving only a frenzy of yellow and orange and red, and on my left the moon continues to rise, lighting up the waves.

The gas has been turned back on for my visit as everything in this house runs on gas. Instead of light bulbs there are small gas mantles to light with an ignition lighter. There is also the unfamiliar luxury of a fridge, and an oven. But I'm a little uncomfortable with gas in this quantity – I can hear it everywhere, feel the heat the back of the fridge is giving off. As it has been uninhabited for a couple of months, I'm worried the whole place is going to blow up. I step back outside and light a match from the doorstep . . . the place doesn't explode and I feel pretty ridiculous as I watch the match burn down.

It takes a while to settle, to be alone again; as with the gas, I'm looking for risks everywhere. But I've soon forgotten about settling in as the very real emergency of lighting the fire takes precedence. Now the sun has gone down and there is no light in the sky except for the moon and its cool pool reflecting off the sea, it is freezing in here and it is dark. I light some candles and spend a good hour getting the fire going. Eventually, I work out how to light the gas lights.

Very rarely during lockdown do islanders come up this far. There is one man who has lived on Lundy for four years and has never been up to the north end of the island. 'I grew up on Exmoor,' he tells me, 'I know what it's like.' But I grew up not far away, we split most of our weekends between Exmoor and Dartmoor in the winter, I lived on the border of Exmoor National Park in the barn, and yet it was nothing like this. Yes, it is scrub and moorland here – but it is everything else that comes with an isolated island that is rich with myth as well. He's a nice man, a smart man, who says that everyone here is searching for whatever it is we feel is missing from the wider world but, then, he doesn't look. Maybe he already found it.

I'm in heaven cooking on a gas stove again rather than a single-ring hotplate, using more than one pan for the first time in months. I continue to be hypnotised by the huge moon outside the kitchen window. I sit and eat spaghetti in the entirely fire-lit room, acclimatising to the silence, and read some Dorling Kindersley books about pirates and shipwrecks. Just as I'm feeling settled and thinking of going to bed, something interrupts the silence. Something is outside. Highland cattle, I guess, sniffing about outside the wall. It's to be expected. But it sounds much closer than that, although it can't be closer than that because there's a wall between the big animals and myself, and I closed the gate. I made sure I did, exactly for this reason.

I get up to look out the window and am confronted with the long brown face of a horse. I can't tell how many of them there are, because as I go between the low-lit kitchen and the low-lit living room, at each window I am confronted with a horse's nose, sniffing and licking the glass. I love horses but behind the horse staring through the window at me, rubbing its dirty wet nose on the glass, two more horses are kicking each other – they've obviously been here for some time already and are getting restless. As time passes, they only get more restless. More kicking. This is not good. It becomes evident that I am going to have to let them out of the gate they have somehow managed to lock more successfully than I did. The one thing I know, from my own mistakes when riding, is that you do not go round the back of a horse unless you want to get kicked in the head. This is more difficult in practice when there are four wild horses loose in an enclosed space.

I open the door to try to run to the gate, but as soon as I do they turn towards me. I go back inside and strategise. I open the door again; this time, my master plan is to throw some peanuts to try to distract them long enough for me to open the gate. But, for the first time ever, they're not interested in food, at all. They run towards me and a small part of my brain wonders what would happen if I let them come inside. They would tear the place down and it would be magnificent, but expensive. I close the door. We used to herd our friend's chickens and sheep when we were kids, cattle when we were being really stupid. It's not like I haven't urged a large animal in the direction I willed it to go before. I just have to remember how to lose the fear, how to be reckless again. I look out the kitchen window, above the smear of a nose print, at their silhouettes. There's huffing and digging at the ground with hooves. I need to make a move before they start kicking each other again.

I grab a poker and an oven tray. There's another whinny, and this is only going to end in disaster one way or another, I think, as I bang bang bang as hard as possible and slam open the door. It works, a little too well. The horses scatter and gallop round the back. Without wasting a second, I dash to open the gate, thinking the danger has passed. With the gate now open, just as I am running back to the safety of Tibbets, the galloping horses circle the house, stampeding. This is not what I'd had in mind. To avoid getting trampled, I make a hairpin turn halfway to the house and leap back to the open gate. Sprinting, the horses a few steps behind me, I swing round and hide behind the wall as they storm through, manes flying, tails raised, hooves thundering over the ground, away, away towards the sea and out into the night, their silhouettes silver-black in the half-lit landscape.

I'm wired and wide-eyed for about an hour afterwards. It's one of the most spectacular things I have ever seen and it feels like an achievement to have got myself out of a tight spot with unpredictable large animals. I feel potent. My heart rate eventually declines while the moon continues to rise above the roof. The candlelight in the wood-panelled room dwindles; the warm embers of the fire glow. It's time to sleep.

Months without habitation, without warmth, mean that the damp here has swollen the door frame and I can't lock the door – which, as I'm on my own, is causing me anxiety. I've grown accustomed to someone else reassuring me that there's nothing to worry about; now I'm alone again, I must reassure myself. But I don't seem to be listening. *I want to sleep with a knife by my side*, I tell the part of myself that is trying to be reassuring, *just in case*. I don't want to draw the curtains because of what I would miss of the sky, but at the same time I don't want any madmen with axes to have a better view of me. I don't know the islanders that well and anyone can lose their mind at any moment, I've seen it. It takes a while to persuade myself I do not need to sleep with a knife under my pillow, and that I'm far more likely to injure myself that way. I wonder why I didn't have this fear in the barn. Perhaps it's because there the fear had always come from within the walls, and once the source of that fear had gone, the relief was so massive, so penetrating, it didn't even occur to my mind to conjure up something else, something that could come from outside.

Here, I do almost get up to grab a weapon, but it feels a depressing thing to do on what has otherwise been a magical night. I must trust that there is no one on the island – permanent resident or invader – who is going to hurt me. I must fight the urge to grab a knife, and choose rather to believe that I am safe. (As it turns out, I discover on my return that one of the islanders has indeed just bought a massive Celtic axe, but he promises he only plans to use it for decorative purposes or the zombie apocalypse, which is a regular topic of conversation around the fire here.)

When I speak to Sara Maitland about her remote location, she affirms that although isolation makes most dangers less likely, it does mean that feeling vulnerable is both an emotional response and a concrete reality. I certainly feel vulnerable in Tibbets. I wake in the middle of the night with the sense that something has roused me. I look outside the window, dreading a face that does not appear. There are still embers glowing in the fire but they're shrouded in ashy cagoules and the room is cooling. Condensation has collected on all of the windows, and the moisture on the one beside my bed is dripping down onto the old, blackened window frame.

I lie there, thinking of the women I have been reading about – female pirates in the 1700s who dressed up as men to get equal treatment, and of one in particular, Mary Read. While still in the English Navy (dressed as a man), she was the only person in her all-male crew to fight back when they were attacked, and because the rest of the crew showed cowardice by not fighting, she shot them and ran off with the pirate Calico Jack and his pirate lover, Anne Bonny. Ruthless.

But even Mary's not enough to keep my mind from imagining something *out there*. Maybe I shouldn't have slept with the curtains open. I wish I could lock the door. There is something outside again. I can hear it. But this time it's not frustrated or agitated, it's desperate. Exhaling through the heather, howling long and low between the strands of purple moor. Jostling the cliffs and stones. Trying to heave up Tibbetts to look beneath. The wind creature tears its way up the island, searching for what it has lost. It whips and snaps as if to say, *I was tricked! I was tricked, and you took it when I wasn't looking and now I'm here to take it back. Watch as I tear through the land, through the water, and turn the air to stone.* It whips around again, accusing the other direction of theft. *Give it back.* And again it turns, spins – as if taunted by a jeering crowd, the wind creature cannot decide which way to turn, who and what and where to accuse of this theft. North-easterly. No. Westerly. No, now south-easterly! The wind creature will not be confined. The wind creature will have its revenge, for the thing it no longer remembers. Until it does, it whips around and turns its face as if to say, *Was it you?*

I'm unable to fall back to sleep. At around 4 a.m. I notice that the moon has travelled over the house and now beams in through the glass I lie behind, cleansing me with its cool photons like the crystals people put on their windowsills. By the light of the moon I get up and go to the bathroom. In my drowsiness I forget that where you might think there is a flush above the loo, there is in fact, the shower. I flush and am promptly drenched in freezing cold water. I swear a lot and change my clothes, sitting in front of the fire for a good hour or so to dry the wet ones and, underestimating the heat the cooling Wenlock is giving off, burn a huge hole in my prized wool joggers.

The next morning I wake up early, looking as if I have been fired out of a cannon, and watch the sun rise to the left of the room. I go outside and stand cold in the morning wind, staring at the sun over the sea before going back to bed. It's cold in here now without the fire, without radiators. I huddle under a millefeuille of thick woollen blankets and sleep a while longer. The next time I wake, the sun is almost above the building and the light is white and retreating back into the heavens, as if it was given a false start today. There are smears all over the windows from the horses' wet, muddy noses. I get up and look out and see the sea mist coming in. By late morning it has risen and it's like Tibbetts is on top of a mountain rather than on an island: the mist has transformed into thick fog that swathes, sea to clifftop. Above, the sky is clear blue with streaks of cirrus, and the fog that has risen to the lip of the cliffs crawls over them like the dry ice my dad used to bring down from his workshop to add magic to our house parties. Behind a huge tentacle of white smoke crawling up from the sea I can see the silhouette of the church at the other end of the island and that is all.

I have drastically underestimated how much water I consume – on top of drinking water, it's incredible how much one needs for tea, coffee and cooking. I have almost run out of water already and I still have another three days left here on my own. I have two choices: walk all the way back to the village and get some more water, bursting the bubble of solitude, or test the undrinkable water from the tap. I decide on the latter, blow a kiss in the direction of my husband and go for a walk.

Out in the fog my eyes start playing tricks on me. I am sure I can see a bear – but there are no bears here. And yet that big brown thing in front of me looks unmistakably like a bear: there's a Stone Age relic locked within the fog. A few feet away, it transforms into a bull. A reminder that supernatural beasties have often arisen from the imaginations of those living in isolation, cut off from the wider population, as they give physical form to the fears, insecurities and anxieties that break free of the confines of the mind. Lundy's monsters come in human and supernatural forms. It's a place where a moral compass can be left spinning for decades – centuries even, down the generational line – and a place where strange findings, happenings, are never fully explained.

During excavations for the foundations of new farm buildings in 1856 up at Bull's Paradise (a field behind staff accommodation called 'Pigs' and the camping field), two granite sarcophagi ten feet long were discovered. When opened, they were found to contain two skeletons of 'abnormal size' – over eight feet tall and covered in limpet shells. Alongside these extraordinarily large skeletons was a row of standard-sized skeletons, heads to the west, and a Lundy Field Society report from 1998 describes how a mass grave of 'disarticulated' skeletons and some fragments of beads and pottery were also unearthed. At the time of discovery, a letter to *The Times* describes how the giant skeletons 'fell to pieces' when they were unearthed, presumably because of the acidic peat soil on Lundy. What was left of the bones was reburied and apparently lost, but the beads and other accoutrements were taken to Bristol Museum and continue to be examined for clues. They are believed to be pre-Christian, made of similar cobalt glass to that found in the eastern Mediterranean from around 600 to 800 BCE. These skeletons are believed to be from around 250 to 50 BCE. It was posited that the man and woman might have been Vikings. The raven standard of the Viking invader Hubba was flown in Devon, but the first Viking raid on Devon didn't take place until 787 CE, and there has never been any mention of the invaders being of 'abnormal' size; the average height of a Viking man was around five foot eight and the average height of a Viking woman was five foot one. So this theory has been discounted. Meaning no one really knows who, or what, these skeletons were.

On a winter evening by the pub fire, I asked Derek about the giants, in the hope of some juicy monster gossip. 'Is it true about the giants' graves?'

'Yeah,' he replied.

'What, they found actual giants?'

'Yeah, yeah, actual giants,' he said nonchalantly, with no further elaboration.

'Okay. Cool . . .'

The summary in the heritage records of the National Trust says: 'Two cist burials found in Bull's Paradise in 1856 whilst the digging of the farm foundations was being carried out. One cist contained the bones of a very large human, supposedly a giant.'

If you choose to go into the church you will find, to this day, one of the granite pillow stones from the cist resting unassumingly in the porch of the church, next to the swallow shit.

Lundy is the second point of a hypotenuse triangle that stretches between here, Glastonbury Tor and Bedd Arthur ('Arthur's Grave') in the Preseli Hills of North Wales – one of many prehistoric sites in the UK that folklore claims as the resting place of the legendary King Arthur. In legend, this triangle is said to encompasses Annwn, a relic of pagan Celtic mythology. As an otherworld, Annwn is a point where mysterious realms can be entered. Its inhabitants 'have human form but are not strictly human. They are immortals – fairyfolk or demons in one point of view. Some are gods thinly disguised. Living people can enter Annwn and so can spirits of the dead,' Geoffrey Ashe says in *A Guidebook to Arthurian Britain*.

The people on Lundy are exactly as you'd hope: they give off an air of immortality. This is a land without repercussions. I have been drinking here like never before. I have also smoked more rollies than I have since I was about twenty. At least half the island are smokers, and one person vapes. Those who give up smoking start again the next day. It's wild abandon. Surrender to what's fun, what gets you that little bit higher off the ground.

I can get away with this . . . but for how long?

In the eighteenth century, a man called Thomas Benson used Lundy as his own Bermuda triangle, where cargo destined for the Americas disappeared and actions had no consequence. Benson wasn't a needy man – if he had been, it might have gone some way to explaining his actions, but he had inherited a large family fortune by the age of thirty-six and became Sheriff of Devon, and subsequently an MP for Barnstaple. A pretty unremarkable trajectory for a well-heeled man, until Lundy.

Between 1744 and 1752, Benson was entrusted with transporting convicts to Virginia to work on the sugar and tobacco plantations. Telling no one otherwise, instead of shipping the convicts to the Americas he took them to Lundy and kept them there as his own personal slaves – or, as Myrtle Ternstrom puts it more generously in her book *The Lords of Lundy*, 'an unpaid labour force'. It appears they lived between what was then known as 'the old fort', the dilapidated outpost built by Henry III to keep the de Mariscos out, and a cave that was sometimes locked up. When it came to what to say about the missing convicts at the other end, in the Americas, those in charge of the boats would simply claim that they had died from disease or another malady on the voyage, a common occurrence.

At least seventeen convicts who were sentenced to work in the colonies were instead transported to Lundy, suggesting that Benson landed at least two convict loads here in three years. Today, inside Benson's Cave, you can still make out the graffiti with a torch. The few initials carved into the rock suggest that the enslaved people were from the 1749 and 1752 passages. That there is so little graffiti is likely because most would have been illiterate and not even able to etch their initials into the stone.

To Benson, Lundy was a no man's land, where the laws of any given country could not reach him and morality was sunk along with his ships for insurance. Throughout his time smuggling, even when he was caught in the act and another man hanged for his crimes, he maintained that he had done no wrong because the convicts had been transported 'out of the kingdom'. His interpretation of the law was upheld. Lundy's isolation meant it was another world entirely as far as Benson was concerned, a playground where his dark side could run havoc. Some say he wasn't a bad man but rather a man of his time, when the powerful were usually corrupt. The use of the past tense here amuses me.

The use of the past tense when we have recovered from an event, an addiction or a disorder isn't entirely accurate either. Whatever I've hoped to leave behind can resurface in the most unassuming moments, and when it does appear, at first I do not recognise it for what it is, as if it has come in disguise. Solitude can be a risky business. If I am to bend solitude to my advantage, I have to exercise willpower and control my anxiety over the litany of injuries any life is bound to contain. As I find I have more to lose again every year, I have to fight a constant refrain that I don't deserve to be happy and the fear that everything and everyone I love will be taken away in some cruel twist of fate. I try to reassure myself that, even if that did happen, I know how to survive things now; I hope I could navigate the worst of it. Every day, there will always be the choice to give in to fear or to choose courage. I knew this the instant I was left alone in the barn and I made the decision to thrive. *Sink or swim, baby, sink or swim.*

'Leaving the Yellow House', a short story by Saul Bellow, tells of a self-destructive seventy-two-year-old woman called Hattie Waggoner who lives in the isolated desert town of Sego Desert Lake, Utah. Hattie is a woman who, when I first read this story in the barn, I had a lot of sympathy for. In the desert, alone, her isolation permits her to drink as much as she likes: 'She had lived by delays; she had meant to stop drinking.' She drinks while at home, she drinks in bars and she drinks while driving, which causes an accident. Her lifetime of denial continues as she claims that the accident was caused by a sneeze when everyone knows she was drunk.

Hattie is laid up after the accident and forced to allow others to look after her while she recuperates. She finds everyone willing to take care of her, but only on the condition that she leave them her yellow house when she dies. While incapacitated, she looks back on her life, the lies she's told, the blame she has placed on others; she sees her failures and her mistakes, she even sees how much she drinks. This clear-eyed evaluation of her life is a bitter pill, and it prompts her to take responsibility, to do something officious and redemptive: she decides to make a will in which she will bequeath the only thing she has to bequeath, her yellow house. Mentally leafing through her list of friends and family, who are all grabbing for what little she has, she decides that, actually, no one is worthy of it. So in a final act of defiance, she leaves it to herself.

Hattie, having had the opportunity to review her checklist of sins and atone for them, looks her demons dead in the eye and chooses to remain exactly as she's always been, drunk and in denial. Which, for many of us, is the outcome of solitude and isolation. For many more, it's the outcome even while surrounded by others, as we end up isolating ourselves to protect our destructive habits. We find ourselves unwilling or unable to change because life has exhausted our last reserves of strength. We allow our demons to consume us. We surrender. Who's to say if that's good or bad, right or wrong, a sin or redemption – giving in is not about morality. It's a hard life, and sometimes it just is.

I'm up at the north end of the island with my head in the sky. The fog is still at island level and the sea to the north-east is invisible, but I can hear the waves crashing. On the north-east side of the island there's a huddle of hidden rocks called the White Horses that churn a vortex of milky, choppy waters below. I turn back towards the landlocked horses and to home, to light a fire before the sun goes down – having learned from the first night's mistake: do it not at a time of emergency, but to prevent it.

Through the sitting room window, the first embers of the sunset are streaked with claws of cloud. They call these 'Tibbettan sunsets', which seems gimmicky until you're looking at one. The winter sky puts on a show, the sun exploding supernova above the sea. Everything all at once. Grey, blue, red, pink, purple, orange, turquoise, yellow, white, black; it's all over the rusty ground and I head outside to watch it from the gate by the orange gas canisters – partly because it's the best view, and partly because I don't want to leave the safety of the barrier wall. The horses have been behaving very edaciously towards me since the first night, and after a couple of days of being chased around and nibbled, I'm tired of it.

The sun becomes a red lunula behind the sea and I can't stay out in the cold. I turn back and walk bang into the moon. Inside, I turn my phone on to take a picture of a candle on the windowsill in front of the palette of the sky, and that's the end of my phone, the battery dies. I have no means of recharging it, and what a relief that is. The things we have as safety nets also tie themselves around us and make us feel like we have something to fear, always, in the back of our mind. I have this in case this happens. But now I have nothing, and so I have no option but to trust that nothing bad will happen; and if it does, I will meet it. Feeling calm, and looking forward to sitting in front of the fire reading about shipwrecks as the night draws down, I go to the bedroom to change out of my muddy clothes, and, just out of curiosity, I look under the beds. There are about a dozen unopened water bottles. I don't think they're meant for me, but I'm drinking them.

The fears that haunted me on my first night alone don't have quite the same power any more, and they'll continue to fade every night I'm here. I start to enjoy the simple pleasure of lighting a fire before the sun leaves the sky completely, getting organised and bowing to the rhythm of the world that is turning. As with many people, I no longer have a watch and am completely reliant on my phone. There is no clock at Tibbetts, as if anyone staying here is encouraged to let time warp a little. I certainly don't know what time it is, but I'm soon able to guess with an accuracy of about twenty minutes as far as the sun goes – I know where it rises and where it sets, and from these points I can make a decent estimation. But with the moon rising at different times every night, later and later, nocturnal hours are harder to calculate and in the end I just go to bed when I am ready.

There is nothing like sleeping in a room with a fire, getting under the covers and having hot embers for company. Tonight, I don't even think of reaching for a knife. I have fought the fear and won. My trophy is this, enjoying the warmth while outside seeps into blackness and stars glitter cold and frozen in the sky. I have remembered how to be alone again, utterly alone. Out here, with no one around me, three-quarters of the way up a tiny rock in the sea, it's more alone than I have ever been. I have no means of communicating with anyone on the island, and it's certainly more alone than I've ever felt. If I screamed, no one would hear me. If a pirate were to crawl through the annals of time and dock at the island, I would have to fight it out alone, as best I could. If one of the islanders went mad, which for some is more probable than others, and went on a violent rampage, I would have to fight it out alone. As I think of these things, after reading too many children's stories of pirates, sleeping on the ground where their bodies were hung to rot, I am reminded that in order to enjoy being alone there are fears the mind conjures that we must overcome, and that battle can be part of the fun. When you are alone like this, with no distractions, no electricity, no phone, no nothing, you have no option but to look your monsters dead in the eye. Look at them until they blink, and ask yourself, can you find them beautiful?

16.

The Ugly Hut

It can be the saving grace of a hard life to ride a bike through summer in the city where you have experienced violence more times than seems reasonable. Riding into the marshes where the river flows under the bridge in late September, I watched the long shadows of Hasidic Jews travel the path and move deeper into the fields over which the cables from electricity pylons hang. I almost forget where I am. I almost lose it all, and maybe here it can never find me. A train is the only reminder that I am no longer in the field next door to where I once lived and there is no going back; there is only moving forwards in search of more beauty. Hunting it like a storm chaser, dedicating my life to finding it, to immersing myself in it and learning to see it in as many places as possible. I will learn that I don't always have to do something drastic or expensive; to change my view sometimes all I need to do is turn around. Beauty is a magic trick, a celestial fluke. The light on the wall will never be bettered and yet it is better every time I see it. The less I have, the more clearly I see beauty, the more I care about it, the more it makes it all worthwhile, and we're losing things all the time. It is the promise, not that I will never fall, but the promise that every fall will be countered. To continue to witness beauty, I would choose madness for as long as the madness would not kill me.

*

It's a grey day in mid-March. The sea is grey, the sky above is bloated with grey clouds that hang into the sea like sacks of fish. There's a slip of orange visible in the furthest reach of the horizon. I have been coming out here every single day for over a hundred days now to see nothing but grey water. Every day the same routine: I take twenty minutes after lunch and walk to the furthest limit of the south-west point and look at the sea through my binoculars. Occasionally the water is broken by a seal or a shag, once there was a fishing boat, usually it's just water. But today it's 2.55 p.m. and I've seen the first dolphin of my life.

I had imagined I'd see the dolphins on a sunny day, imagined the golden light on the water, so I was only going through the motions today when I put on my boots, took out my binoculars and stood out here with my face to the wind. Every shadow of a wave draws my attention, so when another catches my eye a little to my left I can't believe the first rise and disappearance of a dorsal fin. But I can't be mistaken the second, third and fourth times I see the fin, heading way out west.

Suddenly, I see dolphins have designed themselves to resemble the waves that have distracted me every other day. It seems so obvious now, but I never realised it before. Within moments, the dolphin's progress into the horizon makes it indistinguishable from those waves, and yet I stand staring, reminded that beauty is a far more potent force than it is given credit for. At my lowest, it has been the only thing that made me want to stick around, just to see more of it.

Green shoots of ferns burst from the marcescence of their rust-coloured brothers on the east coast path, and two green, feathered leaves rise up from stems like outstretched arms mid-adoration. The warming sun. Bluebells and green bracken sweep the cliffs that were red all winter, like smudges of luminous pastel. Gulls gleefully shit from the sky at 50 mph. Starlings have started nesting in the stones, chirping through the wooden shutters of the garage of the island farm. Gorse creaks in the easterly wind, and on it the odd grey feather of a warbler flutters, threatening to leave for the clear blue sea where the screaming, wheeling sounds of ecstatic oystercatchers echo. Up at Jenny's Cove, puffins emerge from their burrows and pace their porch like proud butlers before returning underground. Rows and rows of guillemots and razorbills impasto the cliffs with streaks of white guano. Violets spring from the earth at every corner, animated by the wind with dancing faces like something out of *The Butterfly Ball* – thousands of them, more here than I've ever seen in a lifetime, like shooting stars.

By spring, I notice a change in my city-boy husband as well. He came not wanting to get mud on his boots and now he plays football with sheep shit. It's a beautiful thing to see, I think, as I kick the rock-hard turd back his way. Under our shit-covered boots, the ground is coming to life. Beetles – dor and minotaur – burrow huge holes. I spot the first oil beetle of the season; once incredibly rare in Devon, they are now a common sight on Lundy. A pin-stripe wolf spider emerges from the heather and scuttles over the granite; 150 species of spider have been recorded on this tiny island. Dean, the warden, seems to enjoy my look of horror when he informs me there is a species of tarantula that lives here. Despite that knowledge, it is good to lie on the grass and get down on the level of the insects, mesmerised by an oil beetle making its slow and laborious progress over blades of grass. I daydream in front of the wandering invertebrate and think about spring on the mainland and all the things you forget, being out here. The motifs of life and its seasons 'out there' are slowly slipping from my mind: wisteria, police cars, ice cream vans, bare legs, signposts, frogspawn, bicycles, Aperol spritz, traffic jams, peonies, dog shit, sirens.

A lot has been slipping from my mind since arriving here. Immersed in the allure of the natural world, it can be easy to lose yourself in it almost completely. With everything putting forward its best self, showing itself in its most spectacular light to attract pollinators or mates, when you look in the mirror you could mistake yourself for a poor imitation. Still, we try to remind ourselves that we are more beautiful in certain lights, just like the cow parsley. If I think myself a part of the natural world, so I will become it.

'The birds had become so familiar with her, that they seemed to heed her almost as little as if she had been a stone,' S. G. Goodrich wrote of his boyhood memories of Sarah Bishop, the 'Hermitress of the Salems', in *Recollections of a Lifetime*. Sarah, a 'considerable beauty' who turned her back on humanity to live like an animal in a cave in North Salem, New York, is said to have achieved a oneness with nature that allowed her to tame a rattlesnake that she kept as a pet. She remained in her cave in the mountains for almost three decades, until the day she died, trapped between two rocks in a frozen bog.

In life, a local paper, the *Telescope*, had visited her hermitage and reported: 'We conversed with her for some time, and found her to be of a sound mind, a religious turn of thought, and entirely happy in her situation. Of this she has given repeated proofs by refusing to quit this dreary abode.' Why would a beautiful, sane woman choose to become a troglodyte? Goodrich reported rumours that Sarah had been raped during the American Revolutionary War, a theory Dr Linda Grant DePauw supports in *Seafaring Women*, claiming Bishop was even captured and imprisoned on a British privateer as 'a communal sex object' until her escape. This would explain why she is often said to have 'dreaded no animal on earth but man'. She didn't want to be seen as beautiful because that had proven dangerous; she didn't want to be seen at all. Bishop kept a depository of rich silks and satins but spent most of her days in rags. She thought herself a part of the natural world, because of a shared connection with it: she was as fearful of mankind as were the 'brute beasts' she existed alongside. Knowing her story, her reaction to society's perception of her beauty, her drive to distance herself from that perception and the society that held it as much as possible becomes understandable. As with any potent force, beauty has its dark side.

I'm walking a circumnavigation of the island on the east path that cuts into the land. There are goats with their kids and Soay sheep with their little brown lambs, stumbling over the uncertain ground with their long legs and tiny bodies. They have arrived much earlier than their hefty white counterparts.

I reach a corner on the path and hear a mother Soay making a lot of noise. She comes forwards, then turns and goes back, over and over again, always stopping at the same point in a small loop, baaing frantically. She's obviously lost her lamb, but it can't be far away because they stick to their mothers like cleaner fish.

As I move closer, treading softly so as not to cause her more distress, I discover why the Soay is crying: her lamb has died. Its small brown body is laid out on the grass. Its mouth is slightly open; a thin blade of dead grass has attached itself to the lamb's bottom lip. The mother is running backwards and forwards, baaing and looking at me frantically, not understanding why her lamb won't get up, and all I can do is show her my empty hands and try to explain to her that 'I don't have it, I'm so sorry.'

While talking to a sheep, I get a message I've been dreading for years: the future of the green hut is at risk. Our cousin handed the keys to the hut back to the estate without consulting anyone else in the family, and shortly afterwards, he died. Within a couple of months, planning on the hut has been announced by the estate. Except for a few dog-eared photos, the hut is the only thing left that holds our history. Built by the carpenters who worked in the nearby Shapland and Petter factory, which is also now falling apart, it is a part of local history; as someone writes into the paper, 'It's a landmark.' What the planning means for the hut is in the hands of the landowners. The problem they have now is that the council sees the hut as having been abandoned over the years, and therefore wants the hut torn down, an outcome the new (more receptive) estate manager professes the landowners want to avoid as much as I do. My having visited the hut and changed the locks when I was at Croyde changes things. As of this moment it is no longer abandoned or condemned, just back in limbo. I say to the estate manager that as long as they don't knock it down, there's hope. I walk on, so consumed in thoughts about the dead lamb and the hut and what it all means that, as I approach the last quarter of the circumnavigation, I don't notice another islander until she says, 'Oh, you caught me talking to myself! How embarrassing.'

She lives on her own here and I remind her who she's talking to – cabin woman, loner girl. 'I was so lost in thought then; I think I was mumbling to myself, wasn't I? I have no idea.'

I have just been having a meaningful conversation with a

sheep. As I try to reassure her that it's normal to talk things through with yourself when there's no one else around, I think of Sarah Bishop, and how, if we spend more time in the natural world than in the human one, it follows that we become less concerned about what people think.

People tend to think that talking to oneself, and indeed talking to anything that is not a human or a pet, is both a dropping of the mask of vanity and a dropping of the mask of sanity. But simply talking to yourself doesn't make you insane; what you say when you're talking does. Once you've been alone for a while you do mutter to yourself, and it's a habit that, once you have developed it, doesn't go away. Talking is a means of listening, of separating thoughts into sentences with a beginning and an end, and breaking down troubles or conundrums into something manageable, whereby we can come to an understanding. Talking things through is still the most efficient means of grounding our thoughts, even if we are alone.

Interestingly, what we tend to find beautiful in the natural world has occurred through mutations – exceptions and alterations to the rule – that are a tool for survival, like the dolphins'. Beauty is originality, and yet insecurity tends to arise from caring about what other people think and striving to be the same. Nietzsche, arch loner and owner of a highly original moustache, suggested that 'vanity is the fear of being original'. If vanity is a fear of being original, then it corresponds that many who have the drive to live alone believe that removing oneself from the crowd and the social posturing it encourages sparks authenticity. Part-time hermit Anne LaBastille believed this. 'Invite a person to a log cabin in the woods for a weekend,' she wrote. 'The true personality emerges every time.' (Not always a good thing.)

We might assume that leaving society is a rejection of vanity, and in many ways it is a rejection of the pre-eminence of human beauty over the beauty of the natural or spiritual world, but that doesn't mean it's not sometimes a little conceited. There is a degree of egotism in the decision of an anchorite or hermit to put themselves in a cell for the rest of their lives in the belief that only God's eyes are worthy, important or worth sacrificing for. In order to get a kick out of being alone – in a cell, in a field, on a mountaintop – it's likely we believe that we are still, in some way, being perceived. But, alone, you are no longer expecting validation to come from anyone else – in the silence it's unlikely you'll find yourself worrying, 'Does God think I'm hot?' Soon, you stop looking for validation and you start seeing yourself as a part of it all, and stop feeling *quite* so insecure.

The racing pigeons that arrive on the island are the only birds that are unwelcome. Nor are they wanted any more by their owners (having got lost and ended up here), so they are mostly ushered out of the tavern, sometimes driven on a quad bike halfway up the island, and end up serving as prey for the falcons. First, one arrives, and then a dozen, then more, and these lost pigeons start to feel like a metaphor. A strong wind blew us here also.

In Spanish, both 'dove' and 'pigeon' are *paloma* – there is no distinction. In the evening light, though the racing pigeons may have lost their way, they have not lost their grace. They wheel in synchronised murmurations over the island, curving out towards the sea. To see something's beauty, its true beauty, we have to see it in its element. A swan is only graceful in the water.

*

The golden oriole arrives on its travels from Africa on a warm spring morning. Males are vivid, lemon-yellow birds with black wings and eyes; females look like yellow thrushes. A notoriously secretive bird, its flutey song flows through our bathroom window and tarries in the sunlight on the sill, and immediately I know something new is here. I've heard its song in Spain in the olive groves, where it drifts through the air amid the gurgles of passing bee-eaters and the clanging of goat bells. Every week, every day, it seems a new migratory bird arrives here, and soon the island is exploding with life and species. Soon, humans will also be returning to it in their droves, hunting for beauty.

The lockdown is finally lifted in mid-April, and on the first day visitors come back onto the island I sit out in the 'ugly hut', writing and staring from dawn until midday when the boat pulls in, wanting to absorb into my being every last moment of the isolation we have become accustomed to. I have mixed emotions about its end. Mostly, I don't want anyone else here, really, is the honest truth. But the numbers are still limited – it won't be that many compared to a typical spring – and I tell myself how the gift of this island being the National Trust's and not under private ownership is that its beauty and tranquillity are open to everyone. And what bliss this will be for someone who has been locked up in a house or a flat all these months. I do feel a little ashamed at wanting to keep the island like this, to preserve this point in time and its timelessness forever, but if you like isolation, if it's been your drive to remove yourself from society, from being appraised, and if you've experienced a total removal for over four months, it's hard not to feel like that. I know I'm not the only one.

At around 4 p.m. I head back to the ugly hut, where I can see the queue of visitors lining up to get back on the boat. As the day trippers leave, the island rolls off the weight and secrecy fills the air again. I watch the boat chug out of the bay and over the sea into an enviable sunset, and let my mind wander over to the mainland, to the moors and the rivers and the country lanes in summer, to Barnstaple estuary, wall to wall with the warbling of wading birds, and I begin to miss it, just a little.

17.

The Swift

It doesn't much look like it on a map, but in my mind the island is the shape of a heart dripping two drops of blood. Hungover one Sunday, I force myself out of the house and for a walk down into the beautiful, calm, late April evening, out towards the bay, heading for the two drips of blood that are the South Light and Rat Island. The air is still, and from the path I can see the water is crystal-clear; since the world started opening up again, a few yachts have begun arriving on the light winds.

We have just moved from the vestry down to a mole hole built into the rock behind the big Georgian mansion in Mill-combe valley, surrounded by daisies and birds and trees. I'm sad to leave the vestry, but since I was so eager to live there, the church and the Landmark Trust have realised they can rent it out to the public as a 'spiritual retreat'. It's a nice idea and I like this turn of events – the valley is also quieter than the church now that visitors have returned. I'm grateful for the seclusion and privacy the wooded valley offers.

I walk past some bird nets that have been put up in the valley. Some of the first people back on to the island are the bird ringers; these nets are up so they can catch and ring the migratory birds that travel through Lundy. Despite a sign telling me not to, I can't help but take a closer look at what birds have been caught. I'm looking at a female blackcap when a man shouts down from the top of the valley, 'I'm coming! Don't worry!'

The man's name is Rob; he's tall and thin and wears a cap and has eyes that are as excited as his voice. He quickly brings me out of my lethargic shell. He's been coming to the island to ring the birds here since 1985, but this morning he has had his best day ever: 'We ringed two hundred birds!'

We've had a week of high spring winds that meant the group was unable to do any ringing, but this morning made it worth the wait. And what better place to come to ring birds – the variety is almost as multifarious as snowflakes. Dunnock, blackcap, wren, robin, cuckoo, blackbird, skylark, swallow, herring gull, black-backed gull, wheatear, guillemot, gannet, puffin, fieldfare, snow bunting, redstart, stonechat, goldfinch, sparrow, starling, raven, rook, buzzard, falcon, merlin, shag, chaffinch, coal tit, chiffchaff, wood pigeon, pink-footed goose, mallard, wagtail, long-tailed tit, meadow pipit, rock pipit, golden plover, great spotted woodpecker, willow warbler, song thrush, storm petrel, whimbrel, Manx shearwater, oystercatcher.

All over the world migrations continue – a reassuring constant after a year that has shaken us and everything we thought we knew. But just as the moon sometimes rises in the day, the times of migrations can no longer be relied upon. The data from the birds ringed and studied here will be shared via computers with data from all over the world, mapping the birds' progress or decline, how they die, what the causes are. It will also record how much climate change is affecting each species, Rob explains. The deserts in Africa are getting wider, the seasons are changing, and the bird's main food source, grubs and caterpillars, is all out of joint.

*

In spring, the airways here are so crammed the birds need allocated flight paths. I watch a herring gull push a wagtail out of the way. But this island is, for many species, just a stop-off, a service station on the intercontinental highway, a place to sing and feed for a few days before carrying on further north, to Wales, Ireland, Scotland and the rest of the UK.

'You've timed your stay here perfectly,' Rob says. I'm unsure whether he means the time of year, or this exact point in time. Deftly holding a willow warbler between his fingers, he explains how much the island has changed over the years he has been coming here – for the better over the last few years thanks to the warden, Dean, who arrived with the understanding that there needs to be shrub and bush and unkempt 'weeds' for the insect life to thrive so the bird life can as well. Everything is thriving now. Although it has been a collective effort over many years to achieve this, and to achieve the island's conservation status, a lot of the work on the ground is done by individuals. Proof that one person can make a huge difference while quietly working away in seeming isolation: that work is connected to the survival of migrating birds all over the world. One of which Rob shows me up close. The willow warbler is light brown and powdered yellow, a dainty thing that has flown over the Sahara to get here. A few female blackcaps have also been caught in this round. I thank Rob and make my way down to the bay to watch the yachts rock in the yellow-blue sea, and wish I had a boat on which to sail to a little island. Or wings.

The next few weeks are busy. The island is making it abundantly clear that she doesn't want us to leave. The housing situation on the mainland has become dire. Suddenly, there is nowhere to rent in North Devon, there is nowhere to rent in the whole of Devon, there is nowhere to rent in Somerset, in Cornwall; we even look at pricey Dorset out of desperation – nothing. The land I think of as home has become inaccessible, so I let myself think about staying on here. It's been made apparent that we could, if we wanted to, but to stay here indefinitely we would have to give up our jobs and start working for the island full-time rather than volunteering tavern and cleaning shifts, which is something neither myself nor my husband is prepared to do, not even for love of the island. We've both worked hard to do the jobs we do now.

The prospect of giving it all up might be tempting, but in my mind the island's beauty, at times, takes on a more malevolent form, as the Dream Eater. People have come here with aspirations of doing one thing – of writing, or making, or being something – and then they've found that the island has taken over. Unless the island and its nature are your life, it will take over your time, your ambition – out here, you wonder: why bother, why strive, it's an easy life if you don't mind a few practical hardships. The freedom here can chain you to its rocks.

In our domestic desperation, I pounce. I try my husband again with the idea of a caravan in a field – maybe it could even be our own field now, I say. But his reply is as close to an unequivocal 'no' as he's ever given me. Despite this disappointment, I keep my eyes on the shore of the mainland and my fingers at the keyboard.

The weather turns in early May. The skies darken and the westerly and south-westerly winds we lacked through April reappear with a vengeance: it's wet, foggy and windy. Boats are cancelled; even replacement helicopters are cancelled. This means that today, the Saturday the ringers are supposed to be leaving the island, they can't. I think about this absent-mindedly as I walk past where they're staying. I'm off for a walk in the weather. Just to feel the rain on my skin and get blown about for a while, to make the fire back home all the sweeter.

Up on the south-west side by a drystone wall, I spot what looks like a lifeless swift. Lying dead still on the soaking grass, its cobble-sized body is saturated with water. It barely moves as I pick it up, but it's alive. It blinks, and I feel its tiny talons latch on to my thumb. I cover it with my hand to keep it warm and dry, and take it to the church porch out of the wind to look at it more closely.

When I get there, I see the winds have undoubtedly wiped the swift out and its feathers are soaked. I take it down to the moth hut – a deserted place full of dead leaves Dean's keeping in order to trap and record moths. It can dry off here, I think, as I open up my hand. But it's too tired to move. It sits on my thumb, and I stroke its little head and chest and tell it that it's going to be okay. I know human intervention is rarely a good thing, it's usually better to let life get on with itself, I can hear people telling me I should be leaving it alone, so I put it on a raised bit of wall in some leaves and prise my hand away from it. It holds on so tightly to my thumb I end up with three tiny cuts. Once out of my hand, it tries and fails to fly. It's like watching an owl swim, but hopeless, heartbreaking. It's not well, I think. And this time I decide I am intervening now, officially. I pick it back up and snuggle it in my hand. It burrows its head into my warm palm.

Around me and the limp swift, swallows glide gracefully through the glassless windows, getting blown about a little even down here. They look strong, though, agile. Not like this little guy.

I walk up to Brambles where the ringers are staying, and there at the window appears Rob, who wasn't there when I walked past half an hour ago, but now he's standing there looking out, as if he's been waiting for my arrival. There is something about this island. With no communication, the person you want to see always appears just at the right moment. As if, after a week or so of outsider decompression, your guard comes down and you become tuned in; as if we're all moving as part of one thing. The synchronicity I could hardly ever obtain in London happens here all the time. And I observe it. If for no other reason than to note it exists. There is such a thing as meaningful coincidence. A phone has never played a part in it. It is people appearing when you need them.

I raise my clutched hand at Rob and he knows immediately I have a bird in there. He leaves the window and rushes to the door. 'It's wiped out,' I say. 'He's too wet and exhausted to fly.'

Rob can only see a black feather. 'What is it, a blackbird?'

'No, a swift.'

His eyes light up. I open my hand a little and he prises the bird expertly from my fingers. 'A swift!' he exclaims, looking at the little body. 'You've done the right thing. We're going to warm him up overnight in a heat bag and feed him – he'd die out here in this.'

They have never ringed a swift before, he says. In all his thirty-five years of coming to the island, this will be the first swift to be ringed here. So when it travels now, they will know it is this one. I'm sad to let it go, but know they have all the equipment to take better care of it than I could. 'You've saved its life,' Rob says again. 'Well done.' He closes the door. I'm pleased, but I don't really believe I've saved anything's life. What a momentous thing that seems.

The wind rages all day and through the night, but calms a little early the next morning. The sea remains white-hot with anger and huge waves crash on the rocks on the west side. The gulls, incredible things that they are, manage the wind like it's an unruly neighbour with a gun. Gracefully. Carefully. Firmly. I have a newfound respect for gulls out here.

Late morning, my husband and I walk up past the moth hut on our way to a windy picnic to watch the waves crash, and come across a heartbreaking scene. The swallows had glided in and out of the hut with grace and agility and ease. They had been looking to make their nests here, but it has not provided enough shelter for them. There was not enough food to be caught. All three beautiful swallows lie dead, a few feet from one another. I can hardly believe it. I pick one up from the pile of leaves I'd put the swift in a few hours earlier. It looks like it could still be alive; its feathers gleam blue and red and white, its tail, shaped like half a mermaid's purse, waves a little in the wind, its eyes are not quite closed. I hold it and rub its chest, hoping I might perform some kind of CPR, and if not that, some magic. I turn to my husband and without thinking say, 'Why can't I bring it back to life?'

As soon as the words are out of my mouth, I'm aware this is an absurd thing to say. But equally, it seems absurd that it's dead. The bird is completely healthy, its feathers shining and reflecting the light, its chin bursting blood red, it should not have died, it is still so full of life. It flew for thousands of miles to get here. Flew over deserts and seas. Over valleys and mountains. And it came here, to this exposed rock where any strong wind on the mainland is exacerbated. And it died.

I have to be persuaded to put it down. I'm upset and frustrated that there's nothing I can do. I'm exhausted from futile house-hunting and early mornings and late nights and news that our old car back on the mainland has rusted and quite literally fallen apart, and everything else that comes with island life in the aftermath of a pandemic, everything else that comes with leaving another life behind. I start crying as I rest it on the ground close to the other two swallows. And in doing so, looking at these three dead birds, I think of the swift yesterday and realise: I did save its life – we did. The number the swift has been ringed with means it will help build a bigger picture of what is happening to swifts all over the world; it will be tracked over thousands of miles for however long its life proves to be. But without an intermediary, its journey would have ended here, like the swallows'. The individual working quietly in the middle of nowhere makes a difference to the world and our understanding of it. Everyone who works here with the intention of making this island a sanctuary for both humans and wildlife has made a difference. Out here, it could become very easy to believe that humanity is a force for the good of the world. We have just forgotten how.

With the abundance of life that comes in spring comes an abundance of death. You see it everywhere – bones, dead rabbits, dead pygmy shrews, gull wings with no body, looking as if they have been left for an angel to wear. But the streams flow again, and it's a relief to hear the water giggling through the primrose woods on the east side; the streams had been silent for over a month now. Everything running dry and the water reserves on the island already getting low. The storm has created chaos; but it will also provide the materials for life to continue.

The wheatears arrived last month, completing their journey from the belt across central Africa stretching from Senegal to Kenya, flying by night under the stars. Wheatears are not, as I had assumed, called wheatears because they like to feed on ears of wheat. Largely insectivorous birds, their name is derived from the folk etymology of 'white arse'. Their little white bums thrive in the gorse and heather and moorlands and on the rocky grounds that are perfect for nesting. Now it seems all the insects they feast on are simply emerging from thin air, as are other things. There is a rumour going about one morning that a sulphur-bellied warbler has arrived on the island. The rumour is confirmed around 11 a.m. This is the first-ever sighting of the bird in the UK. This is big. This means we are in for one of Lundy's infamous twitcher invasions.

By around 3 p.m., men – and they are all men – in khaki, beige and camouflage have arrived with missile-launcher-sized camera lenses on boats they have chartered especially for the occasion. It's like Fashion Week, there's the same buzz, everyone needs to get to the right place at the right time to capture the thing the whole world wants to see, except the main attraction isn't a celebrity tottering out of a party, it's a little bird on a branch. I'd like to see the bird, but feel I can live without it, and too much hype tends to put me off anything. The sulphur-bellied warbler is at risk of being overexposed.

I come back from my afternoon mooch at around 6 p.m. to find a row of thirty men standing on the bank right on top of our roof. The men have come from as far as London and the Midlands in a few hours. Some have travelled further, bombing down the motorways and paying hundreds of pounds to fishing boats to bring them out here in the hope of witnessing, and capturing, the sulphur-bellied warbler. I stand outside our front door for a while with my tiny binos, looking in the direction all the lenses above me are pointing in a vague attempt to see it. I can't, so I take the binos off and just listen to the commotion. A younger guy arrives next to me with a big camera lens.

'Taken any good pictures?' I ask.

'No, not yet. It's been too far away,' he replies, visibly frustrated, and says he saw the warbler come down here.

'I'll follow your lead if you don't mind,' I say.

'Not at all,' he says, not looking at me, immediately running to the opposite side of the big white villa and pointing to a tree next to Millcombe. 'There,' he whispers, 'it's there in the tree.' And there it is: a little brown job in the branches. I have a quick look with my binos and take a very short, very dodgy video of it flying off further down the valley, and actually, I must admit, it's a bit of a thrill to see it, to just happen to be here when it arrives. Rob was right: we timed our stay here perfectly. For the men who arrive the next day, however, there is nothing but disappointment. The warbler left the island overnight, heading who knows where.

Out here, it can be easy to forget that 38 million birds have disappeared from the UK in the last fifty years because of humanity. Isolation can make you forget what's happening in the wider world, while also acting as a barometer. If a species doesn't arrive on this little island, or the numbers are low, it's most likely a sign of something bigger happening elsewhere. Their absence or decline is smoke where somewhere else there is fire. Isolation forces you to observe things in greater detail and with greater clarity, and when you start to observe them you start to see patterns, and when you start to see patterns you are able to observe changes or breaks in the pattern.

Removal from the other world permits one to observe life from a different viewpoint; isolation increases our levels of perception, forcing us to see that, even alone, we are interconnected; that we cannot escape this fact however far away we go. What happens on this island off the North Devon coast can change what happens in the Congo, and vice versa. Away from it all, somehow the connection to it all deepens.

18.

Tell It to the Bees

June is the month of foxgloves and cuckoo spit. Heat shimmers off the land while a huge seventeenth-century-style wooden ship rocks in the bay surrounded by blue glitter, a ghost ship come to take me home. Yesterday, I watched the sun rise for the summer solstice. The red sun chased the moon over the silver side of the island, and the red lit up the waves in front of me. Behind me was the endless flapping of the British flag on the hill. A gull sailed, lean as a Nike tick, out in the offing. The wind blew in my face, ice-cold from the east. When I closed my eyes I saw a thousand red suns.

The day after solstice is a bright day, a completely blue sky overhead and haze across the face of the mainland. It is summer but it's not. The flux began while we slept. There's a cool, crisp wind that carries a prophecy of brown leaves. The birds are dancing with each other, a male and female starling glide from the oak tree down through the valley, jostling together like butterflies. Leaves, wind-burnt from the gales in early May, have refused to let go of their branches and have stayed to see the summer through; they're already brown and will release their grip soon. Goldfinches bob and a blackcap calls for a lover. Joy is in the air. The hardest part is over, for now. The growing is done; now for the effortless decay. A solitary robin flies and lands on a ladder as Adam, a volunteer from Yorkshire who knows about drystone walling and is proud to have broken almost every bone in his body, strims the hedge in the distance.

It's not just the wind; the light has changed, casting long warm shadows before 10 a.m. Moth season has begun. Swallows and swifts swoop low over my head and scythe through the golden dead molinia grass as I procrastinate on the upper east path. Something is rotting in the hedge where new life is cheeping. On the narrow path I stand aside for an elderly lady who starts chatting about islands. She tells me the first island she visited was Skye, and now she and her husband travel to islands all over Britain, and much further afield.

'Island hoppers,' I think out loud.

'Not hoppers!' she insists. 'It takes five days to get to Saint Helena! No, we're not hoppers. I've collected islands all my life.'

'Collected' is an interesting choice of word: collected the experience, kept the memories like attractive stones to finger in your pocket.

As a writer, I sometimes worry that I mentally collect experiences in order to write about them. *Could I use this?* is never far from my mind. In reality, the experiences that happen in the background are the ones I end up writing about, more often than not. The pieces that fit the page are rarely the ones I have consciously collected, because the page doesn't work like that – my page doesn't, anyway – and I suppose that's what keeps it exciting. Initially, I didn't withdraw from society to write about that withdrawal. Withdrawing was just something I did while writing about other things; and writing about other things became so much easier, the more sequestered I became. Creativity seems to prosper in isolation. It's the imaginary friend of the only child.

*

While a life full of distractions might be beneficial for initial inspiration, creativity usually flows from quieter, uninterrupted spaces. Research into the link between solitude and creativity has shown that those who seek solitude tend to be more creative – we've all seen the irritating lists of famous discoveries made and plays written during periods of isolation. But there's rarely any mention as to why.

There's a scientific reason for the correlation between solitude and creativity. There are physical changes that the brain undergoes when someone is on their own: our neural circuits increase and strengthen the part of the brain responsible for imagination to fill the social void. What comes out of being alone might be the theory of relativity, or it might be a selfie, but more often than not what we create in solitude is a means of keeping the lines of communication with the rest of humankind open – we feel a connection to others through our stories, our paintings, our photos, our understanding of the world.

That solitude strengthens the area of imagination goes some way towards explaining why many writers and artists, theoretical physicists and philosophers, musicians – indeed anyone who needs to conjure things from thin air – have lived at least some stretch of their lives in solitude. Excepting the death of a heavily bejewelled tortoise, the reclusive existence of Jean des Esseintes – the protagonist of the classic nineteenth-century novel *Against Nature* – mirrors its author Joris-Karl Huysmans's time in Trappist retreats and life as a Benedictine oblate. Huysmans wrote that he was always trying to escape 'the horrible reality of existence, to leap beyond the confines of thought'.

The urban hermit and writer Julia Holloway said: 'The eremitical life is an excellent mode of life to be a writer, because what you do is you reduce all the false stimuli. With writing you transcend time . . . You arrive at that silence, which is like the silence of a Quaker meeting, where the Spirit speaks.' However, the North Pond Hermit, Christopher Knight, would disagree. Knight likes the reclusive poet Emily Dickinson because she wrote without hope of publication. He thinks that no real hermit would write about their experience as a hermit because it's egotistical. He said this after giving permission for a book to be written about him and his experiences as a hermit, while giving an interview about the books he liked to read while alone. To think you have escaped the ego is the ego's cleverest trap.

On the seashore, whole worlds develop in the rock pools where tidal water stays in pockets. The life that thrives in them does not question its isolation.

'No Man moved Me – till the Tide,' wrote Emily Dickinson. No man moved her much after the tide either, as she spent the last years of her life in complete solitude. ('At home' was even listed on her death certificate as her occupation.) Her poetry thrived in those years. In her solitude she created an outpouring of poems that she requested be burned upon her death. Her sister ignored that request (possibly assuming that if Dickinson had *really* wanted her poems destroyed she would have burned them herself while she was alive), and now we have her prolific oeuvre of more than 1,000 poems that only seem to increase in popularity as time goes on.

There is much speculation as to the reason Dickinson chose extreme seclusion: that she was in love with another woman (her childhood friend and sister-in-law, who lived in the room next door); that there was an unrequited love with a mystery man she called 'master'; and, of course, that she was mad. The only thing we really know, over a century later, is that she did commit herself to solitude. In that state of being, Dickinson wrote poetry that references solitude – what she defined as 'a soul admitted to itself'. It has been suggested that her repetition of the word 'solitude' in her work demonstrates how lonely she was. If this were the case, it would be an interesting choice of word, as 'solitude' tends to imply we are at peace with our aloneness.

In a letter to her friend Abiah Root, Dickinson wrote: 'Does not Eternity appear dreadful to you . . . I often get thinking of it and it seems so dark to me that I almost wish there was no Eternity. To think that we must forever live and never cease to be.' It's almost as if her solitude was preparation.

Living forever and never ceasing to be sounds quite appealing to most of us these days. In working together as a society, we have harnessed the power of medicine and prolonged life expectancy; but we must return our attention to the earth if we are to understand the depths of our nature and hope to make living for such a long time worthwhile. To this end, some go alone into the world. Searching, listening, watching for long enough that they might catch a glimpse of the hunchback of eternity, seemingly in the most godless of places.

I once passed Derek Jarman's Prospect Cottage, a remote fisherman's hut perched alone on the shingle of Dungeness, while filming an advert for a now-defunct t-shirt company. As we drove past in one of the kit vans, I said to myself (as I didn't expect anyone of note to live there): 'Who lives there, I wonder?'

'It was Derek Jarman's house,' Gareth, my cameraman, replied.

The advert featured a vintage car that neither the male model nor anyone else on set knew how to drive. It ended up getting stuck in the shingle, and we had to wait hours for assistance. In those hours, languishing in the run-down pub, I came to the conclusion that Dungeness was godforsaken and that I needed to learn how to drive. As I stood alone outside, smoking and watching the thick mist become fog, I had no idea in which direction the sea lay. There were the doomful towers of a nuclear power station to my right. It was bleak. It was empty. It was a place where time did not exist (certainly as far as breakdown assistance was concerned). But the vacuum is the ancestor of all creation, and a blank canvas is where the imagination thrives. 'You know the task is to fill the empty page,' Derek Jarman wrote, shortly before he died. It had proven to be thus: in the seven years Jarman lived at Prospect Cottage, among other films and shorts, he made *Edward II*, *Wittgenstein*, and *The Garden*, which was filmed at the cottage.

One side of the cottage was decorated with verses from 'The Sunne Rising' by John Donne, the paradoxical metaphysical poet who used alchemy as metaphor and equated lovers with saints:

> Thou, sun, art half as happy as we,
> In that the world's contracted thus.
> Thine age asks ease, and since thy duties be
> To warm the world, that's done in warming us.

Prospect Cottage wasn't just a creative bunker; it was the home of a man dying of AIDS in an age when having the disease was not only a death sentence, but most of society wanted you to feel like a pariah. AIDS and HIV were killing thousands in the UK, and the government had not spent a penny on research to try to help save those afflicted. People were made to feel that it was the ultimate shame, yet Jarman was open about his HIV diagnosis – he said he had to be, for his own self-respect. This rejection of stigma was so powerful that it would lead to an event that was like a trippy myth from old, weird Britain.

In 1991, three years before he died, Derek Jarman was made a saint by a group of queer male 'nuns' known as the Sisters of Perpetual Indulgence. In true chivalric form – and as a dig at an unwitting Ian McKellen for accepting a knighthood from the government during the AIDS crisis – the nuns canonised him as 'Saint Derek Jarman of the Order of the Celluloid Knights'. Prospect Cottage and its garden have since become a place of pilgrimage for thousands of wandering souls.

The last film Jarman wrote at Prospect Cottage came from a new world of isolation. As AIDS ravaged his body, he started losing his eyesight, and as the disease slowly blinded him he began to see flashes of blue light. Jarman had the urge to create something from this – and to keep alive his connection with the world he could hardly see. He made the film *Blue*, a single shot of Yves Klein blue – the colour of immateriality – over which the narration meditates on his descending blindness, his life and death. 'Blue bottle buzzing, lazy days, the sky-blue butterfly sways on the cornflower, lost in the warmth of the blue heat haze . . . blue of my heart, blue of my dreams . . . blue of delphinium days.'

Jarman's love of flowers is evident even in his urban-punk dystopia *Jubilee*, and he once said he should have been a gardener: it shares a similar process with writing. Gardening is preparation as an art form. 'I developed a habit of spending Sundays with seed catalogues and lists of old roses, plotting floral fireworks that wouldn't go off for months,' Olivia Laing writes in *Funny Weather*. Writing is preparation as an art form. When Emily Dickinson wrote about isolation, she did not fear being alone, but rather infinite isolation: the solitude of eternity. It is only through imagination, the companion of solitude, that we can prepare ourselves for eternity. Ernest Hemingway referenced the same thing in his Nobel Prize acceptance speech: 'Writing, at its best, is a lonely life . . . For he does his work alone and if he is a good enough writer he must face eternity, or the lack of it, each day.' Derek Jarman knew he was dying, and he planted flowers that would bloom long after his death. Around the cottage, valerian burst in clouds of deep pink. Thanks to the cottage's current caretakers and Jarman's long-term companion Keith Collins, who cared for Jarman and his garden in the last years of his life, his pharmacopoeia of medicinal plants such as lavender and sea kale still surround the house. Poppies and foxgloves. Colour and visions. 'I want to share this emptiness with you,' Jarman wrote in *The Garden*, as if writing to the foxgloves that would go off like fireworks just a few months after he died.

Bang!

Down in the valley, I've started hearing the strangest noises. The power's off but there's still enough light in the sky to make out the black silhouettes of trees in front of the sea in the dark, moonless, starless night. For lack of owls on the island, there is the Manx shearwater, black seabirds with white underbellies that pass alone and in pairs, *cucaaa*-ing over the house. It's an eerie, unearthly, mammalian, innately nocturnal sound. All the lights except the candles are out. It is the night, and there is nothing – no star, no moonlight – to escape it, only the shearwater to exacerbate it. Little do I know now, but soon I will think I hear the shearwaters back on the mainland through the wind, and I will turn my head to try to hear them better. Lundy will become the mother of my dreams; it is replacing my old home and becoming the land on which every event my subconscious creates takes place. It's growing into a whole world down there. It is taking over.

The rhythm of the island: the waves in and out, the migrations to and from, the lighthouse on and off, the valves in my heart open shut, open shut. The island lulls me into paralysis. I rarely speak to anyone off the island any more. I can feel myself withdrawing into myself, 'a soul admitting to itself' – something my soul is all too good at. I want to talk to no one, not even anyone here. I just want to sit and stare at it all forever. I want to be rocked in this granite cradle, it's sending me to sleep. I let go of all aspirations and dreams. I give up looking for a home on the mainland. My competitive nature has vanished. I'm drinking too much. As if there's a crack in my head, the night seeps into my dreams. I'm not writing as much as I should be. Maybe this is peace, or preparation for it.

I'm not ready.

One morning, out of the blue, I get a message asking if I'd be interested in looking after the horses of a relative of one of my dad's friends in Spain for six weeks. This would give us a date. My initial reaction is 'no'. But I say 'yes'. When I finally write the date that we're to leave Lundy, no one can quite believe it. 'We thought you'd just stay here' – *like everyone else* are the unspoken words. A part of me did too.

19.

The Boundary Lines

'Boundaries. You have to create boundaries.'

Will an ocean do?

Thank you for this book on depression with daffodils on the cover. It is the most depressing thing I have ever seen. I'll read it. The thing is, I couldn't find in its pages where it said I might not be the problem; that maybe there was no more work to be done; that there comes a point where you cannot protect yourself, where your boundaries are laughed down; that the medication won't make the shouting stop; that one day you will hit your own head too hard because you can never make the shouting stop; that sometimes you are depressed for a reason and sometimes – just sometimes – that reason is not you or the chemicals in your brain. That sometimes there is a simple fix. I could not find the page where it said to run. Run for your life. I could not the find the page where it said you will be happy on your own. I did not hear anyone – doctor, nurse or therapist – say you will be safer on your own. Why did no one tell me I would be safer on my own? Safeguarding, maybe. I was depressed, after all, and depressed people are a danger to themselves, left alone. But alone there was no danger.

Draw the boundaries on the map. Chart where my edges are. I touch the sides now. Where once was empty space, now I am there. I get to keep this body for a while, and I want to fill it out. I want to push myself from the small ball cowering in my chest and spread it to the edges. My crown to my toe. I am the boundary line and no one can cross me, unless I let them in.

Solitude saved me. The change was immediate. I knew I would at least be calmer on my own, less afraid of saying the wrong thing in my own home. But I didn't expect it to be a life-changing event. I didn't expect to become happy again. Not on my own. Not like that. And yet it was like this. Maybe timing made it so. Being alone as I was might not have lasted if I hadn't reached the end of the cycle. I had completed the disaster, so I didn't resist my solitude, my removal from society; I embraced it, and, if I am honest, I will never get far enough away from it all for my liking. I continue to crave wider, more ferocious, more unruly boundaries. Sea. Mountains. Desert. Fire. Where else can I become a part of the land, and what elemental force can I dress myself in next?

Can I be satisfied spending my days writing in solitude in a garden shed? Probably not, but I can try. Is it a state of mind or a way of living? Do you become a hermit, or are you always a hermit? The star I am born under, Virgo, is (predictably) the hermit in the tarot; a hunched and wizened old man in a hessian sack crawling over a mountaintop to go and scratch his cilice in peace. Here I am in real life, everything all at once: the hermit, loner, recluse, whatever name you choose to give it, is just one of many facets. That is who I have always been and yet I have become it. And what is it that I became? A hermit? A recluse? A bad anchoress? Or did I simply confirm a lifelong suspicion that I'm just a bit of a loner? Hope Bourne never called herself anything. Despite living a solitary life for decades, she was at pains to resist labels such as 'recluse'. Like the hermit Saint Endelienta, Hope frequently went for walks with people, dropped in on people, she didn't avoid people, but she still preferred to spend most of her time alone.

Anne LaBastille was careful to call herself a 'part-time' hermit. Maybe women are a little more cautious when it comes to calling ourselves one thing or another. Once we are given a label, it is human nature to immediately question and dissect it, and the reason many of us choose to live in solitude is because we are tired of having to justify our existence.

The 1230 work, *Ancrene Wisse*, or *Guide for Anchoresses* says, 'They who love most shall be most blessed, not they who lead the most austere life, for love outweigheth this.' The hermits and recluses who have interested me most have been the dissidents of the genre: Hope Bourne, Anne LaBastille, Endelienta, Harry Hallowes, Shaun Caton, they all behaved in ways we don't expect of a hermit, and, like Mauro Morandi, they had no prior intention of becoming one. Sarah Maitland got a smartphone after decades of resisting the noise that comes with that kind of technology, so that she could see and speak to her granddaughter. Because living an authentic life means reconciling the future we have imagined for ourselves with the life that unfolds in front of us, otherwise we become trapped inside a concept, which we live out for the sake of how others perceive us, or how we think we should conduct ourselves, rather than living. The ornamental hermit of Ashby de la Zouch, who drank and smoked and went to the pub, said it best: that hermits should be 'abettors of freedom', for themselves, for everyone.

I wonder if, with regard to the solitary, people try too hard to define it, to taxonomise it. I've never been inclined to, because I want the definition to expand: the othering of ourselves feels egotistical. And it is society's othering of hermits and those who choose to exist in solitude that makes everyone else feel like spending any real length of time alone isn't something normal people do. We could all spend more time alone, I think. It's true that some of us are more disposed than others towards solitude, but for short periods of time I believe solitude is as vital as company to a human's well-being. Consulting the self is more important now than ever. It has always been imperative that we are informed by the experiences and the opinions of others; but at this point in time, when we are immersed in the thoughts and opinions of others on a daily, hourly basis, it is very hard to hear our own.

Solitude need not be a lofty exercise in enlightenment. Simply to be able to sit with ourselves and our lives is a start; to see how we make ourselves feel when we are alone and whether our life fits us any more is progress. How does it feel? As you sit alone in your kitchen staring at a packet of cornflakes next to the toaster, does the silence whisper, *You are wasting your life.* That's what happened to me. This horrible, mundane realisation that is profound in the extreme to the individual: we only live once, and we're always running out of time. It's the most valuable realisation I ever had, and I had it because I was left alone.

Can you live alone and still live life to the fullest? Of course you can – those were some of the best years of my life. I've never understood why we have this expectation that we should be bored when we're alone. I don't think this assumption shows a lack of imagination, because it doesn't require imagination to see what's around you; I think it demonstrates a lack of perspective, in a cosmic, galactic sense. It demonstrates a certain inability to experience wonder; it's symptomatic of a dulling of the senses, a reluctance to get lost in the world and experience mental and physical unity with the planet, a state that is achieved when we are at our most present – more often than not, we reach that state when we are alone. But if someone comes along and asks to walk to the end with you, there is no pride in saying either yes or no, there is only pride in walking to the end smiling.

Can I take you with me? Can I share this emptiness with you?

If the love is good, it will thrive in isolation. It does not require the constant diversion of others – but it does not object to the diversion of others, either, welcomes it sporadically. It is not so fragile it will implode on itself. Although I had doubts as to whether my husband would take to remote island life after thirty-six years in cities – except for a few months down in Devon with me beforehand – I had no doubt David and I would get along fine. But I had no idea how close we would become and the extent to which we would thrive. How seamlessly we would work together, how seamlessly we would work apart. How could I? I'd never experienced such a thing. I will have to work to maintain my independence now. It's something I can never afford to lose. The fewer people we love, the deeper they are within us and the harder it is not to fall apart when life again reminds us that, although intrinsically interconnected, through all states of energy and being, we experience this alone. That's not a bad thing. It can't be a bad thing. It's the beauty of all things.

In the days, weeks, months and years of sitting on my own, I may have only learned one thing: I have come to realise that I don't really know what forgiveness means. I forgive the people I love in an instant. What it is, or it was, is forgotten, absolved, loved away. It is forgotten – that's what it is, isn't it? Forgiveness, true forgiveness, is forgetting.

And then we forget things we have not forgiven. During times of stress and anxiety, increased cortisol levels affect the memory. We forget things. If you have ever been in an argument or an accident, you might find it hard to recollect the exact details. There will be cubes of time that you can inhabit, but you will find yourself unable to move forwards or backwards. Sometimes our mind forgets it for us. It wipes it clean to save us the torment – a survival technique. And then it reappears in flashbacks and nightmares. So, simply because we forget, or cannot remember, does not mean we forgive.

What is forgiveness, then? For me, forgiveness can never be a thought process. Forgiveness is an emotional and physical process. It tends to require one to be of sound mind, but other than that, there is no logic involved. It is through the body, not the mind, that we forgive. If forgiveness is to be penetrating, total, reaching even the unconscious, then muscle memory must forget also. The body walks the mind further and further away from the scene of the crime. The body says: *Only when I am far enough away will I allow these cells of mine to regenerate, only then will I give you a new life. Only when the body is safe will you sleep all night.*

Can you be grateful for something having happened that at the same time you wish had never had to happen? It's just something I was going through. So sad that I saw everything as if it was underwater. But since the barn it's been like I'm high all the time, even when I'm not. Clouds take my breath away. A wind-bent tree takes me back a thousand years to a life I never had. A leaf falling brings me to tears. It is ridiculous to live like this, so constantly blown away by it all. I ripped off the skin of my old life and I walk around without one now. When the wind creature comes searching, I raise my hands in surrender and dare it to carry me away. It rushes left to right, west to east, grass to star, blowing gulls out of their roosts over the sea like spume, searching for what it has lost. I took it. I took what it searches for. I collected it like a stone to skim across the river.

Carry the body to an island of the dead. She is forgiven who forgives herself.

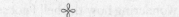

The honeysuckle is at its sweetest at 1.30 a.m. on the walk home down the valley, but its scent is no competition for the light I hold in my hand. Owing to the current water shortage caused by a leak somewhere in the tanks and a lack of rain, a dodgy new borehole has been opened up, so I'm grappling three bottles of drinking water while my phone's torch guides us home. The electric's off now and the moon is waning. The night is dark except for what comes from my hand. As I stumble, I realise the tavern has been cunningly built as far away from the cliffs as possible, and after a Walter Hicks – the Navy-strength rum – you can see why.

Moths of all sizes have started fluttering around the light I hold, landing on my hand. Burnet moths, common wave moths, silver footmen, honeysuckle moths, buff ermines, so many I cannot make them out. Within a minute my hand is covered, there is no skin visible, my fist is just a vibrating mass of powdered wings with hundreds more moths flying around me and my hand. The mass becomes so swarm-like through the long grass in the field behind the pub that I'm scared I'm going to breathe them in.

When I get to our house, I turn off my torch and the moths disappear in an instant, like a spell retracted by its master. I don't want to go back inside, the night is too magnificent. Outside, I lie alone out on the gravel and look up at the stars. This was something I used to do at our old house: lie on the gravel of our drive and look into the infinite simply because it was there. I stare until I doze, and I doze until I am woken by the sensation of the world spinning. The earth is rotating too fast. I rum-stumble in the candlelight, covered in dust, and into a warm bed, wondering how the hell I got so lucky.

It's ten days before we are to leave and I know now why the island has such a pull on me. Yes, it is magnificently beautiful, but so are many other places. That's not it. The reason the island has such a pull on me, why I'm reluctant to leave, is because there is nowhere on this rock I cannot go. I can walk and go anywhere I want, nothing and nowhere is off limits, nowhere is out of bounds, nowhere is private land – for everyone, staff and visitor, there are no 'Keep Out' signs, no estates we have to avoid, the only thing stopping me is the sea, and when I want to go there, I can. I head down to the beach in the evening. The blue sea, crystal aquamarine, is somehow still freezing. A swimming costume was a nice idea but I'm glad I've packed my wetsuit, which I climb into on a rock. I will microdose the water cure a little every day until we leave, and my aim tonight is only to get my head under, and once I do, once the freezing water that has leaked through the suit begins to warm and my hands and toes become accustomed to the cold, I swim out further, and then a little further, and then I decide I will swim out to the sailboats and the yachts moored out in the bay until I become a dot. I look back to the shore and wonder if this is as close to no man's land as I'm going to get in the UK.

The months have slipped into the fields, songbirds have turned into butterflies and the ravens into moths. We will be leaving under a waning moon. As the illuminated portion of the moon is decreasing, you are supposed to make room for the new, let go, reflect and make space, as an advert for an app on my phone informs me. Make space for what, I wonder? Although I have the islander Helen's words ringing in my ears – 'Nothing else compares to it' – I'm ready to leave. The island has changed, and huge dark shadows of high-rise cruise ships drift past like dark hands reaching into the unconscious. It's very ominous.

Smaller cruise ships arrive on what seems to be a weekly basis. The wild land we arrived on has become Disneyland, and dozens of black, motorised RIBs (small inflatable boats) leave the mothership for the coast of the island, scouring it like assassination teams; it feels like a very pathetic invasion. I sit on a rock at a place I've dubbed 'Selkie Cove' – what was, just a few months ago, a quiet spot with only seals, razorbills and the occasional gannet or shag for company, but where now three black RIBs pass me by and the elderly passengers look at me and wave at me like I'm a seal. I think of an older man who talked to me on the east path a few weeks ago about diurnal variations, how extreme they have been this year, and sang me a rhyme as we tried to identify whether the black bird in the distance was a cormorant or a shag.

> The common cormorant or shag
> Lays eggs inside a paper bag.

The rhyme didn't help us identify the bird, but it made me laugh and I was glad to share this place with him. So I try to tell myself not to be such a bitch, that this is how they enjoy nature and there is nothing wrong with that. But I can't convince myself. It's an inauthentic, detached way of experiencing nature. Not a part of it. Not even setting foot on this island. I end up peeing in plain sight of the cruise ship and sticking my middle finger up as the loud tannoy dings and bings across the whole island, announcing when dinner will be ready. Fuck off.

Nature, including remote nature, should be accessible to all, and fair play to Lundy, they have done an excellent job at making it so. The 'Trampers' (all-terrain mobility scooters) mean those with disabilities and health difficulties can explore the island from north end to south. So, actually, there is no excuse for this kind of thing any more, this thing polluting faster than its rate of knots, destroying the wildlife faster than its passengers can look at it from their little black RIBs before heading back to the ship. I feel trapped by the dozens of cursory eyes that pass over me as if I were an ornament: a plastic bridge in a goldfish bowl. It's time I should be leaving.

When Endelienta left Lundy for the hamlet of Trentinney in North Cornwall, she would have left the island hoping to return for rest and meditation; she had built a chapel here, after all. She wanted to leave the island not because of an influx of cruise ships on its coast, but to join her soon-to-be-headless brother Nectan in leading the pagan stronghold of Devon and Cornwall into Christianity. At Trentinney, she lived in a low-key anchorage and subsisted entirely on the milk of her cow and on water from two nearby wells. She met one of her many sisters, Saint Dilic, regularly for walks, and where they trod the grass grew greener. When her cow wandered from this green grass into the Lord of Trentinney's land, he killed it. Endelienta's supposed godfather, King Arthur, had the landowner killed in turn. The story goes that she regretted the death so much that she brought him back to life. It does not befit a woman to wish someone dead, but who's to say she didn't, just for a moment. *Holy mother Endelyn, gentle anchoress who did not forget to pray even for your enemies, pray unto Christ our God for us sinners!*

Because she was murdered, icons show her raising the palm of the martyr, as does the only medieval rosary that survived the Reformation, which happens to have her engraved on an 'Ave' bead. Devon and Cornwall being remote, they were one of the last Catholic strongholds – as they had been the last of the pagan strongholds – along with Yorkshire and the north of England during the Reformation. It is believed her bones were hidden somewhere in the church that was built in her name in the Cornish parish of St Endellion – also named after her – so as not to be destroyed with everything else. When they constructed her church, it was built with granite from Lundy, because no other stone would have been good enough. Lundy's granite was its main export for a whole five years between 1863 and 1868. Supposedly, some of the South Bank in London was built using Lundy granite, but only a bit, because it wasn't deemed good-enough quality. One man's trash is another man's treasure.

> The thief left it behind:
> the moon
> at my window.

> Ryōkan, the penniless Zen monk

There's no way of knowing what time of year Endelienta left Lundy – but, for sure, whether summer or winter or spring or autumn, the journey on her ship would have been a less comfortable one than mine will be. Though it would have been quieter, her leaving more personal. I will leave the island with a hundred day trippers, reminding me that my leaving is as generic as everyone else's who has ever left. The island being so small, everyone feels as if they have a claim on it. Ash, one of the islanders, says that in a normal, non-pandemic summer, when there are two hundred or more visitors a day, Lundy can be special to everyone, but it can be no more special to one person than it is to another. Despite the connection I feel to this place, almost as if it's a living entity with a mercurial personality, it's not mine, either. Everyone tries to carve their life into the rock but the stone erodes with time. Lundy was not any of the lords' or the invaders', nor the Bronze Age farmers', it was not the Welsh wizards', nor the kings' or the Knights Templars', and it was not Endelienta's either; ultimately, it is not even the National Trust's. As the centuries wear on and the sea and the wind continue to bite into her sides, Lundy will disappear.

After her first visit, Endelienta would return until there came the day when she left and never came back. How did she feel on that day, as she watched the island wane and melt into the blue horizon? Did she press her stomach against the prow and lean a little into the salt spray to better see the dolphins that have been chasing our ships for centuries? The wooden oars creak.

Mid-July. The rains come just before we leave, to remind us of the Lundy we knew – our Lundy, my Lundy, the wild Lundy that did not have a soul, that had no cruise ships stalking its banks, only the wind. As the final twenty-four hours tick on, I walk the island again. For the last week I have been walking the island every single day. Covering as much distance as my mind will absorb. Burning it into the brain, every movement of every thing. We move, things change. A swallow shoots past what is now the butterfly path; most of the swallows have moved onto the mainland now and it's time for me to follow. The sycamore and oak by my side rustle timidly with their hard-won new leaves, knowing the full terror the wind can inflict when they have something to lose. Turning the corner on the road down to the beach, there are the lights from the red and white lobster-pot boat I saw with great regularity over the more remote months. One of the fishermen is shouting, 'I can't do it!'

You can. You always do.

I bump into Dean the warden on one of his walks. 'Seen anything cool?' I ask.

'Always,' he replies, smiling.

Orange-tip butterflies flit between one another's bodies and the flowers. The honeysuckle on the east path is crawling with green, crackle-glazed figeater beetles, reaching, straining from one flower to the next and sometimes falling to the ground. Their green-orange backs are iridescent as a TVR Tuscan. Ravens rise and fall over each other, and somewhere near the herring gulls a peregrine falcon screeches. Flowering golden grasses shimmy to the song of skylarks. The red beadlet flowers of dock leaves blush the fields. There is what the sea delivers when the wind is up; angry, the ocean throws up its dead. Large vertebrae appear on the shore, jaws of unidentified carnivores. A dead sheep washes up alongside some deflated helium birthday balloons that lie golden and ridiculous on the shingle beach beside the swollen body of the sheep. It's not one of the island's flock, it's been in the water too long; its eyes have long gone, its wool has completely disappeared from most of its body, and all that is left is a cling-film-thin membrane between the very depths of it and us. An emerald-green emperor dragon-fly crosses the fields near the lake of Pondsbury. It's mating season. Everything that was once so new I must soon leave behind. Everything that over winter, spring and summer we have come to know, every path, combe, rock and bay, every promontory and cove. This world we have seen every day for three-quarters of a year, suddenly we will see no more. The blackbird in the quarry with a white tail feather – a freak, a dream of nature. Below, hair rubbed off by Highland cattle is tickled by purple and yellow woody nightshade flowers that seem so unreal for an English plant. It creeps below the pussy willow and a strange, white, dead algal pool. Crested clouds are blurred like sand dunes in the wind. A wood pigeon flies over the sea. I saw bats here for the first time last night, by the cow parsley. There's always more to see.

Over the fields to the west side of the island. The ancient, Irish side where the sea is at its biggest, its oldest. Marching down to the Battery as if I am being pulled. Down to where I've spent sunsets from December to July with my feet hang-ing off the edge of the world. Where the distance between the coves is the widest and the gulls' call is amplified, as the booming from the two fog cannons I sit between must have been. I have spent the stillest summer nights here, but tonight it's like winter again. The sheepdogs will be barking up at Pigs. The rising wind sits on its counterweight lever with the sun; the moon through the leaves on the trees in the valley, and a white moth dancing illuminated against the half-darkness. I watch the night drawn over the sea. A freezing wind brings a rain cloud smashing over the ocean as the sun sets in ascensionic rays of light. It's coming this way. The land, the woodland, the marshland, the farmland, the moorland, all the land is grateful for the coming rain. In my head are the words of the swimmer from *Masquerade*: 'Stand at the water's edge a little before the Sun sets in the west, and you will see a yellow carpet. If you can run its length before the sun has time to set, you will reach your destination.' A great dark cloud with a haze of drizzle passes over the grey sea where the yellow carpet should be, driving into the face of the ocean, pouring back into its past: a wall of time and water. I race up the steps of the Battery as fast as I can to avoid the coming downpour, which might just pass me by if I'm lucky.

Epilogue

Eyes down. Eyes down. Eyes down. I must not become so distracted by the moon rising blood-red above the ocean that I lose my footing on the rocky ground beneath my feet. Eyes down. Eyes down. Eyes down. There's a luminous red rock in the sky and the island is empty. A quick look back to see the church, then forwards into the light as the Worm Moon rises, becoming huge and orange like a low-hanging fruit. A myth of a moon, this.

I arrive at the ancient castle and its drystone walls and reach for my husband's hand. The wind whips south-westerly round the old fortress and mist comes in over the sea. The moon continues to rise, yellow now, like a second sun. The light so bright it illuminates the mist at ground level and all around us is orange-yellow light, like that exhibition at the Tate Modern the name of which I've forgotten. There is the sound of oystercatchers down in the bay, their screams echoing through the cliffs. Where the currents converge, the rippling of water widens and flattens into a lake of gold in the middle of the sea. The beam of the southern lighthouse strobes the grass.

The oystercatchers calm, and there's not a sound now but the sea hitting the rocks. It's strange, the moon is so bright that I have a shadow, yet everything is still dark, as if the world has been turned upside down, or we are standing a billion years in the future witnessing our dying sun in our dust-shattered atmosphere, and this is the last of the light that we live by on Earth.

It was through my shadow that I entered this life.

We are in agreement, the moon and I, the score is settled. I have paid my dues. I tear my eyes from its light; dragging them west, I notice a bright blue star shimmering. It is Rigel, a blue supergiant pulsing in the constellation of Orion, the Hunter – his left knee. Its name comes from an Arabic word meaning 'the left leg of the giant'. A smaller blue supergiant, Saiph, makes up the Hunter's right knee. Rigel is more luminous than the sun; it's only blue because of its distance from us. Blue is the last colour we see before darkness. One day, this gigantic white-blue mass of energy will end in a supernova, the most powerful stellar explosion, visible even on earth. When the Hunter's left knee ruptures it will create either a black hole or a metal-rich neutron star, or it will completely destroy itself. We never know what trauma will do.

The moon continues to wind through the sky, becoming paler as it rises, until it appears as blue as a supergiant through the droplets of mist it illuminates. It's time to go home. Home. Home is wherever we are, we tell each other; we take it with us everywhere. We are walking back to our home for now, a church on an empty island surrounded by stars. And they say there's no such thing as magic.

Acknowledgements

For someone who considers herself a loner, I appreciate the irony of having so many people to thank. There are so many people I am grateful to. There are those who directly contributed to this book, and others who contributed to the journey within it (it was a long road).

Thank you to Farmer John Mitchell for sitting with me over many pots of tea and being so generous with your time and your recollections of Hope Bourne. Thank you to Shaun Caton for your vivid and moving retelling of your time as the blue hermit with Paul. Thank you, Sara Maitland, for taking the time to have a frank and in-depth conversation about solitude and why we crave it. Thank you for imparting your wisdom, advice and humour. Thank you so much to Radha Case for fielding all my queries about hikikomori from halfway across the world.

Thank you to J. C. Hughes and Harriet Wilson for putting me on the Hope Bourne trail in the first place. Julius Beltrame: thank you for taking an interest in this subject and for putting me in touch with your friend and ornamental hermit. Thank you to Ashley Howe for being patient with a novice twitcher and showing me the sulphur-bellied warbler. Thank you to Judith Clark and Alethea Creighton of the Shobo-an Zen Centre for checking my interpretation of my ad hoc Zen readings. Thank you to Laura Rothwell for giving me my lifeline. Thank you to Anthea and Ian Davidson for talking about Lundy pirates that day.

On Lundy, my eternal thanks and gratitude to the Landmark Trust and the Diocese of Exeter, in particular to Derek Green, Rob Waterfield and Reverend Jane Skinner for taking that leap of faith and letting us come to Lundy (and stay there for so long). Thank you to Jackie at the Lundy Shore Office, who chatted to me instead of shutting me down, and first suggested The Vestry. Thank you to the incredible Old Light conservationists, Rachel and Charlie, for imparting so much knowledge and letting me wield a trowel. Also to Phil, for all the ghost stories. Thank you to everyone who was on the island during that lockdown: Sue, Helen, Alice, Ash, Kobe, Pete, Jo Girl, Joe Boy, Tina, Stritch, John, Jon, Philippa, Pia, Dean, Zoe, Rosie, Fiona, Dave, Tom, Julie, Kevin – may he rest in peace – Matt and Sam. It was magic.

Thank you to Gus Brown and Tom Lloyd-Williams at Aevitas Creative Management UK. Thank you to my agent, Max Edwards. I wouldn't be writing these acknowledgements without you. Thank you for finding me, thank you for seeing that I had a story to tell, the story I'd been too busy living to take notice of. Thank you for being such a wonderful (and fun) agent.

To my editor, Zennor Compton: thank you. Thank you for being the only editor this book could have had. Thank you for welcoming strangeness, for being whip-smart, emotionally intelligent, and for your instinct that said to dig deeper. I couldn't have asked for anything more. And to the team at Penguin Random House for bringing this book into being, particularly Laurie Ip Fung Chun, Gemma Wain, Callum Crute, Nicky Nevin, Lucy Thorne, Klara Zak, Sam Rees-Williams, Olivia Allen, Daisy Saunders, thank you.

Thank you so much to the early readers of this book for their support: Stu Hennigan, Joanna Pocock, Jon Dunn, Weird Walk,

The Fence, Rob Palk, Catherine Taylor, Tom Vowler, Niall Griffiths, Cal Flyn, M. John Harrison, and Tristan Gooley.

Thank you Kit Williams for creating *Masquerade*, for your influence on the way I see the world and its inhabitants, and for allowing me to use your words in my book. Thank you to Basilisk Communications for the gift of Derek Jarman's beautiful words. Thank you to Picador and Pan Macmillan for their generosity.

At London Metropolitan University, thank you to Anne Karpf for taking a punt on me, for being an inspiration to your students, for teaching me the importance of editing myself and showing me the creativity that non-fiction has to offer. Thank you also to Nico de Oliveira, for agreeing to have me as your sole student. Those lessons are precious to me. You taught me to think more objectively; cosmically, even.

Thank you also to the bursary team at London Met for awarding me some financial support to help me complete the degree. Niall Griffiths and Jenni Fagan, thank you both for giving me a vital confidence boost when I was at an early stage in my writing on the Arvon course at Lumb Bank. Thanks also to the Arvon Foundation for awarding me the grant that allowed me to take part. Thank you to the Society of Authors, for your generous grant that has helped give me time to finish this book. Thank you to my schoolteachers who were kind – you know who you are. Thank you to all the editors who have published my work – I doubt I'd be writing this without your support.

Thank you to all of my friends, especially to Alex Waespi, Lexxi and Ben Duffy, and Kat Aedy, not only for being beautiful, kind and supportive friends, but also for letting me sleep on your sofas for an interminably long time and never once making me feel unwelcome or ashamed. I don't know if I could have completed the master's without your support. I'll always be grateful to you. Thank you to Jemima Kelly for your encouragement and enthusiasm in all walks of life, including writing. Thank you for lighting up my landline. Thank you to Ben Fogg for always being straight up.

Thank you to Allegra Winton for dancing to Paul Simon with me when I was down and out. Thank you to my school friends who remain my friends, it means a lot (you weirdos). Thank you to Joseph, for taking care of me that night, and many other times. Thank you to Lauren Backhouse for turning that corner when I've never needed to see a friendly face more. Thank you to Louis, for being encouraging about my writing from the very beginning, when the grammar and spelling were particularly atrocious. Your encouragement, without a doubt, helped me get here. Thank you to Tena Strok for saving me from someone's fucking box room. I cherish our time in that beautiful townhouse. Thank you also for letting me hold the exhibition of my illuminated manuscripts in your magical shop – what a trip!

Thank you to Shenagh Cameron for also always being a voice of reason, and being the voice encouraging me to get a qualification. You were right. Thank you to Angie Barry and Alistair Findlay for your love, care and much-valued silliness, and for giving me counsel. Thank you to those who are no longer with us, in particular to Judi Allette, my godmother, a safe haven and giver of rum, who I wish was here to see this. Thank you to my grandparents and every ancestor who helped pave the way for this life.

Ninette, thank you from the bottom of my heart for giving me the platform that led me here. Thank you for seeing me when so many wouldn't even have noticed me. I am eternally grateful for your kindness, support and generosity, for giving me hope, for showing me that you can rebuild a life, and for making me laugh.

Thank you to my new family, particularly Rose, Malcolm, Emma and Amelia (and Lilly), for making me feel so welcome and at ease.

Thank you, Charlotte Collins, for always guiding me and giving me sound advice, and continuing to give it even when I seem to be ignoring it. Thank you for taking me in so many times, for letting me sleep on your sofa (and your bed) so many times and for so long. Thank you for being my big sister; I will always look up to you.

Thank you to my parents, Susan Kingsford and John Fitton, for filling our world with magic, for building the house of dreams, for being like no one else and never wanting to be, for showing me that the most fun is had with the outsiders, and for making me see life in such a way that I continue to be inspired by it. My greatest stroke of luck was to be your child.

David, where do I begin? How do you thank someone for restoring their faith in human beings? Thank you for your unwavering love, support, and belief in me and my work; for trusting me with this; for trusting me. Thank you for being someone I can trust with my life. Thank you for making me laugh when I am sad. Thank you for making me feel safe. Thank you for never judging me. Thank you for being open to new experiences. Thank you for moving to Devon with me, and not leaving again when they slurry the fields next door. Thank you for being patient. Heart, body and soul, I thank you.

If anyone reading this is inclined to make a donation to help fund research into LAM disease and support people with LAM, the details can be found here: https://lamaction.org/donate/

About the Author

Jade Angeles Fitton is a writer, journalist, and award-winning producer. Her work has appeared in the likes of the *Guardian*, *Independent*, *Vogue*, *Times Literary Supplement*, *New Statesman* and the *Financial Times*. Her poetry has been published in a number of magazines including *The Moth*. She lives in rural Devon with her husband and ghost dog.